JAN 13 1986

B As81C 1985
Carrick, Peter.
A tribute to F

D0122365

PHOENIX PUBLIC LIBRARY
PHOENIX, ARIZONA

DEMCO

A TRIBUTE TO

Fred Astaire

A TRIBUTE TO

by

Peter Carrick

Salem House
Salem, New Hampshire

3 1730 02105 7877

PHOENIX PUBLIC LIBRARY

© Peter Carrick 1984
First published in the United States
by Salem House in 1985.
A member of the Merrimack Publishers' Circle,
47 Pelham Road, Salem, NH 03079.

ISBN 0 88162 081 5

Printed and bound in Great Britain

For my late mother and father, who took me as a small boy to see Fred Astaire movies, and to my own family, with whom I have shared this latest Astaire experience.

Contents

List of Illustrations   9

Acknowledgements   11

1   The man and the magic   13

2   Following in Adele's footsteps   17

3   Talk of the town — in New York and London   30

4   Leaving the stage behind   40

5   'Making a stab at Hollywood'   47

6   Stepping out with Ginger   62

7   Just one darn film after another   81

8   Change Partners   98

9   The Band Wagon   121

10   Getting to know the man   126

11   The march of time   135

12   Entertainer of the century   146

Chronology   159

Appendices   163

Index   180

List of Illustrations

Between pages 32 and 33

1 Fred and Adele in *Stop Flirting,* 1923
2 Fred and Adele in *Funny Face,* 1927/1928
3 Fred and the former Mrs Phyllis Potter after their wedding in 1933
4 A youthful looking Fred with co-star Claire Luce in *The Gay Divorce,* 1933
5 Starring with Ginger for the first time in *Flying Down to Rio,* 1933
6 'The Continental' from Fred and Ginger's second film, *The Gay Divorcee* (*The Gay Divorce* in UK)
7 Astaire and Rogers in the 'I'll be Hard to Handle' sequence from the 1935 production of *Roberta*
8 Top billing as Fred and Ginger's names appear above the title for the first time in *Top Hat*
9 Fred and Ginger in *Top Hat*
10 Fred wearing top hat, white tie and tails from *Top Hat*
11 A nautical flavour as Fred taps it out in the 1936 production of *Follow the Fleet*
12 'Bojangles of Harlem' was a featured sequence in *Swing Time,* 1936, in which Fred paid tribute to Bill Robinson
13 Fred and Ginger on roller skates in *Shall We Dance,* 1937
14 The famous golf ball scene from *Carefree*

Between pages 96 and 97

15 Pandro Berman
16 Fred and Phyllis arrive in Ireland and are greeted by their brother-in-law Lord Charles Cavendish, 1939
17 *Broadway Melody of 1940* with Eleanor Powell and George Murphy
18 Fred with bandleader/conductor Johnny Green
19 In *Second Chorus,* 1940 with co-star Paulette Goddard
20 Fred with Rita Hayworth in *You'll Never Get Rich*
21 Joan Leslie was seventeen and Fred almost forty-four when they danced together in *The Sky's the Limit*

22   Lady Adele Cavendish arrives back in the United States, 1945

23   The two Freds share a joke

24   Ann Miller

25   Fred and horse — a shot from *Easter Parade*

26   The tramps number from *Easter Parade* with Judy Garland

27   Fred relaxing with co-stars Ann Miller and Peter Lawford. Composer and lyricist Irving Berlin playing piano

28   Together again! Fred and Ginger in *The Barkleys of Broadway,* 1949

29   Fred with Cyd Charisse in *The Band Wagon,* 1953

Between pages 128 and 129

30   With co-star Jack Buchanan from *The Band Wagon*

31   The world's greatest song-and-dance man relaxes between takes of *The Band Wagon*

32   'Dancing in the Dark' dance sequence from *The Band Wagon.* Fred and Cyd Charisse

33   In *Daddy Long Legs* with Leslie Caron

34   Fred in flight

35   Fred escorts his daughter to a debutantes ball in Los Angeles

36   Fred with co-star Audrey Hepburn during shooting of *Funny Face,* 1957

37   Fred and Cyd Charisse together again in *Silk Stockings,* 1957

38   Cyd Charisse in *Silk Stockings*

39   *On the Beach* gave Fred his first non-singing, non-dancing role

40   *The Midas Run,* 1969 (*A Run on Gold* in UK) with Sir Ralph Richardson

41   Fred with Jennifer Jones in *The Towering Inferno,* 1975

42   Fred and Adele photographed in New York, 1972

43   Fred at seventy-seven

44   With Cyd Charisse, Leslie Caron and Gene Kelly

45   With his second wife Robyn Smith soon after their marriage

The photographs in this book are reproduced by kind permission of:
The Raymond Mander & Joe Mitchenson Theatre Collection 1, 4;
Popperfoto, 2, 6, 18, 28, 42, 44, 45; Keystone Press Agency, 3, 16, 22, 35, 43; National Film Archive Stills Library, 5, 7, 8, 9, 10, 11, 12, 13, 14, 15, 17, 19, 20, 21, 23, 24, 25, 26, 27, 29, 30, 31, 32, 33, 34, 36, 37, 38, 39, 40, 41.

Acknowledgements

Scores of people, both inside and outside the world of entertainment, have helped me with *A Tribute to Fred Astaire* by providing material, showing enthusiasm for the project and by sharing with me their views and knowledge of Fred Astaire. I am particularly indebted to Her Majesty Queen Elizabeth The Queen Mother. I am also grateful to Fiona Allison, Lionel Blair, David Boyce, Robert Brandon, John Buckledee, Peter Cliffe, Barry Edwards, Dickie Henderson, David Lewin, the anonymous Fleet Street journalist whose exclusive telephone interview and personal knowledge was so useful in the preparation of chapter 11, and to colleagues in the BBC and Orbis Publishing Ltd and on the *TV Times Magazine.*

My special thanks go to Melanie Kindley, who helped me considerably, and who typed the manuscript, to Sheena Atkinson for all her help, and to Paul Smith.

For permission to include extracts from published material I am grateful to the BBC (*The Fred Astaire Story*), Orbis Publishing Ltd (*The Movie*), the Hamlyn Publishing Group Limited (*Fred Astaire* by Benny Green), A.D. Peters & Co Ltd (*Steps in Time* by Fred Astaire) and John Farquharson Ltd (*Bring on the Empty Horses* by David Niven).

Other sources of reference were *The RKO Story* (Octopus Books) by Richard B. Jewell with Vernon Harbin, *The MGM Story* (Octopus Books) by John Douglas Eames, *Fred Astaire* (W.H. Allen) by Michael Freedland, *Gotta Sing, Gotta Dance* (Hamlyn Publishing Group Ltd) by John Kobal, *The Twenties* (William Heinemann Ltd) by Alan Jenkins, and newspapers and film magazines too numerous to record individually.

ONE

The man and the magic

No dancer in the entire history of the silver screen won greater fame than Fred Astaire. Yet all through his career he was the most casual and disarming 'Hollywood Great' of them all. He wasn't ambitious, didn't plot or direct his career, and shrugged off setbacks and stalemates with the same charming detachment as he accepted his greatest triumphs.

When sister Adele left the successful brother and sister stage act to get married in 1932, he admitted that his career came to a halt mostly because he did nothing about it. Later, when Hollywood beckoned, he stayed in New York. When finally he travelled to California his ambition was meagre and success unexpected. 'I decided to make a stab at Hollywood and the movies. Frankly, I didn't think I had much of a chance, but I would try', is how he put it.

After finishing work on his first film with Ginger Rogers, *Flying Down to Rio,* he didn't even bother to stay around long enough to see a full run-through. As the movie capital buzzed with excitement on seeing the amazing 'Carioca' dance sequence, Fred was in London appearing on stage in *Gay Divorce* at the Palace Theatre, convinced that the preview of the film must have flopped and his movie career was already at an end. Though welcomed enthusiastically as a movie star on his return to America, he didn't even see the film for the first time until some weeks later — sneaking in unnoticed as a paying customer at a small theatre in Augusta, South Carolina.

Always, it seems, he was content to let events take their course, leaving others to take the initiatives which advanced his career. At times he would stop and wonder what to do next — then play golf or spend a day at the races. At forty-eight, not having danced professionally for two years, he took over Gene Kelly's role in the 1948 movie *Easter Parade* with Judy Garland, Peter Lawford and Ann Miller. He admitted that he had been thinking about telling MGM that he wanted to return to the screen, but didn't know if they would want him. Then came the urgent call from the studio asking if he would consider taking over from Gene Kelly, who had broken an ankle in mid-rehearsal. Even then he telephoned Kelly direct to make sure he really wasn't fit enough to carry on, before accepting the part.

Seven years later, and after completing work on *The Band Wagon* with Cyd Charisse, Oscar Levant, Nanette Fabray and Jack Buchanan, Fred was resigned to retirement once more, since nobody seemed to want him to do another film. This time it was left to studio boss Darryl Zanuck, who saw him by chance in a restaurant one day, to approach Fred's agent with the idea of a musical version of *Daddy Long Legs.* Astaire subsequently starred in this film with Leslie Caron and Terry Moore. Another time, after admitting that he wasn't concerned whether he worked or not, it was his first wife Phyllis who told him to take a serious look at his career. Only then did he sit down to study a part already offered to him and then decide to take it.

Women, incidentally, have played a significant part in his life. It was his mother, not his father, who left the family home in Omaha in the American midwest, to take their two young children to live in New York. This was so they could learn dancing from the experts and break into vaudeville. Though Fred's father was determined to get his children into show business (it was the money he earned back in Omaha which paid for those vital early years of learning in New York), it was their mother who was close at hand to influence their day-to-day lives.

After his mother, it was sister Adele who became his biggest influence. In their early teens Adele, a little older and then a fraction taller, made most of the decisions and Fred admitted he was happy enough to follow on behind.

After Adele married and left show business it was his wife Phyllis, whom he married in 1933, who inspired him to go solo. Later, in Hollywood to make the movie *Flying Down to Rio,* it was women again who sign-posted his career. He has talked about the kindness and encouragement of Joan Crawford, with whom he made his film debut in *Dancing Lady.* That same year, 1933, saw the first of the Fred Astaire-Ginger Rogers epics and it was with Ginger over the next sixteen years that his prodigious reputation as the movie world's supreme song-and-dance man was made. After the tragically early death of Phyllis in 1954, his mother moved more into his life again and continued to run the Hollywood household. With his second marriage in 1980 to former professional jockey, Robyn Smith, less than half his age, emerged the latest female influence in his life.

Yet however persuasive those influences, Fred Astaire was always very much his own man when it came to dancing. What others might have considered astute for his professional future didn't always interest him; seldom did he look beyond the next picture. This curious detachment was matched later by an almost absurd and sometimes irritating failure to come to terms with his own gigantic reputation. Cynics might even claim he made a mockery of modesty, but Fred's closest friends will tell you that he genuinely hated the star-spangled razzmatazz of Hollywood and the superficial publicity machine. He always remained faintly embarrassed and surprised when confronted by the reality of his enormous success.

Today that attitude seems incongruous but in the 1930s when he went to try his hand in films, his lack of confidence was not surprising. Hollywood heroes then were tall, hunky, handsomely cast in the traditional 'beefcake' mould. Fred certainly did not fit into this category and when he first saw himself on screen he was horrified. By the standards of the times that now legendary assessment of Fred Astaire's first screen test is perhaps understandable: 'Losing hair. Can't sing. Can dance a little'. Even David O. Selznick, then head of production at RKO, admitted to doubts about his 'enormous ears and bad chin line' but was impressed by his 'tremendous charm'.

Meantime, Fred seemed happy enough to let the future sort itself out and concentrated on what he did best of all — dancing. Indeed, his 'distant' attitude to the careful development of his career was in dramatic contrast to the devotion he applied to his dancing. This he always took seriously and on stage, in rehearsal, working through difficult routines, nobody was tougher or more dedicated. Disciplined, indefatigable, he was obsessive in his quest for perfection. Dance director Hermes Pan, who worked with Astaire on the majority of his musical films, said: 'Fred is such a perfectionist. A lot of people might just look and say, "Oh, it's good enough", but it wasn't with him because he was striving for perfection. That's why he's Fred Astaire and other people are not.' Irving Berlin, who wrote the music and the lyrics for six of Astaire's most popular movies said he worked harder than anyone he knew to get one step right.

The intricate and complicated 'Waltz in Swing Time' duet from the sixth film he did with Ginger Rogers and released in 1936, lasted over two and a half minutes and the entire number was photographed in one complete take. It is still considered an epic and memorable performance. In *Top Hat,* which even Astaire admitted was a 'good picture', he rehearsed one important sequence for two months, polishing and perfecting. The result is one of the classic film song-and-dance routines of all time, forever to be associated with Astaire: 'Top Hat, White Tie and Tails'.

Like most perfectionists, the demands he sometimes made on associates were not always easy to bear. After his partnership with Ginger Rogers ended, Eleanor Powell, Paulette Goddard, Rita Hayworth, Joan Leslie, Judy Garland, Vera-Ellen, Leslie Caron, Audrey Hepburn and Cyd Charisse were among a succession of talented singer-dancers to co-star with him, and some viewed the prospect with hesitation. But generally, Astaire's forward reputation as being difficult to work with was not sustained when rehearsals began, though he demanded high standards, hard work and an ability to match his style.

As a popular dancer on film, Fred Astaire is incomparable. Gene Kelly's 'Singin' in the Rain' from the film of the same name has emerged as perhaps the greatest music sequence on film. But despite its impact, it is Fred Astaire whom most people immediately think of when the film musical is mentioned. Fred was the more instinctive dancer, more fluid, relaxed, and with a greater natural technique. As Benny Green once wrote: 'People understood that there would never be anybody with whom to compare him, to duplicate the range of his achievement, least of all to replace him.'

Commentators and observers have repeatedly tried to analyze his success and to pin-point the reasons for his enormous popularity. In any conclusion, words like talent, style, technique, professionalism, charm, personality must never be too far from the surface. But while others tried desperately to arrive at deep and fundamental assessments, Fred Astaire himself has not helped matters because of his continued preference to live a private, quiet life. Now eighty-five years old, in 1984, he does by all accounts live very much in the present and the future, and finds talking about the past — particularly his own — irritatingly boring. His policy is not to give interviews, but in his autobiography, *Steps in Time,* first published in 1960, he has the complete answer for all those who have tried to psychoanalyze his success. He says: 'I am often asked to expound on the history and the philosophy of "the dance" about which I have disappointingly little to say . . . I don't know how it all started and I don't want to know. I have no desire to prove anything by it. I have never used it as an outlet or as a means of expressing myself. I just dance.'

With Fred Astaire . . . who needs more?

TWO

Following in Adele's footsteps

If you want to break into show business, a name like Frederick Austerlitz doesn't really help. Not that the four-year-old son of an Austrian immigrant to the United States was all that ambitious in 1903. But his father certainly was ... particularly for his two children. So when his five-year-old daughter Adele began to show as much talent at local dance school as any five-year-old can — and she was desperately stage struck into the bargain — he was determined she should be given her chance. She had a natural stage talent and unusual ability for one so young.

Omaha, Nebraska, where the family lived, was not exactly ideal as a springboard to a stage career, so in 1904, Adele and her mother travelled to New York in search of fame and fortune. Young Frederick, as he himself put it later, simply went along for the ride. Or so he thought. It was only after they got to New York that Fred realised that he, as well as Adele, was to attend dance class daily and soon the talent of Adele Astaire (the adopted name) and kid brother Fred began to show through.

Fred was born on 10 May 1899, four years after his father, also Frederic (no k) Austerlitz who was born in Vienna, arrived in America and settled in Omaha, where he had friends. A former officer in the Austro-Hungarian Army, Mr Austerlitz had two brothers, Otto and Ernest, who were also serving officers. In the United States Mr Austerlitz worked first in the leather business and then as a successful beer salesman, concentrating on a trade in which his family had been involved for years. In 1896 he married attractive schoolteacher Ann Geilus while she was still in her teens. Daughter Adele was born in 1897. A son, born eighteeen months later, was christened Frederick, the k being added because it sounded more American. Fred said later that he had a sensational mother — gentle, softly-spoken and retiring — and his enormous affection for her continued throughout her long life.

But she was not musical, nor had she any theatrical background. Any inherited interest or talent in that direction must have come from Mr Austerlitz for, although he did not perform publicly, he played piano and enjoyed music and theatre. For him to see potential talent in Adele at such an early age was a delight and, despite the sacrifices that were necessary, he knew that New York City provided the best chance for her to develop a stage career. He remained in Omaha and sent money to finance their stay but also visited them from time to time. Fred's future at this stage was, by all accounts, of secondary importance. It simply seemed right and sensible that he should be with his mother and elder sister, rather than his father. After all, he was only five years old.

The odds on making the grade in New York were slim. For one thing Mrs Austerlitz had never visited the city before and didn't know anyone there. She didn't even have one single letter of introduction. In the circumstances, the move itself was an act of bravery or, if it failed, utter folly. But giving Adele her chance was what mattered most and a sensible arrangement made before the party left Omaha was the enrolment of both Adele and Fred at Claude Alvienne's Dancing School on Eighth Avenue. Though selected at random from a theatrical trade paper, it turned out to be a good choice. Adele and Fred were quickly made to feel at home. By all accounts, Mr Alvienne was a kind, fatherly individual and both Adele and Fred took to him instantly. His wife, who was also involved with the school, was a former stage dancer. More importantly, the two ran a good school and could look back on a number of former pupils who had made a good career for themselves on the stage. Adele and Fred were given a solid grounding, both in stagework and drama, as well as in dancing. After a while they were able to dance in school concerts. One of these was *Cyrano de Bergerac*, but Adele took the lead while Fred, because he was three inches shorter than his sister, had to make do with the part of the girl Cyrano was in love with, Roxane.

Days were full. After dance and drama lessons at Alvienne's, the young Astaires would hurry to their rented home to normal school lessons given by their mother. It wasn't for several years that they attended their first public school. Any spare time was spent playing and going to the theatre occasionally. They saw one musical comedy, starring a famous Danish ballet-dancer, twenty-eight times! It was all part of their theatrical education. These happy days at Alvienne's provided the background to Fred's first conscious moves towards dancing and an appreciation of rhythm and movement. But he wasn't at all keen to dance, being much more fascinated by the way Mr Alvienne beat out the time with a stick on the back of a chair. Their school recitals gave performance experience to the youngsters and in one Adele and Fred played bride and groom — Adele in white satin and Fred, prophetic by some thirty years, in top hat, white tie and tails. This act was a solid twelve minutes of unashamed novelty, child enthusiasm and charm. It incorporated duet and solo numbers with all kinds of elaborate props, but it also led, after they had been at Alvienne's for about a year, to their first professional engagement in New Jersey. As an opening act they fared well, received fifty dollars for a split-week engagement, and read their first complimentary press notice in the local paper: 'The Astaires are the greatest child act in vaudeville.' It was a proud moment for Mr Austerlitz when he read that cutting back in Omaha.

In those less cynical days it wasn't hard for cute youngsters with a novelty act and enthusiasm to claim a 'good hand', and further small-time engagements followed. Their father now advanced their career directly, coming over to New York frequently, making contacts 'in the business' and ferreting for openings. He had a good personality and made friends easily. In the meantime, the act improved, the presentation was polished and when he thought they were ready, Mr Austerlitz brought one of his important contacts to see his children perform. The result was a twenty-week touring engagement at an astronomic 150 dollars a week. For a sister and brother barely nine and seven years old, it was a fortune. They loved the excitement of being on tour, travelling by train from one town to another, the pace and movement of it all.

Their act, worked out in infinite detail by Mr Alvienne, was overly elaborate, even for a child act in those days. A couple of giant prop wedding cakes were the 'show stopping' feature. They were all of six feet across and two feet tall and incorporated startling devices like flashing lights and novelty musical bells. Against the giant cakes, which lit up, Adele and Fred played a mini bride and groom number. At one stage Fred was dressed up as a lobster, Adele at another stage as a glass of champagne. It was all highly improbable, but gradually their act developed. The novelty items, which required elaborate and often cumbersome props and equipment, were eased out, the performance was streamlined, but the songs and the dancing were retained. Success continued and the Astaires played to enthusiastic audiences all over America.

They were mostly insignificant dates in small town vaudeville theatres and Adele and Fred shared the bill with all kinds of acts — jugglers, tumblers, comics, ventriloquists, illusionists, contortionists and singers. It was all valuable experience and gave Fred a flavour of the big time. The greatest thrill was when they appeared in their hometown of Omaha. They were greeted as top liners! Even at nine and seven they were already seasoned performers.

But problems were on the way. There was a strong and well-intentioned move by the 'Gerry' organization to protect children from exploitation and cruelty in all forms and at about this time they began to turn their attention to child performers, making it difficult for anyone under fourteen to get bookings in many cities. The Astaires short-circuited the system, as did countless other theatrically ambitious youngsters, by lying about their ages. To add conviction, Fred started wearing long trousers at an early age! In the end Mrs Austerlitz pleaded her children's cause, saying how dedicated they were, and Adele and Fred were allowed to continue.

The second problem was more crucial. Kids grow out of the cute stage and the Astaires, as did movie stars like Mickey Rooney, Jackie Cooper, Deanna Durban and Judy Garland a generation later, found it tough bridging the gap from child stars to adult performers. Troublesome also was the way Adele grew faster than Fred, making the dancing they did together at times awkward and uneasy. They also outgrew their material. Bookings dried up and their highly successful careers as child stars came to an end. Mr Austerlitz travelled to New York to deal with the crisis. Through a contact they took over a house in nearby New Jersey and although they had no idea of giving up the stage for good, they retired temporarily and for the first time attended normal school for a formal education. Fred can't have been too upset because not long before he had seen a report on their act from one of the theatres at which they had appeared. It said: 'The girl seems to have talent but the boy can do nothing!'. They were out of show business for two years. Enrolment at Ned Wayburn's famous dancing school on West Forty-fourth Street in New York was the start of their second stab at the theatre.

Wayburn ran one of the most outstanding theatrical dancing schools in the whole of the United States and Fred and Adele learned a lot over the next six months. Both were devoted pupils and Fred also started working out at a local gym. Their mother, as dedicated as ever to their cause, paid Wayburn more than 1,000 dollars for a specially written act for them to perform. It seemed to be a well-balanced act incorporating dancing, music, singing and comic dialogue. Fred even danced and played piano simultaneously, but even with novelty and Wayburn's influence, it was hard to get back into the business. When they did get their big break, at Proctors, a major theatre in New York, they flopped badly and after only one performance were taken off altogether. After enjoying so much success as youngsters, this was a devastating blow. Engagements were hard to come by and when they did get on stage Adele and Fred made little impact. They endured the slow handclap, pennies being thrown on stage and restless critical audiences. Their failure came at the worst possible time. Prohibition threatened Nebraska, their father was in danger of losing his job and the money from home dried up. To make ends meet they had to lower their sights and forget about trying to break into the big theatres in New York and the major cities. As Fred reports in his autobiography, *Steps in Time:* 'We played every rat trap and chicken coop in the Middle West for about two years and at one place we had to climb a ladder to get to our dressing rooms because the trained seals on the bill had the only downstairs dressing room!'

It was a tough period, but fortunes began to change, first when Mr Austerlitz sought the aid of an important vaudeville star of the day, Aurelia Coccia, and his wife; then again when manager Lew Golder managed to get them a touring engagement at an impressive 175 dollars a week. Coccia influenced their act by making them realize the importance of showmanship, and by training and coaching them over some six months. They were required to adjust their approach and learn new things, but Fred said later that he considered Aurelia Coccia had more influence on his dancing than anyone else in his career. Out went the old novelty routines and jaded dialogue, to be replaced by an uncompromising song-and-dance act. New songs and dance routines had to be learned and the act kept fresh with the regular introduction of new material. Two numbers had Fred playing the piano.

Not all dates were successful and there was a particularly sticky patch when a strike in the theatrical profession left them without work for several months. Mrs Austerlitz pawned some of her jewellery to help them survive.

It was three more years before the break Adele and Fred longed for came. With the 175 dollars a week deal which Lew Golder had negotiated for them came the expertise of Max Hayes, an influential agent who worked with Golder to get them noticed. Pay went up to 225 dollars a week and then, filling in at emergency notice for a top-line act which couldn't appear, to 350 dollars. With a good position on the bill, the Astaires virtually stopped the show at every performance. They made such an impact in their next engagement, at the important Palace Theatre in Chicago, that they took six curtain calls and were called back when halfway to their dressing rooms to acknowledge the prolonged reception, with Adele self-consciously thanking everyone 'from the bottom of our hearts'.

It was now some ten years since Mrs Austerlitz had taken her two small children on that somewhat perilous journey to New York in search of fame and fortune on stage. Although the talented brother and sister were still only in their mid-teens, they had gained enormous experience, developed the art and skills of their trade, and were true veterans of American vaudeville. On the way they had brushed shoulders with some of the most famous names in the business, both present and future. Douglas Fairbanks senior topped the bill once while they struggled with the terrifyingly depressing opening slot. The audience not yet settled could still be heard clattering through the auditorium to claim their seats. Another was Bill Robinson, the great coloured performer and the legendary father of tap-dance on film. Early cinemagoers will recall his delightful film sequences with Shirley Temple. Bill was perhaps approaching his peak then and Fred Astaire developed a deep respect and affection for him. Even Sophie Tucker once shared the programme with the Astaires, though her billing was somewhat bolder.

For a number of weeks they had worked on the same bill as Eduardo and Elisa Cansino and Fred said he watched them at almost every show. Little did any of them realize that in thirty years time Fred would be making a couple of important Hollywood movies with their beautiful and talented daughter, Rita Hayworth.

As still comparatively young performers, Adele and Fred Astaire got on well together and this mutual friendship and affection continued through their joint stage career and far beyond. Their professional standards were high, yet they had a lot of fun, both on and off stage. They learned to take the hard knocks and downturns philosophically — even when they were once replaced by a dog act!

He called her Delly and didn't seem to mind in the least that press notices during these years mostly credited her with the greater talent. Certainly Adele bubbled with personality and charm and it wasn't surprising that she grabbed most of the limelight, for as they approached their vaudeville peak she was almost twenty and naturally flattered by admiring glances and male attention. They were now playing bigger dates at more important theatres in larger cities such as St Louis, Buffalo, Pittsburg, Detroit and Chicago, but their ambition to play the Palace in New York eluded them. Press notices were good and around this time, Fred, casual and easy-going, had an uncharacteristic rush of blood to the head and in one extraordinary flourish, reproduced a selection of their glowing newspaper reports in a full-page advertisement on the back of the magazine *Variety*. Whether this influenced events is not known, but soon afterwards a well-known theatrical agent called Rufus LeMaire offered the Astaires an important booking in a Lee Shubert musical. It would be their first appearance in a Broadway musical comedy and they eagerly turned their backs on vaudeville for ever.

This was an enormous move forward, but the next few shows were not all rip-roaring successes. In *Over the Top,* which opened in November 1917 at the 44th Street Theatre, theirs was considered one of the more talented performances in a mediocre offering which, until it went out on the road with a new name in the top role, attracted only limited business. But it was important because the influential impresario, Charles Dillingham, saw the show in Washington and signed up Fred and Adele for *Apple Blossoms.* It was a big break and the salary of 550 dollars a week for just two featured dances and no dialogue was 200 dollars more than they had been getting. But first they were committed to do *The Passing Show of 1918.* Their chance to go into this show came after a representative from the famous Shubert brothers, then among the most influential impresarios of the day, visited them backstage and invited them there and then to sign for *The Passing Show of 1918,* scheduled for the Winter Garden Theatre on Broadway. Fred was just seventeen and impressed, for Lee and John Shubert had made a name for discovering and promoting talent, including Al Jolson. They were billed at that time as 'Fred and Adele Astaire, New Songs and Smart Dances'.

There was an anxious moment in terms of their careers when Fred became old enough for the Army draft. He had even received his reporting notice, but the war ended just in time and he didn't have to go. *Passing Show* was a tuneful and colourful extravaganza which ran for 125 performances on Broadway. It had an exceptionally large cast with many popular comedians of the day, including Willie and Eugene Howard as the stars. Fred and Adele's act was still grossly unsophisticated by later standards and at one point they were dressed up in bird costumes, with a chorus of 'chicks' behind them. Fred and Adele received good press notices and advanced their reputation considerably. As they moved into *Apple Blossoms,* which opened in October 1919, the future looked so hopeful that when they were able to ride in Dillingham's brand new Rolls-Royce, Adele turned to Fred and said: 'We ought to get one.' They were now doing so well that they moved, with their mother, into a suite in the Hotel Majestic which overlooked Central Park.

But the Roller had to wait awhile as a different kind of Royce had entered their lives. He was the British choreographer, Edward Royce, who later developed a routine specially for them which became known as the 'run-around' and which they used in almost all of their shows in the 1920s. It was an outstanding success. Others who drifted into their orbit at about this time included Fritz Kreisler, who once stepped in as their rehearsal pianist, as did the great George Gershwin on another occasion. Soon an unknown shop assistant called Alex A. Aarons, who nonetheless knew a lot about show business, would spark off an idea which later Fred would utilize profitably; and none other than the inimitable Noel Coward, then in the bloom of his early career, was the first to predict an enormous success for the Astaires in England and encouraged them to go to London.

Apple Blossoms was a winner. Charles Dillingham was a natural showman and his new operetta opened in New York with a flourish. Praise for Fred and Adele from the critics was unstinting — 'the biggest hit they've ever made', proclaimed the *Evening World*. 'Vastly entertaining dances by the two Astaires', reported the *New York Times*. It wasn't long before Fred and Adele knew they were contributing to that showbiz phenomenon, 'the Broadway hit', and they took their opportunity by keeping their act crisp and sparkling. After the New York run of 256 performances, *Apple Blossoms* went on a highly successful tour, eventually coming to the end of its road in the spring of 1921. Determined to repeat the success formula, Dillingham put the Astaires in *The Love Letter,* another operetta, but this time the magic key wouldn't turn the golden lock, despite good choreography by 'Teddy' Royce. The show, doomed despite the early optimism, ran for only 31 performances, but for Fred and Adele it was a personal triumph and their act repeatedly stopped the show.

A tour followed the short New York run, but although business was reasonable, it was an expensive show to put on the road and Dillingham couldn't make money from it. Nobody gave much for its chances, but in the meantime Fred had unexpectedly met the young and enthusiastic Alex Aarons, whose father was with a firm of theatrical producers and theatre owners. Alex had produced George Gershwin's first musical show, *La La Lucille,* and looked upon the Astaires as ideal candidates for another show he intended producing. When *The Love Letter* closed after its unexpectedly short run, Dillingham had nothing lined up for Fred and Adele, so arrangements were quickly made for them to be 'loaned out' to Alex Aarons for his forthcoming show, *For Goodness Sake.*

After the flop of *The Love Letter,* Fred and Adele were nervous when *For Goodness Sake* opened at the Lyric Theatre on Broadway. Unlike the Dillingham show, they had a lot to do, but they had rehearsed well and, along with dance director Allan Foster, produced some new dance specialities. It all worked perfectly. They received an enormous reception, the critics were enthusiastic and Fred, who in this show began for the first time to do some of his own staging and choreography, later reckoned that *For Goodness Sake* was probably the most significant step forward in their careers up to that time. They both enjoyed working with Alex Aarons and became close friends with him and Ella, his wife. Charles Dillingham, though, had no intention of losing the talents of the Astaires and by the time *For Goodness Sake* closed, was ready with a very promising follow-up called *The Bunch and Judy*. This was built around the Astaires with music by no less a talent than Jerome Kern, and with Teddy Royce handling the dance routines. It seemed certain to be a major hit, but show business demonstrated its capriciousness and, despite Dillingham's wide experience, obvious talent and theatrical flair, this latest show failed and closed in New York after only a few weeks.

Aarons now steps into the story once more, again to play a significant role. The idea was to take *For Goodness Sake* to London, where Aarons was convinced it would do well, but Fred and Adele were still committed to a final fling with *The Bunch and Judy,* which Dillingham now tried out on tour. It did no better and finally closed.

It was curious that Fred and Adele Astaire had the misfortune to suffer two of Charles Dillingham's failures, for his reputation in the business was considerable and he was one of the most influential and successful impressarios of the day. In both *The Love Letter* and *The Bunch and Judy,* the Astaires had scored a personal triumph, but no matter how good an artist's performance, nor how well liked he is by audiences and critics, it simply isn't helpful to be associated with shows that flop. In *The Bunch and Judy,* Fred and Adele between them had been paid 1,000 dollars a week. But after the show closed, Dillingham decided to let his option on them lapse. It would have brought them 1,250 dollars a week the following season and 1,500 dollars a week the season after. They bore no malice as he released them from their contract, realizing that Dillingham had really very little alternative. They understood the situation but had no immediate plans.

One or two offers were dangled, but Fred and Adele, still depressed from *The Bunch and Judy,* didn't respond, mainly because they knew Alex Aarons was trying to make arrangements for *For Goodness Sake* to open in London. Both Fred and Adele were keen to go to Europe and delighted when Aarons told them definitely that the deal was on.

London theatre audiences took to the Astaires immediately and gave them an overwhelming reception. The show, suitably Anglicized and bearing the new title, *Stop Flirting,* went to Liverpool, Glasgow and Edinburgh, before opening in London at the old Shaftesbury Theatre. It was a memorable debut and Fred and Adele's number, 'Oh Gee, Oh Gosh, Oh Golly, I Love You', in the middle of the second act stopped the show. From then it was success all the way and the performance ended with speeches of thanks from the stage and an enthusiastic party at Claridge's Hotel with Noel Coward, Gertrude Lawrence and Tallulah Bankhead among the many celebrities present. In *Steps in Time,* Fred recalls the scene: 'When we left the stage door, the Gallery First Nighters were en masse, some standing on top of our car, some on the hood — all over the place.' Six months later, when the show and the Astaires were the talk and the toast of London, Fred asked one fan how many times he had seen the show and was astonished to be told, '114 times'!

By now Fred was twenty-four, Adele twenty-five, and their act had matured. They were more adult, more professional, their dancing and their routines more sophisticated and polished. Fred played piano, they could be serious or funny, but it was all still a long way from the magical RKO film musicals which came, surprisingly, only a decade later, but after Adele had retired and Fred had Ginger as his partner.

In Hollywood, later in life, Fred Astaire shunned party-going and publicity, and is still almost anti-social in his determination to lead a quiet, private life. In London, during the run of *Stop Flirting,* was, however, one time when he seemed positively to revel in going out with Adele to parties and nightclubs. The famous Savoy Grill was a favourite rendezvous for supper, he spent weekends in the country with friends, enjoyed the sights of London and was perhaps more extrovert and relaxed than at any other time in his career. He and Adele quickly became part of the London society scene. He also found time for the horses. His first bet, on a horse called Tiger Rose, came home at four to one and he finished the day with extra cash in his pocket. It was the start of a life-long passion.

The pattern of his early career on stage allowed him to develop his interest in racing. Theatres at that time were not air-conditioned so in the steamy heat of American summers, even successful shows would suffer from falling attendances. It was quite normal for theatres to close down during the hot months and when this happened Fred and Adele would take off and spend a few weeks holidaying and relaxing generally. Adele was never very keen, but Fred would often spend a pleasant day at the race-track. It was in these days, incidentally, that Fred first indulged in his other life-time passions of golf and a whole series of card games.

In London, with a long-running show in prospect, Fred's appetite for racing was stimulated when he discovered that the sponsor of his show and a man who was prominent in London's theatreland, Sir Alfred Butt MP, kept horses and was a serious racegoer. They attended several meetings together. He could exchange racing gossip with George, his newly appointed English valet whose gift for dropping 'h's' was unrivalled, for George, too, was keen on the horses. Fred became such a regular supporter of the race game that while in London he had accounts with several of the prominent bookmaking companies, among them Ladbrokes.

It was one of the most exhilarating periods of Fred Astaire's life. *Stop Flirting* had opened on 30 May 1923, at a time when London unquestionably led the theatrical world in glamour, energy, style, status and success. Regular theatre-goers would see the show time and again. Fred and Adele took to them as friends and would exchange good natured banter with them across the footlights. It was also a time when the British aristocracy considered it smart and fashionable to go out to the theatre. After the show had transferred to the nearby Queen's Theatre, it was seen for the first time by the young Prince of Wales. His presence sent a buzz of excitement round the theatre and threw backstage preparations into turmoil. It was occasion enough for a member of the Royal Family to attend a theatrical performance, but the Prince of Wales was, into the bargain, a colourful and magnetic personality in his own right. Thirteen years later the Prince was to pitch the British Constitution into turmoil and to focus the attention of the world on to Buckingham Palace as he abdicated as King Edward VIII; but in the twenties he was concerned with changing the image of Royalty and in closing the gap which separated the Palace from the people. He mixed with ordinary people and enjoyed himself sharing their interests and habits. He enjoyed the theatre and, evidently, *Stop Flirting,* for he was there with his party again a few nights later and this time invited Fred and Adele to join him for supper at a well known London club after the show.

Typically reticent in later life, Fred Astaire remained guarded about his friendship with the British Royal Family, but it is well known that Queen Elizabeth, now the beloved Queen Mother, was always a great admirer. Some time after the present Queen Elizabeth was born, he and Adele received a personally written note from the Queen Mother, then the Duchess of York, inviting them to 'come and see the baby' and to stay for lunch; and when later the Duke and Duchess sailed out for an official tour of Australia, Fred and Adele sent a box of roses to the ship.

Meantime, *Stop Flirting* continued its successful run and after moving to the Strand Theatre, played as usual to capacity houses. Almost from the start the 'Oompah Trot' had been a show stopper. The run-around finish, which was now a trade mark of the Astaires, had first been suggested by the brilliant Teddy Royce for the show *The Love Letter* more than two years before. As choreographer to the show he had wanted some kind of comedy routine at one point. The words could be nonsense — so much the better if they were — and the dance routine a bit crazy, but clever. He got Adele to extend her arms forwards as if she were grabbing the handlebars of a bicycle and then told her to run around in a large circle singing 'oompah, oompah' repeatedly. He then told Fred to join her and together, shoulder to shoulder, they continued the circling. This was then tagged on to the end of a 'fun' number labelled 'Upside Down' and Fred and Adele performed the run-around oompah bit before finally running off-stage to complete the act.

All these years later, it sounds embarrassingly tame and uninspired, but in the early 1920s it was a stroke of pure genius and it brought the house down. Like many other novelty dances and routines which followed, it was exactly right for its time and in England it proved to be a sensation. Nicknamed 'The Oompah Trot', it was ideal therapy and relaxation for a nation caught between the end of a major war and an international economic depression, and it became a fashionable craze all over London with the nightclub regulars. It was so successful that Fred and Adele used it for ten years and featured it in five of their shows.

Another interesting musical point about *Stop Flirting* was the introduction of a George Gershwin number. 'I'll Build a Stairway to Paradise' not only added focus and dimension to an otherwise lightweight ensemble number, but also became a major hit song in its own right. The Astaires and Gershwin first crossed paths as they struggled for recognition in the United States. Fred and George struck up an instant friendship when the aspiring composer was a song plugger for Remicks, the New York publisher. Fred and Adele had ambitions to star in musical comedy. Gershwin wanted to write one and they day-dreamed together about the day when Gershwin would write a hit show for the Astaires to star in, not knowing just how prophetic they were being. A close friendship developed and often they would all go out together. But that first Gershwin show for the Astaires was still some years ahead. Meantime Fred and Adele Astaire enjoyed being the darlings of the London stage and were in constant demand for publicity gimmicks, product endorsements, personal appearances; they even made a gramophone record for the celebrated His Master's Voice label.

It seemed that London's theatreland would never tire of their endearing qualities as Fred and Adele continued their hectic life. As well as taking the show to Birmingham when the Strand Theatre had to honour a previous commitment, they enjoyed a weekend with Prince George; saw the sights of Paris on their first-ever visit to the French capital; and met all kinds of celebrities including Lord and Lady Louis Mountbatten, newspaper proprietor Esmond Harmsworth, Douglas Fairbanks, Mary Pickford, and Noel Coward.

Fred admitted that he and Adele didn't find much time for developing new ideas for their professional act. They were just too busy having fun and enjoying themselves. 'We adored London and all that was happening to us,' he said. But quietly he was a little disturbed that he couldn't persuade Adele to rehearse more. He was always the more serious of the two. Adele was easy-going, but in any case it didn't matter. Fred rehearsed on his own when he felt the need and the show continued to be a huge success anyway.

It seemed that *Stop Flirting* would go on for ever and certainly the London crowds didn't want the Astaires to leave, but professionally Fred and Adele acknowledged it would be wrong for them to be away from the United States for much longer in case they were forgotten there altogether. Adele was also feeling the strain and had been advised by her doctors to rest. They decided to make the break and *Stop Flirting* finally put up the shutters. It had run for an astonishing 418 performances and before the final curtain the atmosphere was deeply emotional with the audience joining in with the well-known songs and singing 'Auld Lang Syne' with the cast.

Yet the visit, for all the success, joy and fame it brought to Fred and Adele, was marred by one bitterly sad experience. For it was while they were in London that their much-loved father died. He had not been well for some time and as reports of his health gave cause for concern, Mrs Austerlitz, who had chaperoned her children to London though they were now adult, returned to America to look after him. After his death she rejoined Fred and Adele in London but was far from well herself and had to be treated in a nursing home for a few weeks.

Although Fred and Adele had spent considerable time away from their father they knew they had been seldom from his thoughts and that he had viewed their success with deep pride. He lived long enough to know how successful they had been in London and knew that all the early planning, ambition and sacrifices had brought the results they sought. But more was yet to come.

And it began almost as soon as they got back to New York.

THREE

Talk of the town– in New York and London

It was in 1915 that the undiscovered George Gershwin daydreamed about writing a hit Broadway musical for his then equally struggling friend, Fred Astaire, to star in. The dream came to life nine years later, soon after Fred and Adele's return to New York following their triumphant stay in London. *Lady, Be Good!* opened at the Liberty Theatre in New York on 1 December 1924 and ran for 330 performances. George Gershwin wrote the music, brother Ira the lyrics, and the show was produced by Alex A. Aarons and Vinton Freedley.

The plot, typically trite for a musical, concerned a brother and sister dance team turned out of their home because they couldn't pay the rent, and the various situations they found themselves in before meeting wealthy partners who solve the problem. Hardly inspiring, so it's not surprising, perhaps, that at first Fred almost turned down the idea. The show's provisional title can't have helped: during early rehearsals it was seriously contemplated as *Black-Eyed Susan!* But *Lady, Be Good!* had a modern format, some good comedy, the enchantment of Fred and Adele Astaire, and an inspiring score by George Gershwin. And it was an unqualified success. The title song was to become an Astaire classic, one of a number of songs which in later years he made his very own. Yet in the show, 'Lady, Be Good!' was sung by character comedian Walter Catlett, then a well-known stage performer and who, like Astaire, was later to make a name for himself in Hollywood.

Another great number which was destined to stand the test of time and become a standard of popular music was 'Fascinating Rhythm'. In the show it was a Fred and Adele dance number which owed much of its success to an idea of George Gershwin's. Dance director Sammy Lee had been striving with Fred and Adele to find a high-spot finish to the dance sequence of 'Fascinating Rhythm', but they had failed to come up with anything particularly inspiring. George then hit on the idea of repeating the last dance step over and over again, while also moving to the side, until the dancers finally disappeared off stage to conclude the sequence. Fred was doubtful because the step, in his own words, 'was a complicated precision rhythm thing in which we kicked out simultaneously as we crossed back and forth in front of each other with arm pulls and heads back'. Like the 'oompah' routine earlier, however, it was a huge success. It wasn't long before the 'repeat step' became a successful exit ploy for many dancers and certainly in *Lady, Be Good!* it always brought loud applause.

It is also said that Gershwin wrote 'The Man I Love' for Adele Astaire to sing in *Lady, Be Good!,* but according to Ira Gershwin, it was taken out because it tended to slow things up. The show was significant in a number of respects. It was the first time that George and Ira Gershwin had worked together on a Broadway show; the first time Aarons and Freedley had co-produced the same show; the first time George Gershwin and the Astaires had worked together on a much hoped-for Broadway hit; and, most significant of all perhaps, *Lady, Be Good!* was the background to Fred Astaire's first major solo dance.

Until then he had always danced with Adele in their shows. Fred's solo was the number 'The Half of It, Dearie, Blues', which was more of a song than a dance until he worked out a tap routine for it. Gershwin was so impressed that he often played piano for Fred at the private rehearsals which the latter insisted on doing to meet his own highly critical standards.

Lady, Be Good! was the first of a new style of Broadway musical — more sophisticated, more fluent, more professional. It heralded the era of the great American popular song and the haunting, lilting melodies of such astonishingly prolific and talented composers as Cole Porter, Jerome Kern, Irving Berlin and, of course, Gershwin himself. All were to have a profound effect on Fred Astaire's career in the years to come, and, of course, he on theirs.

Another feature in *Lady, Be Good!* was the speciality playing of the two pit orchestra pianos by Phil Ohman and Vic Arden. The audience loved it so much that an impromptu concert would sometimes develop after the show for the fans who refused to go home and Fred reckoned this 'two piano' novelty had much to do with the show's overall success.

Opening night at the Liberty brought lots of curtain calls, a self-conscious speech of thanks from the stage by Adele, and something of the adulation they had enjoyed in London. Press notices were good, especially for Adele, who continued to capture the bigger share of the publicity limelight. Life was satisfying for the Astaires, who were now being paid a joint salary of 1,750 dollars a week, which went up to 2,000 dollars a week once the show went on the road. They were big Broadway hits and *Lady, Be Good!* continued its success until it closed in New York in September 1925. A successful short tour followed, then it was back to England where the show opened in London at the Empire Theatre on 14 April 1926.

London theatreland was quick to prove it still remembered the Astaires. Fred had approached the show in typical fashion and once in London had begun serious rehearsal. He often worked late into the night. Not even the smallest item was left to chance and on the opening night the London audience responded with an enormous reception. The warmth of the welcome for Fred and Adele was greater than had been shown to any other American star and as the show developed, audience enthusiasm and delight mounted. The first night was a huge success and *Lady, Be Good!* continued for 326 performances. It had been three years since their earlier triumph in London with *Stop Flirting*. Their impact had been so great that *Lady, Be Good!* too, it seemed, could have continued to run for ever. But this time it was not left to the Astaires to bring down the final curtain because they didn't want American audiences to forget them. The decision was made for them and they even had to pull the theatre down to get them out! *Lady, Be Good!* continued to run until the old Empire Theatre in Leicester Square closed its doors prior to being demolished to make way for a cinema. The London production was soon booked solidly, well into the future. The General Strike posed something of a threat, but somehow the audiences got to the theatre, and, in the best tradition of the business, the show went on. This time in London, as before with *Stop Flirting,* both Fred and Adele Astaire were thrilled and excited by their success on stage and by their ready acceptance as Americans into the British social scene. They were the toast of London town.

As celebrities, they were invited to all the most important social occasions, introduced to all the biggest names in town, and developed a warm friendship with members of the British Royal Family. Their mother, who was always close at hand on their visits to London, was as fascinated and thrilled as the delighted British public. With a long run in prospect, Fred was also able to settle down and spend some time at the races. He mixed with influential owners and soon knew all the most important and successful jockeys and trainers. Good friendships were established. For £500 he bought a half share in a racehorse and was thrilled at last to be an owner; a long held ambition realized. Soon he owned a few

Fred and sister Adele in *Stop Flirting* at the Shaftesbury Theatre, London, 1923.

Funny Face, New York 1927 and London 1928, gave the Astaires seven featured musical numbers. With music and lyrics by the Gershwins, it was highly successful on both sides of the Atlantic.

Fred and the former Mrs Phyllis Potter after their wedding at the Brooklyn Supreme Court in 1933. It was to be a blissfully happy marriage.

A youthful looking Fred Astaire with co star Claire Luce in *The Gay Divorce* at the Palace Theatre, London, 1933/34.

Fred and Ginger together on film for the first time in *Flying Down to Rio* in 1933. Pictured is the famous 'Carioca' sequence, with seven grand pianos and a galaxy of supporting dancers.

'The Continental', from Fred and Ginger's second film together, *The Gay Divorcee* (*The Gay Divorce* in UK). It was a worthy successor to 'The Carioca'.

The 'togetherness' of Astaire and Rogers in 'I'll be Hard to Handle' from the 1935 production of *Roberta*.

opposite
The special chemistry which existed between Astaire and Rogers was well in evidence in *Top Hat*, despite the problems caused by Ginger's dress. It covered Fred in feathers.

Top billing as Fred and Ginger's names appear above the title for the first time in *Top Hat*.

Fred Astaire personified—the elegant tails, the white tie and that shining top hat worn at just the right angle. *Top Hat*, with a musical score by Irving Berlin, was for many people the best-ever Astaire-Rogers movie.

A nautical flavour as Fred taps it out on deck in the 1936 production of *Follow the Fleet*. Irving Berlin was again responsible for both the music and the lyrics.

'Bojangles of Harlem', with Fred paying tribute to noted coloured tap-dancer Bill Robinson, was a featured sequence in *Swing Time* (1936). 'Pick Yourself Up', 'The Way You Look Tonight' and 'A Fine Romance' all became Astaire standards.

The 1937 production of *Shall We Dance* included the memorable roller skating sequence. The film was sheer escapism as Fred, a ballet dancer, falls for a musical comedy star played by Ginger. For all the success of the partnership, neither was keen to prolong it and had no regrets when it ended two years later.

The famous golf ball scene from *Carefree*. The film was also notable for Fred and Ginger's first screen kiss and such Irving Berlin numbers as 'I Used To Be Colour Blind', 'The Yam' and, most of all, for 'Change Partners'.

more, and then a half share in a mare enabled him to go into breeding.

It's hard to say what makes a man like Fred Astaire take to racing. In the early days particularly — though his interest could have hardened perhaps later in life — he always seemed more fascinated and delighted by the fun of going to the races than by any extra money he might make from it. Doubtless the occasional wins were welcome, but the twinkle in the eye and that easy smile came more from the *idea* of success than in pocketing his winnings. He became so involved that during the running of *Lady, Be Good!* Fred had three jockeys racing for him, one no less a figure than Harry Wragg.

A great tribute to *Lady, Be Good!* and a particular thrill for the Astaires was the performance on 9 August 1926, when the show was honoured by the presence of His Majesty King George V and Queen Mary seated in the royal box. By this time the Prince of Wales, the Duke of York and the younger Prince George, now a close friend, had all seen the show, the Prince of Wales a number of times. It was thanks to Fred that His Royal Highness was there at that final nostalgic performance before the workmen moved in to pull the old theatre down. The Prince had only just returned to London and wanted to bring a party to bid a fond farewell to the hit show and the old theatre. Could Fred arrange a box? It wasn't easy, but Fred put the word round and with the help and co-operation of others, the Prince got his box and his party shared an emotional moment with a house packed to the last seat. It was a gala occasion with all the social notables there to share an historic theatrical experience. Setting the example was an exuberant Prince of Wales in full evening dress, so delighted and enthusiastic that he was seen to be on his feet and joining in at the back of the box as Fred and Adele did the familiar, show-stopping 'run-around'. Later the Astaires attended an impromptu supper party at St James's Palace at the invitation of the Prince of Wales and which went on until four in the morning, with Fred demonstrating to the Prince the latest dance sensation, the Black Bottom.

Fred Astaire's most memorable film roles with Ginger Rogers a decade later portrayed him as an easy-going, casual, carefree song-and-dance man. His true personality fell short of the film image. According to Adele he was a constant worrier. Those who worked with him knew him as an uncompromising perfectionist. He shunned publicity, disliked being interviewed, and made no secret, particularly in later life, of his near contempt for the media. Some said he was naturally shy and reserved and genuinely embarrassed at talking about himself and his career. But perhaps in London, in the 1920s, he came nearer in real life to the character of his most famous screen roles than at any other time in his life. He seemed to enjoy party-going and mixed well. Days were busy, life hectic and varied. After the old Empire closed, *Lady, Be Good!* embarked on a short tour of the provinces with similar success, but already George Gershwin had signed with Aarons and Freedley for a new show for the Astaires, provisionally called *Smarty,* back in America. Leaving London was hard after such glittering success, but as they boarded the SS *Homeric* for the transatlantic trip they did have some consolations. They had been paid well and their first Rolls-Royce was on its way back to America with them.

Early days of *Smarty* were a monumental let-down after the triumph of London, particularly as so much was expected of it. The Gershwins were responsible for the score, Robert Benchley did the words and a brand new theatre called the Alvin was ready for them. But nothing seemed to go right and in the run-up dates prior to the much-heralded New York opening, audiences were poor and reaction cool. Major re-writes became essential if the show was to be saved. Benchley slaved but finally gave up, being committed by this time to another project. New writers Fred Thompson and Paul Gerard Smith were brought in, scrapped most of what had been done and started again, almost from scratch. While this was going on, the disconsolate cast were struggling with the original version and playing to meagre and unresponsive audiences in Philadelphia and Washington. The new version finally emerged with a new title and when *Funny Face* opened in New York at the Alvin Theatre on 22 November 1927, it was another instant hit for the Astaires.

The plot again was thin, but that didn't matter. Audiences came to see Fred and Adele Astaire, dancing, singing and making fun. *Funny Face* completed 250 performances on Broadway before opening in England at London's Prince's Theatre where it ran for another 263 shatteringly successful performances. The final score by George Gershwin, with brother Ira providing the lyrics, was outstanding after all the earlier doubts and problems. ''S Wonderful' was to emerge as a popular standard and although Adele sang it in *Funny Face* it was subsequently to be a song synonymous with Fred.

The relaxed, casual sentiment and easy-flowing melody were just right for his debonair style of presentation. Inconceivably, looking back, Ira Gershwin had trouble with the lyrics of the song. In some quarters they were considered a little too suggestive, and one critic went so far as to point out that it included an obscene phrase. He told Ira it just wasn't possible to use the word 'amorous'.

Less popular but nonetheless a fine melody, perhaps underrated by all except the serious student of Gershwin melody, was 'My One and Only', which Fred sang in New York with the delicious Gertrude MacDonald. Fred and Adele's familiar 'run-around' sequence was featured in a novelty number called 'The Babbitt and the Bromide' and the successful duo-piano arrangement was retained from *Lady, Be Good!* The original pianists Phil Ohman and Vic Arden appeared in the American presentation, Jacques Frey and Mario Braggiotti in London. The show was reckoned to have a fairly heavy comedy line, provided by William Kent (who also appeared in *Lady, Be Good!*), and Victor Moore, who later became a very famous funny man both on stage and in films. In London Sidney Howard took over the Victor Moore part and the famous Leslie Henson the William Kent role. Both were featured in what 1920s analyst Alan Jenkins described as 'one of the great "drunk" scenes of all time'.

An incident at the end of the American run of *Funny Face* had caused anxiety on Broadway. One weekend in July 1928 the Astaires were enjoying themselves as house-guests of a well-known millionaire playboy at his estate just outside New York. Adele jumped at the chance to take a ride with her host in his new speed-boat. It was a sunny day and the water was calm, but suddenly the boat blew up. Adele was taken to hospital immediately with serious burns and stayed there for several days. The word got about that her career was over and she wouldn't work again, but the rumours were scotched when it was announced that Adele would go to London with Fred and their mother as planned for the opening there of *Funny Face.*

In 1928, when *Funny Face* opened in London, musical comedy in the traditional mould continued to be popular. The society crowd was still important and audiences attended the theatre in evening dress before enjoying a good dinner at some fashionable restaurant. The pattern on stage was hardly more flexible and, no matter what the storyline, included good chorus numbers, some tap-dancing, plenty of comedy and, if possible, a 'drunk' scene. But the format was changing and Jenkins reckons that *Funny Face* was one of the last American musical comedies of its kind to come to London. Not known then was a truth far more significant for the Astaire brother and sister partnership, for *Funny Face* was destined to be the last show in London in which Fred and Adele would appear together, and the last-ever London show for Adele.

In the meantime, the Astaires had become the 1920s version of the modern-style transatlantic commuter and when *Funny Face* closed in London after 263 performances (thirteen more than in New York) they were soon sailing for home yet again for another show on Broadway.

It is true to say that in the 1920s no Americans had more impact on the London theatre scene than Fred and Adele Astaire. In a sense they pioneered the popular trend, though many years in advance, of top American stars appearing in the West End. These were happy, energetic and jubilant days for the Astaires and if Fred in later life ever did look back on his career — though he steadfastly refused to admit it! — then it must have been with pleasure, happiness and contentment on the days he spent in Britain.

Sharing their enormous success, and in no small part responsible for it, was producer Alex Aarons. He had the vision to recognize potential talent and had brought Fred and Adele together professionally with George Gershwin in a phenomenally successful partnership. He had guided and shaped their careers, and had the happy knack of blending astuteness and luck in shows which, for Fred and Adele, were outstanding winners. He and Fred were great friends over many years. The bond of trust was so great that in the early days no contract existed between them. Fred once said he signed their first contract on the lid of a luggage trunk on board ship as they were waiting to disembark at New York after their first major success in London.

But now their sequence of success together was sadly to end. The legendary American impresario Florenz Ziegfeld made no secret of his interest in the Astaires. He was a big man in the business even then and his Ziegfeld Follies had set a vital and imaginative trend in musical extravaganzas. Ziegfeld had approached Fred and Adele during the New York production of *Funny Face,* wanting them to stay on Broadway when the run ended, but Aarons was already in England fixing up the London production and the Astaires didn't want to sever connections without talking to him first. Reluctantly, they declined the Ziegfeld offer, pointing out that they might well be available in 1929 after the London production of *Funny Face.*

Alex Aarons got to know about the meeting on his return to America and, in Fred's own words, 'hit the ceiling'. Fred pointed out that he thought the change would be good for his and Adele's careers and, in any event, he didn't see it as a permanent arrangement. The idea was that the Astaires would return to Alex after doing the Ziegfeld show with an even more formidable reputation and that would also benefit Aarons. Aarons remained unconvinced. He felt that despite Ziegfeld's reputation and obvious talent, he wouldn't know how to handle Fred and Adele to get the best from them. Neither, of course, did he want his biggest stars to desert him.

But Fred was excited by Ziegfeld's interest and thrilled to receive, during the latter part of the London run of *Funny Face,* a cable from Ziegfeld mentioning 'a wonderful idea for you to co-star with Marilyn Miller'. This young lady was considered in the late 1920s as 'New York's Queen of the Musical' and her reputation was such that when Fred and Adele arrived back in New York, she was doing the ultimate chic and fashionable thing — making a picture over in Hollywood.

The Ziegfeld association theoretically should have brought Fred and Adele another major hit. It wasn't for the lack of trying or investment that Alex Aarons' worst fears were to be realized. Ziegfeld bought an original idea from Noel Coward and hired Louis Bromfield and William McGuire to write it and shape it for the Broadway stage. Provisionally titled *Tom, Dick and Harry,* the show finally emerged as *Smiles,* but Fred, in his autobiography some years later, was to describe the whole sorry experience as 'devastating'. Bromfield, who had at one time been considered a writer of some promise, did not apparently produce the anticipated blockbuster of a script, while McGuire, whose reputation as a drinker preceded him, seemed not to have mended his ways significantly. When you add to these two crippling influences a rather weak story about a Salvation Army girl adopted and brought up by a Frenchman, German and an Italian; composer Vincent Youmans struggling to produce his best material; and Flo Ziegfeld's alleged motive in putting on the show in the first place — his infatuation with Marilyn Miller, according to one report — it is perhaps surprising that the show got completed at all.

It very nearly wasn't and one source went so far as to say that the script had only been half written by the time work started on it. Certainly, a disastrous tryout in Boston on 28 October 1930 prompted panic re-writes and revisions of all kinds and the company stayed there an extra week trying to pull things together. *Smiles* opened at the Ziegfeld Theatre on Broadway on 18 November 1930. It ran for just sixty-three performances and closed, having lost for its backers according to one estimate, more than half a million dollars.

Nonetheless, *Smiles* was significant in one respect. Fred's ingenious choreography for 'Say, Young Man of Manhattan', a number which was virtually lost in *Smiles,* was later used with phenomenal success in the film *Top Hat.* He used a cane in the form of a gun, shooting down a long line of male dancers dressed in white tie and tails and, of course, top hats. As each of them fell to the ground, he emphasized the action with a loud tap. The idea apparently came to Fred at four o'clock one morning as he lay in bed awake and he had leaped out of bed, grabbed an umbrella and worked out the routine there and then. Five years later Fred mentioned it to Irving Berlin. He wrote the song *Top Hat* specially for the number, and *Top Hat* was used as the title for the picture.

Despite the disaster of *Smiles,* the professional reputation of Fred and Adele Astaire remained intact. Fred, ever the perfectionist, considered his own performance 'inadequate', but most of the critics were not prepared to share that view, and songwriters Arthur Schwartz and Howard Dietz weren't put off as they looked towards the casting of their new show, *The Band Wagon.* But before leaving *Smiles,* mention should be made of the significant names in the cast list. Harmonica player Larry Adler appeared in the show and produced one or two bright spots, and way down at the bottom of the cast list were also the names of Bob Hope and Virginia Bruce.

A short trip to Europe helped Fred and Adele sweep the disaster of *Smiles* away, but before sailing they signed to do *The Band Wagon* on their return. The prospect was exciting. It was booked into the New Amsterdam Theatre on Broadway, where the Astaires had always wanted to work, Arthur Schwartz and Howard Dietz were a respected and talented songwriting team, some important names had already agreed to appear, and, perhaps most important of all, the concept of the show in the revue format was fresh and original. It even incorporated the very first revolving stage. Fred and Adele saw it as being ideal in casting away the shadows of *Smiles.* Another flop immediately after *Smiles* might have hindered their career, so the timing was good, luck played its part, and Fred and Adele looked forward to *The Band Wagon.* They even celebrated by dropping their old 'run around' routine.

The Band Wagon was to prove the perfect antidote. It was everything that *Smiles* was not. Rehearsals developed well. The organization was smooth and professional. Schwartz and Dietz proved to be diligent and uncomplicated, as well as being gifted and able, and there were no major last minute re-writes to worry about. Fred, particularly, was busy in the show, appearing in numerous sketches along with his dance numbers. *The Band Wagon* was later to be judged as one of the best revues ever to appear on Broadway and certainly the immediate reaction of the critics was enthusiastic; box office takings were also very healthy. It played on Broadway for 260 performances before taking to the road on a successful tour. Then, with little fuss, hardly any display of emotion, and only a few brief tears, Adele Astaire retired from the theatre on 5 March 1932, after her performance in *The Band Wagon* at the Illinois Theatre in Chicago. She was married in May that year though Fred, because he was still appearing in *The Band Wagon* (and now partnered by Vera Marsh), was unable to be there.

Fred enjoyed *The Band Wagon* immensely. Although there was no story to worry about, there was a lot for Fred to do — character bits, comedy, various skits as well as singing and dancing. The musical score was tuneful and enjoyable, but the song which was to become one of the most famous standards of all time was said to have been rushed out by Arthur Schwartz, one morning long before daybreak in a matter of minutes. Howard Dietz had written the lyrics after reading a book called 'Dancers in the Dark'. In *The Band Wagon,* 'Dancing in the Dark', as the combined Dietz-Schwartz effort finally emerged, was a dance number for Fred and Tilly Losch. Nobody guessed then just what an impact the song was to make on popular music.

When the final curtain dropped on *The Band Wagon,* Fred found himself alone and undecided professionally. Privately, he was not in the least disturbed. A lady named Phyllis Potter had suddenly come into his life during the run of *The Band Wagon,* and Fred has to thank his interest in golf for bringing them together, and his other passion — racing — for giving him his first sight of her. The latter was at Belmont Park, but they weren't introduced, though Fred knew Phyllis's uncle, Henry Bull, over some years as president of the Turf and Field Club. The fateful meeting took place at the luxury home of Mrs Graham Fair Vanderbilt one Sunday afternoon. A tournament held on her private golf course adjacent to her home was preceded by luncheon, and Fred and his friend Charlie Payson shared a table with Phyllis and her friend Dorothy Fell. Fred was captivated, but Phyllis was a popular lady and, as Fred later explained, had so many beaux that he had to mow them down, one at a time.

Phyllis was twenty-three and had a young son, Peter, by a former marriage. She had been brought up by Mr and Mrs Henry Bull. The stage was new territory for her, but after some lengthy persuasion, she agreed to go to see Fred in *The Band Wagon* and thought he was very good. From then on Fred systematically pursued her though at first she appeared reluctant to change her lifestyle, and was seen by Fred in the company of a succession of escorts. Fred's career hung in the balance, as he drifted along in a kind of vacuum. He wanted Phyllis much more than his career and finally he got what he wanted. They were married on 12 July 1933.

FOUR

Leaving the stage behind

Fred Astaire was almost thirty years old when his sister left the partnership to get married. It was all of twenty-five years since old man Austerlitz had packed them off with their mother to New York City to seek their fame and fortune in the theatre. In all that time Fred had never had another stage partner, yet when Adele left he was remarkably unprepared. It wasn't as if the parting was unexpected. Adele had made no secret of her wish to marry when the right man came into her life. She never pretended to be as dedicated or disciplined as Fred. In a sense she didn't have to be because as she grew older she wasn't ambitious to continue on the stage for the rest of her life. And once she retired to marry, she never returned.

Adele had grown into an attractive personality, fun-loving and vivacious, and had not gone short of boyfriends when she wanted them. She had even been engaged before. She found the grind of rehearsal harder to sustain than Fred and didn't worry about, or work on, their routines always with quite the same devotion. A number of times he spoke to her when he felt she was falling short and there is the classic case during the New York run of *Funny Face* when Adele arrived at the theatre later than usual, having had what was described as a cocktail too many. Fred had to hold the curtain for five minutes while he stuffed smelling salts under her nose. He 'carried' her for much of the first number, but pulling her around in the dances was harder and less convincing. He made light of it for the audience, who seemed not too disturbed, if somewhat puzzled, by what might have appeared to be an unusually individualistic performance that evening. In the wings waiting to take their bow at the end of the number he slapped her sharply on both cheeks before dragging her out on stage again, telling her to take her bow . . . and smile.

Fred quickly forgave this isolated lapse by Adele. On himself, he would have been much harder, though his self-discipline and dedication would have made such an incident, in his case, unthinkable.

Fred admitted that he and Adele had talked about the future; that they both understood that one day she would very likely want to get married, and at that point the end of the partnership would be in sight. But curiously, he never worked out what he might do if and when that happened, despite his entire career hanging on it. He seemed far more concerned in Adele's general welfare, in helping her to brush off particularly insistent, though unwanted, 'stage door' admirers and, as they grew older, in hoping that when the time came she would choose the right man with whom to share the rest of her life.

Surely the signs were highly recognizable as he witnessed her relationship with Lord Charles Cavendish blossom. The pair had first met on the closing night of *Funny Face* in London. It called for a celebration and well-wishers crowded into Adele's dressing-room. Among them was Lord Charles Cavendish. Nothing much seriously happened until he went to America to work. He had gone there to join a New York banking company called J.P. Morgan and was soon seeing Adele regularly. He was seven years younger than Adele, but it was obvious that they were deeply attracted to each other and might even have married sooner had *Smiles* been a success. As it was, Adele didn't want to end her stage career with a miserable failure, but prior to the opening of *The Band Wagon* on Broadway, she did tell Fred that the romance had been developing over the past six months or so, and that it was serious. She wanted to retire and, if possible, at the peak of her career. *The Band Wagon* was clearly to satisfy that ambition.

There was also a nasty situation to deal with following the failure of *Smiles*. Both Fred and Adele liked Flo Ziegfeld as a person. He was flamboyant, a colourful character with an expansive personality and an easy way of spending money. But it could be argued that his general lack of control over the production of *Smiles* had contributed substantially to its downfall. Perhaps his first mistake was to buy only the outline of the basic Noel Coward story. His next was in engaging writer William Anthony McGuire, who, it was reported, spent most of his time drinking and chasing the show's chorus girls. Ziegfeld himself continued to display more interest in his leading lady, Marilyn Miller, than in the problems of the show — an infatuation which was finally to end in his sending Miss Miller for what was declared to be routine medical treatment but which those in the know knew to be an abortion.

But Fred and Adele's problem was that they were owed wages from Ziegfeld for *Smiles*. They sued him, claiming 10,000 dollars for wages they insisted they had not received. They reckoned they had received only 2,000 of the 12,000 dollars due to them when the show opened. In the end, they were awarded 4,000 dollars. Both Fred and Adele had lost heavily in the Wall Street Crash, and money, for all their success, was important to them. However, Adele now had other more lasting things on her mind.

Charles Cavendish was the second son of the Duke of Devonshire, a member of the British aristocracy, and Fred and he became firm friends. The wedding was a big affair at the Devonshire's classical and magnificent mansion of Chatsworth in Derbyshire, the ceremony itself being held in the tiny church. Fred said that he never felt upset about the prospect of Adele's retirement and, considering all their time together, they parted professionally without ceremony and with a matter-of-factness that seems extraordinary. Adele never again seemed to yearn for the lost glamour of the footlights, while Fred, the life he had known for twenty years severed, seemed content to abandon himself to whatever future happened to come along. He wasn't sad, didn't seem disappointed and displayed little if any sense of ambition. Parting, as he said later, was not a sad affair. 'There were a few tears, but we soon laughed our way out of it.'

He put far more into his pursuit of Phyllis and quite early on was talking to her about marriage, though she considered they had not known each other long enough. In the meantime, *The Band Wagon* ran its natural course, after which Fred's career came to a temporary halt. It wasn't that he didn't receive offers. Flo Ziegfeld for one tried to sign him up. Instead he went to Europe, visited Adele and Charles at their new home at Lismore Castle in Ireland and then went on to London. Phyllis was in London and was furious when he said he didn't care whether he worked or not. She told him that if he had any serious thoughts about marrying her, he had better do something positive about his career.

He sailed back to the United States, having pledged to look seriously at an offer he had previously received to feature in a musical called *Gay Divorce*. When he was told that Cole Porter had agreed to do the score, he signed immediately. There was some time before rehearsals began, so he took himself off to Europe again to be with Phyllis.

Gay Divorce was a formidable test for Fred Astaire. He was without Adele for the first time and he could be sure that the critics would examine his performance minutely and would not pass over a good story for any personal feelings of friendship towards him. Claire Luce, an attractive blonde and extremely competent dancer, was his new partner and no less vulnerable because the comparisons with Adele would be inevitable. In the circumstances, the quality or otherwise of the music was of secondary importance even to a quizzical audience who were equally eager to make their judgements.

Adding to the tension was Fred's own dilemma. He had signed to do *Gay Divorce* quickly enough after Phyllis's intervention, but he was unsure about his professional future. Adele's departure had brought a natural break in the familiar rhythm. Times were changing anyway. Dancing was what he knew, what he enjoyed doing, but he seemed less stimulated by the prospect of continuing in the theatre.

Meantime, *Gay Divorce* opened at the Ethel Barrymore Theatre on Broadway on 29 November 1932. Produced by Dwight Deere Wiman and Tom Weatherly and directed by Howard Lindsay, both music and lyrics were by Cole Porter. The show was to be special because it provided the first public hearing of Porter's haunting 'Night and Day'. Fred worked well with dance director Carl Randall and for 'Night and Day' produced a routine which he felt was fresh and different from the kind of thing he had done with Adele. In the circumstances, opening night was nerve-racking. The critics had a field day. They made it clear that in their opinion Adele's absence left Fred wanting. The press notice most often quoted read: 'Fred Astaire stops every now and then to look off-stage towards the wings as if he were hoping his titled sister, Adele, would come out and rescue him.' But perhaps this was more a criticism of the plot or the show than it was of Astaire.

Considering the impact that he was to make later both as a singer and an actor, this comment is interesting: 'But as an actor and a singer, Astaire does not approach the perfection he achieves with his feet. In *Gay Divorce* it must be recorded that he has perhaps taken on too much of a task.'

Critics are not always reliable prophets. Certainly, you'd be hard pressed to claim that *Gay Divorce* was one of the greatest musicals of all time, but neither was it a desperate flop. It ran for a very creditable 248 performances on Broadway, only two short of *Funny Face,* and went on to add another 108 performances when it moved to the Palace Theatre in London. The showbiz writers, positively light-headed and certainly blinded at the prospect of what they saw to be the somewhat freakish spectacle of Fred on stage for the first time without Adele, failed almost to a man to recognize the phenomenal potential in Cole Porter's haunting melody, 'Night and Day'. The public, on the other hand, were more perceptive, knowing and objective. They made 'Night and

Day' one of the greatest popular classics of all time and a song which, as the years rolled by, was identified strongly with Astaire.

Looking back nearly fifty years, it's hard to quantify Astaire's first performance without his sister, in *Gay Divorce*. Critics seem largely to have been unimpressed. Some paying customers were doubtless drawn by the novelty of seeing Fred without Adele. Those who helped pull the strings without being fully in the spotlight appear to have harboured some anxiety at the prospect.

Composer Arthur Schwartz, for instance, tried to prepare the way. By the time he and Howard Dietz got around to producing the score for *The Band Wagon,* Adele had already told them it would be her last show. 'That was why we built *The Band Wagon* more around Fred,' said Schwartz. 'Until then Fred had always been the stereotyped black tie and tails semi-society man, the handsome playboy type, while Adele was the comedienne who also sang and danced with him,' explained Schwartz. Anticipating the stage void resulting from Adele's departure, Schwartz and Dietz developed Fred's performance, giving him a bigger bite at the comedy and cutting back the sophistication. In one sketch they even cast him as a hunchbacked beggar, who waited at the stage door for a big star. Explained Arthur Schwartz some years later: 'It turned into a fantasy sequence in which he imagined himself dancing with her. That was a real risk considering Fred's image.' Yet it became one of the big successes of *The Band Wagon.*

Someone who had no doubts about Fred's ability to carry on successfully without his sister was Adele herself. She more than anyone was in a position to assess her brother's individual talent, his dedication and his sheer professionalism. After seeing his success in *Gay Divorce,* she summed up her attitude neatly: 'I must have been a drawback for years,' she remarked.

There was a gap of a few months between the closing of *Gay Divorce* in America and its opening in Britain into which were crammed three major events for Astaire. He took his first steps in Hollywood though, typically, he was doubtful that he could build a future career in the movies. He also married Phyllis Potter which gave him enormous pleasure and delight, but once in London preparing for the opening, he was saddened by the news that Adele had lost the baby she and Charles Cavendish had been expecting.

But the enthusiasm of the West End's first-nighters was a tonic. They gave him and his new co-star Claire Luce a warm-hearted welcome and showed him without reservation that he was still one of their favourite Americans. That first performance was seen by one of Fred's greatest admirers and a firm friend, Prince George,

who was among numerous backstage visitors after the show to con-
gratulate him on what had all the signs of yet another outstanding
success. But just when Fred particularly wanted to make a good
impression because Prince George was out front, the worst happened.
During a difficult and complicated routine they stumbled and
Fred's heart skipped a beat, though nothing amiss was noticed by
the audience. But for poor Claire Luce the repercussions were far
more serious. She hurt a hip in the fall and, although she was able to
continue for the remainder of the run of the show, it continued to
trouble her and was sadly to put an end to her career.

As Fred was later to indicate, everyone seemed to feel that *Gay
Divorce* was a good choice for his first 'solo' appearance. 'No one
said anything about my being unable to carry on without Adele. I
felt that the difficult obstacle had been surmounted.'

Fred had agreed to a maximum six months with *Gay Divorce* in
Britain and that first performance gave every indication that it was
to be another major hit for the likeable American whom British
audiences had taken so much into their hearts. When Adele saw the
show with her husband some weeks later it was the first time she
had seen Fred from out front as a member of an audience. The
show went perfectly. Fred was in fine form and said he threw in lots
of extra bits for Adele's benefit, and was proud when the audience,
who knew Adele was present, clapped her at the intermission and
she stood to acknowledge the applause with a 'little bow and a wave
to the gallery'.

It was while he was in London that his future career was beginning to take shape in Hollywood. For a while Astaire was oblivious
to the success of the first tentative steps he had made in the movies
just a few months before. He was virtually certain he had made little
if any impact there, but as the news of his success began to filter
through to London, it added to the joyous time he had in England
while playing *Gay Divorce.* One day a cable arrived which hinted
strongly at the impact he had made on his short sojourn in
Hollywood. Another time Fred and Phyllis bumped into Douglas
Fairbanks senior while having supper in the Savoy Grill. 'What do
you mean by revolutionizing the movie industry?' is how Fairbanks
greeted Astaire. He had just seen *Flying Down to Rio,* Fred's first
major film, and thought it was terrific. 'You've got something
absolutely new,' he said.

These were particularly happy months for Fred. He had pursued
and won the girl he loved; captivated audiences left him in no doubt
that he was an outstanding success without the support of Adele;
and it looked as though the doubts and uncertainties about the way

his career might develop were being solved for him. The news coming out of Hollywood continued to be enthusiastic which promised well for the future.

It was appropriate that Fred Astaire's stage career should end on a highly successful note in the West End of London. The enormous success he and Adele had enjoyed as a team had given them both a special kind of affection for British audiences and they had shown conclusively that they loved him just as much even if Adele was not there with him. One of his lasting memories from the 1920s and early 1930s spent in London was the friendships established with members of the British Royal Family. A particular thrill was the performance he and Claire Luce gave of 'Night and Day' at the Theatre Royal in Drury Lane at the Royal Command Performance, and in later years Queen Elizabeth, wife of George VI, made no secret of her admiration and enjoyment of the Astaires.

FIVE

'Making a stab at Hollywood'

For all his phenomenal success Fred Astaire never gave much thought to carving out a career for himself. By 1933 he was finely balanced professionally. Without Adele he had no zest for stage work, yet had no positive idea what he should do instead.

Hollywood came up with the answer and virtually made up his mind for him. With the coming of the 'talkies' a few years earlier, the movies had extended its vistas prodigiously. There was now the added dimension of sound so that it was possible to talk and sing on film as well as dance and act. This led quickly to one of the greatest money-spinning film phenomena of all time, 'the Hollywood musical'.

The beginnings were tentative and modest enough with low budget offerings which simply added song and dance to a normal storyline. The deliberately created 'musical' followed as a natural development and once the enormous potential of the all-singing, all-dancing formula was recognized, Hollywood squeezed it dry. For more than a decade it seemed that every other film was a musical. Budgets soared as the staging became ever more elaborate and the major studios elbowed each other out of the way, presenting one extravaganza after another. They were enormous and elaborate productions, none more so than those astonishing and often bizarre Busby Berkeley film fantasies featuring scores of gorgeous showgirls in bathing-costumes or glamorous gowns. As the music echoed round the cinema, the girls would form geometric patterns on elaborate stairways, or group themselves around swimming-pools. Sequence movements predominated and the girls smiled beautifully and moved gracefully. Unusual camera angles from high above, and from below the waterline of the giant tanks used to stage some of the aquatic sequences, picked out the kaleidoscopic patterns as the girls glided from one formation to another. This was film-making at its most unconventional and it offered escapism from the depression and gloom of the 1930s.

Hollywood had a sharp eye for new talent, a near insatiable

appetite, and had already poached New York for many of its Broadway stars, Ginger Rogers among them, who was first attracted to the film colony in 1930. Astaire's first contact with the industry had been as early as 1931 when he and Adele had done a short sequence as a screen test for a proposed cinema version of *Funny Face*. Later, during the American run of *Gay Divorce,* the idea of movie work was suggested to Fred by Mervyn Le Roy, a director with Warner Brothers. He had seen the show and thought it would make a good film, but back in Hollywood his enthusiasm was not shared by film boss Jack Warner and the idea, at that time, came to nothing.

The trouble was that Fred didn't look too much like the conventional Hollywood hero. His face was too thin and bony, his hair already receding, and altogether he seemed too lightweight for a film career. Not that Fred was bothered. By now he was besotted with Phyllis Potter and his ambition to marry her as soon as possible meant much more to him than deciding what course his career should take.

When the big chance came, it was deceptively casual and informal. One day Fred, who by now had virtually decided to leave the stage and 'make a stab at Hollywood and the movies', bumped into Eddie McIlvaine, an old friend who was currently associated with Leland Hayward. Astaire and Hayward had first met during Fred and Adele's stage days when Hayward, then in the agency business, had booked them into their first night-club engagement at what was at the time reputed to be a record 5,000 dollars a week for a six-week period. Hayward by now was influential in film circles and, having talked with McIlvaine, recommended Fred to David Selznick, head of RKO Radio. Selznick had on schedule a big musical called *Flying Down to Rio,* with music by the celebrated Vincent Youmans, and agreed that Astaire might fit in well.

Just one complication could have threatened Fred's Hollywood debut, as Hayward called round to Astaire's dressing-room at the theatre to give him the good news. Fred was committed to the London production of *Gay Divorce* after the show had closed in America. But fortunately there seemed enough time for him to go to Hollywood for the filming after closing *Gay Divorce* in New York and before moving on to London for the scheduled opening later in the year. Contracts were signed and, flushed with success, Fred asked Phyllis to marry him. She hesitated, not wishing to be rushed into marriage on the basis of Fred's impending departure to Hollywood. So Fred suggested he go out to Hollywood on his own, do the picture, and they should be married when he got back. In

Steps in Time Fred describes Phyllis's reaction like this: 'She said, "No, that's not good. If you go away from me to Hollywood, you'll start running around with some of those girls out there and, whether you do or not, I'd always think you did, so we'd better get married right now, as soon as possible".'

But there was more to it than that. Phyllis Potter's unhappy marriage to a Wall Street stockbroker had ended in a Reno divorce in early 1932 and she had been given custody of their three-year-old son, Peter. Phyllis, however, was anxious to have Peter with her for more of the time and went back to court for permission. Once she had been granted what amounted to virtual total custody of Peter by the Supreme Court in Brooklyn on 12 July 1933, she felt the way was then clear to marry Fred. In quite a dramatic sequence of events, the judge, who only minutes earlier had granted Phyllis additional custody of Peter, performed the marriage ceremony in the court library. A celebration at Fred's New York apartment was followed by a one-day honeymoon on a friend's yacht cruising up the Hudson River. On 14 July, Mr and Mrs Astaire boarded a commercial flight to California and after twenty-six hours arrived at Burbank Airport. Fred had no thought of being an overnight success in Hollywood. He was very doubtful about making the grade at all, but by now, having mentally jettisoned his stage career, he was looking more and more towards films as solving the problem of what to do next. He could also do with the money after his and Adele's losses following the Wall Street Crash.

Friends and colleagues back in New York hadn't been encouraging. Most were sure that, after spending so many years on the stage, he would miss the immediate audience reaction and the instant applause of the theatre. Surprisingly, he soon found he missed none of it. He took easily and naturally to working in a film studio environment and almost from the start enjoyed performing for the cameras more than for a theatre audience.

Moreover, he took almost instinctively to what he called the 'simplicity of Hollywood home life, if you chose to have it that way'. He and Phyllis would go to bed early and get up early, a routine dictated by early starts at the studio. He said later in *Steps in Time:* 'The weather was beautiful, and I never failed to appreciate those nice mornings. The feeling has never changed. I am always glad to get back.'

Events had taken a hectic turn after Fred had signed his contract with RKO. His scheduled film, *Flying Down to Rio,* was not yet ready for him to work on, so he found himself loaned out to MGM for a guest appearance in a major Joan Crawford-Clark Gable movie called *Dancing Lady.* Other Hollywood favourites of the day in the cast were Franchot Tone, Nelson Eddy and Robert Benchley. The storyline featured Crawford as a chorus girl who becomes a big star. Fred played himself in what he described as a backstage yarn in which the dance director, played by Clark Gable, says to the leading lady: 'I've got Fred Astaire here from New York to dance with you — Oh Fred, would you come here please?' — and out came Fred to be seen for the very first time on the silver screen.

Fred was depressed and demoralized when he saw those first shots of himself because he looked so thin and angular. But people whose opinions were more professionally important seemed happy enough with the results. His first weeks in Hollywood were happy, exciting, hectic and successful. Thrust immediately into the production of *Dancing Lady,* he was given no time to ease himself gently towards new techniques and a dramatically different working environment. The way they did things seemed disjointed and disorganized against the structured, more formal precision-rehearsed routines of the Broadway stage, but Astaire responded enthusiastically and was a quick learner.

Friends on the set helped him settle. Jerry Asher of MGM's publicity department, says Fred, 'sensed very quickly the difficulties of a greenhorn, fresh from the New York stage' and helped him enormously as he worked to acclimatize himself to the vastness of the studio lot and the pressures of what would now be called 'media demands'. When it came to shooting the dance sequences with Joan Crawford, dance director Sammy Lee, an old friend from Broadway days, was helpful and understanding, and Fred later gratefully acknowledged the patience of his first film director, Bob Leonard.

Being new he didn't say much, hardly expressed an opinion, but in the dance sequences particularly, he noticed how things were done and even in those first weeks began to work out his own ideas and how he might apply them should he ever get the chance.

Joan Crawford, even by then established as a big star with numerous films behind her, was, it seems, kind and considerate, despite the accusations of toughness and eccentricity made many years later in her biography, written by her daughter. She invited Fred and Phyllis to her home a number of times and seems to have made a genuine attempt to make the newcomers feel at home.

Influencing everything, of course, was Fred's utter delight and supreme contentment at being married to Phyllis. They were devoted to each other and, although Phyllis took longer to settle in Hollywood, they were both soon to look upon the film capital as home. Their wedding bliss blossomed into a model marriage, unscathed by gossip or scandal, and admired by close friends and associates alike. The late David Niven, who was to become a lifelong friend, saw them as the ideal couple. In *Bring on the Empty Horses* he said that the combination of Fred and Phyllis was a joy to behold. 'Theirs was the prototype of a gloriously happy marriage,' he wrote.

Fred's work on *Dancing Lady* lasted several weeks. His was a relatively small part, but it was perfect for getting to know the ways of film-making and for building up confidence in a totally new method of working. Against the criteria of film-making, *Dancing Lady* found it hard to stand beside the best of the Busby Berkeley musical extravaganzas. Despite its lavish budget, it has been criticized by some commentators for ponderousness and static camera work.

But in 1933, when the film went out on release, Hollywood was beginning to approach its golden years and the film studios' main concern was to satisfy a lavish hunger at the box-office. Picture-going was soon to become a habit. Audiences saw a movie once or twice a week, sometimes more often than that. They didn't wait for a good film to come along. It was the way the Western World spent a night out.

Though perhaps falling short by critical standards, *Dancing Lady* nonetheless was a major hit, making a lot of money for MGM and giving Fred the obvious advantage of being part of an outstanding box-office success on his film debut.

By the time Astaire moved on to the RKO set, the cast of *Flying Down to Rio* had not been completed and it was a couple of days before he heard for the first time that his partner was likely to be Ginger Rogers.

But Fred worried that Ginger might not want to dance with him. She had been in Hollywood for three years and was something of a veteran in film-making. More particularly, he knew she had ambitions to develop her career as a dramatic actress and wondered how she would react to the prospect of doing another musical. Ginger wasn't keen, but after explaining that she had really wanted to continue with straight roles, said happily enough, 'But I guess it'll turn out all right.'

What an understatement! It was the start of an astonishing partnership which took them in whirlwind fashion from one enormous success to another over the next six years and, after a few years' lapse, to their final fling together in 1949. But in *Flying Down to Rio* they were not yet big stars and, though featured dancers, were cast behind the raven-haired beauty of Dolores Del Rio and her handsome co-star, Gene Raymond.

Released on 20 December 1933, the film itself was not an epic, although RKO billed it as a 'musical extravaganza staged in the clouds' and 'a romance that soars to the skies on the wings of a song'. To some degree the claims were justified because the film had a number of speciality sequences and visual novelties devised by dance director Dave Gould, and featured chorus girls dancing on the wings of a plane. The plot for such a musical extravaganza was characteristically slim and cast Astaire as a dancer and Rogers as a band-singer. Together they helped bandleader-aviator (hence the aeroplane sequence) Gene Raymond to impress and thereby win the girl he loved, Dolores Del Rio, by staging an aerial opening for her father's new hotel. The film ran for just short of one and half hours, but the plot was incidental if, by today's standards, tedious. Much more important was Vincent Youman's tuneful score. Fred joined Dolores Del Rio for the title song, 'Orchids in the Moonlight', and Ginger had a rather undistinguished solo, but by far the most outstanding sequence in the entire film was to be the electrifying dance routine, 'The Carioca'.

This scene, which was to mean so much to Fred Astaire and Ginger Rogers's film careers, became a classic and at the time was exceptional. Seen today, it is particularly interesting for the way it demonstrates how their dance style developed and became more relaxed over the years. In 'The Carioca', taken at a furious pace, the impeccably-timed pauses and the 'light and shade' of their later offerings are absent, though technically it is brilliant, with Astaire and Rogers literally 'dancing' almost every step.

Though typically extravagant, glamorous and exciting, the scene had to fight for audience notice with the much more visually dramatic aerial sequences. No one at the time, least of all Fred and Ginger, considered 'The Carioca' sequence, in movie terms, in any way exceptional. The dance, as so often happened in the movies in those days, had been put together hurriedly and Astaire was to admit, when he found to his astonishment that the film was playing to packed houses, that he felt he had barely scratched the surface in *Rio* and that there was still so much more that could be done with dance on film.

'The Carioca' was a blend of rumba and Brazilian rhythms, the two main sequences timed minutely by Hermes Pan, the film's assistant dance director, who worked jointly with Astaire on most of the film's dance numbers. *Flying Down to Rio* brought Astaire and Pan together for the first time, though the former Broadway dancer had worked with Ginger Rogers two years earlier. In her Broadway debut, a show called *Top Speed,* he had been in the singing chorus. It was to be a significant association, for once RKO saw the box-office success of 'The Carioca', they didn't hesitate to bring the two together again. Hermes Pan was engaged as assistant to dance director Dave Gould once more in *The Gay Divorcee* and then was promoted to dance director for the next Astaire-Rogers offering, *Roberta.* The two were to work together many times and invariably with enormous success. They shared an obsession for working dance routines through to perfection and the two were to become firm friends in private life.

The scene in *Flying Down to Rio* which launched Fred Astaire and Ginger Rogers on their sensational screen partnership had, if not 'a cast of thousands', at least sixty or seventy cast members on stage. The elaborate centrepiece was seven grand pianos formed into a circle with seven pianists at the keyboards. Fred and Ginger danced 'The Carioca' on the tops of the pianos — he establishing the debonair image which became his trade mark, in elegant evening suit with buttonhole.

No technicolour process then, of course, but for all that the scene was every bit as spectacular as those Busby Berkeley musicals by which all standards were then set. There were few difficulties. Pan and Astaire worked out the routines jointly and, although Ginger had little part in the choreography, she proved more than adequate in executing the demanding dance sequences. 'The Carioca' took four minutes of film time, but somebody estimated that one hundred hours were spent rehearsing it. Pan said later that Astaire was always happier dancing by himself or with a partner, rather than in big chorus numbers, and with Ginger the chemistry seemed to work from the start. Assessing their 'togetherness', writer Philip Jenkinson explained that no matter how complicated the steps, Ginger not only kept up, 'but provided a perfect foil for Astaire's delicate body and hand movements. Going over and over the carefully planned routines that Fred and Pan had devised, she quickly caught on to the Astaire secret: to dance with the *whole* body. Arms, shoulders, neck and head became as important as the legs and feet. Her hand movements, at first a little unsure, soon adopted the flowing sinuous rhythms of the footwork.'

The film wasn't intended to advance Ginger's dramatic career over much and at the start she had consoled herself by agreeing with Fred that it should be a lot of fun. That's how she approached it and although her standards had matched the dictates of perfectionist Fred, when shooting ended they parted happily at the conclusion of what they both considered to be a pleasant and enjoyable interlude in their careers. Fred didn't honestly think *Flying Down to Rio* would be a success. He thought maybe it would stand a better chance if some of the dancing was deleted and told Ginger that he didn't reckon their sort of dancing in pictures would catch on.

Fred and Phyllis didn't stay around long enough to see a complete running of the film — Fred had seen a number of clips and that had been enough to fill him with apprehension. He genuinely didn't give much for his long term chances in Hollywood, and on the day before leaving for London and rehearsals of the stage show *Gay Divorce,* confided in RKO executive producer Pandro Berman that he didn't expect to be back. Berman dismissed the idea and said Fred had a great chance. He promised he would cable Fred once the film had been previewed, and admitted to an idea for making a film version of *Gay Divorce,* featuring Fred, of course. He was, indeed, to do very much more than that for, in the years ahead, it would be Pandro S. Berman who hired the talents of people like Irving Berlin, Cole Porter, Jerome Kern and, of course, the Gershwins to produce those magical musical scores for the most successful Fred Astaire-Ginger Rogers films.

Fred and Phyllis left for Europe, via New York, while Ginger resumed her normal schedule for RKO, starring in no fewer than five films in 1934 before being brought together once more with Fred Astaire in a 'successful recipe as before' follow-up. What with the rehearsals and then the London success of *Gay Divorce,* Fred had little time to dwell on the success or otherwise of *Rio.* Without sister Adele for the first time in his stage career, he nonetheless, as we have seen, captivated London audiences and enjoyed once more enormous success with West End regulars.

With no word from Hollywood, and both Fred and Phyllis now convinced that *Rio* must have flopped, the all-important cable arrived from Pandro Berman. There was no doubt, Fred had been a success in the preview of *Rio.* Fred and Phyllis celebrated, but more good news followed. They heard from Leland Hayward that RKO had taken up the option they had on Fred and that Pandro Berman was hot-footing it to London to see *Gay Divorce* with the intention, if he was impressed, of making it into a film for Fred and Ginger to do next. Meantime, *Dancing Lady* had been released and was already doing good business.

Not long ago, it seemed, Fred Astaire, without sister Adele, didn't have much of a future in the theatre, according to the New York critics, though in London the reaction had been enthusiastically different. Now it didn't really matter. If he could make it in the long term in films he didn't expect to return to the stage. All that was over and he was delighted. *Flying Down to Rio* opened at Radio City Music Hall in New York and shortly after went on countrywide release. Box-office receipts were excellent and therefore it was a life-saver for RKO whose financial position was critical. They had backed *Rio* as a last fling. If it had failed, they would almost certainly have gone out of business immediately. But *Rio's* success was all RKO had been waiting for and Pan Berman rushed over to London to make plans for Fred's next film. He saw *Gay Divorce* and satisfied himself that it could not only be adapted into a motion picture, but that the film would be better than the stage show.

Rio didn't open in London before *Gay Divorce* closed there, but Fred's psychological 'high' took a nasty jolt when Phyllis insisted, when *Dancing Lady* opened at the Empire, Leicester Square, on their going to see it. On screen he thought he looked a disaster. That's probably why he turned down the theatre's invitation to put on a private showing of *Rio* — though he said later that he knew *Gay Divorce* would be closing soon and he preferred to see the film in New York in a public theatre with the audience there.

At the end of the London run he returned to the United States and in New York found himself greeted as a film star. By this time *Flying Down to Rio* had moved out of town and Fred and Phyllis couldn't find a showing anywhere. Not until they were snatching a few days' rest with Phyllis's family at Aiken in South Carolina was there a chance for Fred to see the film. Phyllis saw it billed in a local paper at an off-beat theatre in nearby Augusta and literally dragged him there. They paid to get in, and passed through the box-office unnoticed. They both enjoyed the film, but on the way out, a youngster recognized Astaire and soon there was a crowd around. Fred said later that this is the kind of thing which shows you've made some sort of impact in the movies and went on: 'I needed it. I always need a lot of convincing about the acceptance of my work.'

Back in California, Astaire was soon once more into the excitement and general disorder of movie-making. Committing *Gay Divorce* to film provided the opportunity for change and re-writes. Since the plot centred around Ginger's screen divorce, director Mark Sandrich altered the title to the more attractively-sounding *The Gay Divorcee,* though the stage title was retained for British audiences. Fred's part was also built up and to give him more scope, was re-written with him cast as a dancer, not a writer as in the original. Only one of Cole Porter's stage songs was retained, the haunting 'Night and Day'. Ginger's ambitions were still centred on straight, dramatic roles, but she was unhappy about some of the mediocre material she had appeared in since *Rio,* so she viewed her second teaming with Astaire with a little more enthusiasm. In any event, she didn't see her partnership with Fred as an on-going thing. Indeed, no one at the time had any idea of the impact they would make together in the movies. In the unreal world of Hollywood, it was enough to know that you had enjoyed one important success and that, because of it, the formula was to be repeated in the hope of hitting the jackpot once more.

A good cast was assembled for *The Gay Divorcee.* Supporting Astaire and Rogers were Alice Brady, Edward Everett Horton, Erik Rhodes and Eric Blore — names that were destined to become closely associated with the Astaire-Rogers musicals yet to come. And the film is additionally significant because it featured in a minor part the delicious Betty Grable, who was herself to become a big name in film musicals in the 1940s (and whose legs were reputedly insured at Lloyds for one and a quarter million dollars at the height of her career).

The perpetually worried and nervous Edward Everett Horton played a lawyer acting for Ginger in her pending divorce who has fixed up a meeting with a professional co-respondent (Erik Rhodes). The plot takes off and the song-and-dance numbers develop when she is introduced to Astaire, playing a dancer, who misunderstands the situation and, as he falls in love with her, the complications seem endless before everything works out to a 'happy ever after' ending. Hardly a heavy plot, but who cared when the singing and the dancing were really all that mattered. The musical score was pleasant and listenable with an excellent little cameo sequence for Betty Grable and Edward Everett Horton called 'Let's k-k-knock K-nees', but the outstanding dance routines were the Astaire-Rogers 'Night and Day' duet and a song called 'The Continental', which turned out to be the new film's blockbuster. Written by Herb Magidson and Con Conrad, it did for *The Gay Divorcee* what 'The Carioca' had done for *Flying Down to Rio.*

'The Continental' was a vast production number used as a finale to the film and lasted seventeen minutes, said to be one of the longest numbers based on one song ever filmed. It wasn't short on presentable extravagance either, with a large chorus dressed immaculately in black and white, fifteen separate variations on the main theme and, from Fred and Ginger, three set pieces interspersed, as Philip Jenkinson has described, with 'further mass tap and shuffle'.

'The Continental' was a worthy successor to 'The Carioca'. The clever use of black and white in the dancers' outfits was devastating, and Fred and Ginger's routine was an even greater sensation than their performances in 'The Carioca'. 'The Continental' was soon on its way to becoming a standard classic, to be forever associated with Astaire.

Film critic and showbiz writer, the late Dick Richards, said 'The Continental' 'folded up the film in a speedy, tingling mass of dancers, with Fred and Ginger naturally dominating it, and helped tremendously by swift, imaginative cutting and sparkling camera work. Their exit from the hotel ballroom could hardly have been better designed to make their admirers long impatiently for their next film'.

Against the pulsating excitement of 'The Continental', the superbly interpreted 'Night and Day' should not be undervalued. In its own way it was a classic, choreographed sensitively by Hermes Pan in a series of long takes which were superbly elegant and free flowing, with finely balanced and graceful twirls and sensitive movements. In 'Night and Day' Hermes Pan reckoned Fred had produced a 'gem of its own kind' and although he didn't see the stage version he was sure, since the film kept in many of the steps and sequences from the stage routine, it must have been among the most memorable numbers Astaire ever did.

Years later, Fred admitted to being more than a little anxious about the 'Night and Day' sequence, because it was long and he doubted whether his singing would be able to do justice to the memorable Cole Porter lyrics. But in the end he went so far as to say that he thought that particular number had perhaps contributed more than anything else to the success, certainly, of the stage show. By comparison, Pan described work on 'The Continental' as blood, sweat and tears. 'We used to work from ten in the morning till ten at night and no overtime — it was really a tough job,' he remarked.

Astaire was much happier with his and Ginger's dance routines in *The Gay Divorcee* than ever he was with those in *Rio*. The success of *Rio* had already given him some measure of status and when he asked for more time to plan and rehearse the numbers, the studio listened and told him to take whatever time he wanted. Six weeks' solid rehearsal preceded the shooting of those remarkable dance sequences and, typically, he didn't compromise, allowing Ginger plenty of time to get the more tricky movements, including the complicated table dance which he had lifted from the stage show, absolutely right.

At first he had been nervous about working with Ginger again. Producer Pandro Berman put it stronger. 'Most of my efforts were devoted to getting Fred to work with Ginger in *The Gay Divorcee* . . . because he said she wasn't English and didn't belong . . . and he didn't want to make a second picture with somebody that he had already worked with.' It's true. On a personal level Fred and Ginger got along fine, but professionally he did have strong reservations, explaining that she was basically a Charleston dancer and hadn't any experience of the kind of dances featured in 'Night and Day'. 'On the stage in New York I did it with Claire Luce and it was her style which had suggested to me the whole pattern of the "Night and Day" dance,' explained Fred some years later. 'Claire was a beautiful mover. The dance was designed largely for the way she moved and it was something Ginger hadn't done.'

In the end Fred had no misgivings about Ginger. 'By the time we got Ginger into this thing she just sold it beautifully — that's all I can say. She knew how to sell it.'

It was in *The Gay Divorcee* that the professional relationship with Hermes Pan was forged. Each admired the other's work immensely, they approached situations in the same way, inspired confidence in one another, and in the end Fred and Ginger worked it so that he did all the pictures they did for RKO. Pan, who was born in Tennessee of Greek extraction, was a brilliant dance director, particularly when working with Astaire. Born in 1905, he was never trained formally in dancing, but was enthusiastic for a career in show business. Before going out to Hollywood, he appeared in the chorus of a number of New York shows, but his talent developed alongside Fred and together they were a remarkable combination. He became a family friend of the Astaires.

Fred, of course, was still something of a novice in the business of making films, but he was learning fast. So, for that matter, was Ginger, but in a different way. Acting, moving and speaking in front of the cameras is where Ginger helped him most of all, because in this department his experience on a film set was still limited. He, along with Hermes Pan, who showed infinite patience, helped Ginger enormously when it came to the musical numbers. The routines were new and, compared with what had gone on before, in the Busby Berkeley musicals for instance, they were excessively demanding, and Fred's standards of execution were as painfully high as ever they had been.

Alongside all that, Fred still grappled with technicalities of movie-making which were still unfamiliar to him and in *Steps in Time* he makes interesting observations about this. For instance, he said that in his earlier films he found it difficult working with a fifty-piece orchestra while they were at one end of the set and he at the other. 'This separation was technically necessary to control the sound properly when picked up "live" on set. Most of the dance numbers in my first four pictures at RKO were made that way. Techniques have advanced hugely since then and films are not made that way any more.'

He also found it hard to reconcile his instinctively precise and orderly approach to his work, his almost obsessional pre-occupation with getting the numbers perfect, with having lots of unfinished dances, as he put it, 'hanging over my head as we progressed through the dialogue and story of the film'. Some of the problems arose from Astaire's own insistence on making every segment of every routine as near to perfection as possible. He applied the same standards throughout everything he did and once said that an audience might not notice the less important numbers so much, but those too have to be thoroughly and completely presented.

This time, when the filming was completed, the way ahead had already been plotted. Half way through shooting *The Gay Divorcee,* the studio announced that a follow-up film had already been scheduled. Adapted from another stage play, *Roberta* was to team Fred with Ginger yet again and Pandro Berman was to produce. Berman, in fact, was by far the main force and influence in the joint careers of Astaire and Rogers at this stage. He above all others recognized the enormous potential in their screen partnership and had not been deflected despite opposition from inside RKO. He said later that he knew after buying *The Gay Divorcee* and *Roberta* that the partnership was a gold mine.

Astaire-Rogers fans could not possibly bear to think about what might — or directly, what might *not* — have happened had not the far-sighted Berman been close at hand in Hollywood when Astaire left for Europe at the end of the shooting of *Rio.* Back in Hollywood, when Berman suggested to Louis Brock, who had produced *Flying Down to Rio,* that he did a follow-up by adapting *Gay Divorce* for the screen, he didn't want to know and there the matter — and possibly the, as yet, unestablished partnership of Astaire and Rogers — might have ended. Berman, however, as well as being in an executive position at RKO and ostensibly at any rate in charge of production, was still doing some independent producing. It was after Louis Brock turned down *The Gay Divorcee* that Berman decided to follow it up anyway, went to London on holiday, saw the show a number of times, talked to Astaire about it, and because Louis Brock wasn't interested, decided to make the film himself.

He saw enough potential on the set of *The Gay Divorcee* to collar the partnership again for *Roberta* and by this time Fred Astaire and

Ginger Rogers, whether they realized it or not, were already well on their way to subordinating their individual identities, in film terms, for the sake of a brilliant new screen entity. Starring in *Roberta* was Irene Dunne, who sang one of the film's all-time great musical successes, 'Smoke Gets in Your Eyes', by Jerome Kern and Otto Harbach. This beautiful and haunting ballad was also used for an immaculately performed dance duet with Ginger, displaying a subtle sensuality in a low-cut black satin dress tightly fitting to show her elegant figure, and Fred, resplendent as always in evening dress with white carnation buttonhole, black patent leather shoes and, of course, just that precise touch of cuff showing beneath the sleeves.

Fred and Hermes Pan, who incidentally was billed for the first time as dance director in *Roberta* — and not before time — produced a dreamy, exceptionally slow sequence — Ginger wondered if it might not be too slow — but their feeling for the mood of the song and the way it should be put over was absolutely right. Fred said it was a very good song to dance to and it remained one of his all-time favourites. Other unforgettable songs from the film were 'I Won't Dance' and 'Lovely to Look At', both by Dorothy Fields and Jerome Kern.

The screenplay had been adapted from the stage musical, *Roberta,* which itself had been taken from the Alice Duer Miller novel, *Gowns by Roberta.* The plot of the film was typically frail, but in any event took a poor second place to the work of Astaire and Rogers. Their interpretation of 'I'll be Hard to Handle' was sheer perfection and every bit as exciting as 'The Continental'. The British writer, Benny Green, in his book on Fred Astaire, put his finger on the charm and appeal of the partnership when he wrote that by this time 'the Astaire-Rogers duets had already evolved into mobile character sketches, in which the theme of the plot, the pursuit of the girl by the boy and the courting of her through dance, was expressed in terpsichorean terms. It was this thematic element in the duets which rendered the partnership unique.' Cinema history can produce other dance duos, but certainly, Fred and Ginger were the first of their own special kind and, frankly, nobody did it better.

Roberta also featured Randolph Scott (loaned from Paramount) and Lucille Ball, making her first appearance in an RKO movie, almost hidden away in a parade of fashion models.

Pandro Berman spent heavily to secure the rights of *Roberta* for RKO, but box-office receipts underlined his perception and wisdom, for it made a profit of 770,000 dollars, contributing handsomely to

RKO's first profitable year since 1930. More importantly, it served to materialize not only the Astaire-Rogers partnership, but also the production package of Hermes Pan as dance director, Van Nest Polglase as art director and Berman himself, producer. Collectively they were now poised to make movie history with a string of films which made legends of Fred Astaire and Ginger Rogers.

In *Roberta,* however, they were not quite there. Some critics complained they weren't on screen long enough and, surprisingly in view of the enormous impact they made with 'The Carioca', 'The Continental' and the delectable 'Night and Day', they still lacked top billing.

Both shortcomings were to disappear later that year (1935) when Pandro Berman brought them together once more in a film which was arguably to turn out to be the finest, and certainly the most profitable, of all the Astaire-Rogers offerings, *Top Hat.*

SIX

Stepping out with Ginger

Fred Astaire's first three films for RKO not only made box-office stars of himself and Ginger Rogers, but helped to salvage the studio's flagging fortunes. 1932, when he signed that first film contract, was the worst in movie history. The Depression devastated the industry. Cinema audiences, which in 1930 were running as high as 110 million a week in the United States alone, slumped to little more than half that by 1932. That year Warner Brothers lost fourteen million dollars, Paramount suffered a crushing deficit of twenty-one million dollars and crashed into bankruptcy, and RKO turned in losses of ten million dollars. This was on top of a five and a half million dollar deficit and, as a result, RKO collapsed financially early in 1933 and for a time teetered on the verge of extinction. The receiver took control, slashed costs, and kept the company going. One of the sacrifices was the brilliant David O. Selznick, who had joined RKO the year before and whose outstanding perception had recruited an abundance of talent, both in front of and behind the camera. He packed his bags after a row about who had the final say in production. Other major names to depart included director George Cukor, who had been brought in by Selznick and who now accompanied him to MGM, and Constance Bennett, one of the studio's top stars.

In 1933, when Merian C. Cooper took over from Selznick and began making cheaper films more quickly, the studio was literally in chaos. But benefiting from the further talent of Pandro Berman, who took control when Cooper spent long periods away from the studio because of ill-health (and was finally to quit in mid-1934), RKO began slowly to claw its way out of the abyss. As the Depression eased, and with the benefit of two major successes — *King Kong* and *Little Women* — losses were cut to a little more than four million dollars in 1933.

The year 1934 proved crucial to the fortunes of RKO and film fashions played their part in the studio's recovery. Instigated by Warner Brothers' successful *Forty Second Street* and *Gold Diggers of 1933,* both of which incidentally starred Ginger Rogers, the film musical was making a major come-back and RKO were well placed to jump on the bandwagon. Encouraged by the success of a minor musical called *Melody Cruise,* which had Phil Harris and Betty Grable in the cast, RKO put their hands more deeply into their pockets to finance the somewhat speculative venture, *Flying Down to Rio,* which brought Fred Astaire and Ginger Rogers together for the first time. This film, along with *Melody Cruise* and one or two other titles, grossed well at the box-office and helped ease the tensions and anxieties in the studio. Helped considerably by the success of *The Gay Divorcee,* which was among RKO's most profitable films of the year, studio losses in 1934 were slashed to less than 311,000 dollars. In 1935 RKO moved into the black for the first time in five years with a vintage performance which left them showing a profit of more than 684,000 dollars. The main reason for the turnround was the enormous success of the two Astaire-Rogers movies, *Top Hat* and *Roberta.*

But back in 1932 Fred Astaire wasn't over-concerned about RKO's liquidity. It is doubtful if he even gave it a thought. After all, business was only just beginning to piece itself together again after the colossal disaster of the Depression. With millions in the United States still looking for work, you didn't bother to find out if a company was financially stable before taking on a job. In any case, Fred had nothing to lose. He had decided to put the stage behind him and wanted to see if he could get into the movie business. To be offered a picture at all was opportunity enough and more than he had dared to expect, in spite of his king-sized reputation as a stage star.

The timing, the appalling economic situation apart, was impeccable. The good fortune which took Fred Astaire to Hollywood just as a new dawn was beginning to break over screen musicals was matched only by the monumental coincidence which brought him and Ginger Rogers together. So easily the pairing might never have taken place. At first, a girl called Dorothy Jordan was pencilled in for the part of Astaire's partner in *Flying Down to Rio* but when she married producer Merian C. Cooper and pulled out, studio chiefs started desperately casting around for a replacement. Time was short for by this time Fred was already on the set. Then Ginger Rogers was put forward for the part, initially by whom, precisely, is not totally clear.

What *is* clear is that the astute — and the same — Merian Cooper, top tycoon at RKO, had earlier played an important cameo role in the scenario which was later to bring Astaire and Rogers together. Had Harry Cohn, famous egotistical boss of

Columbia Pictures, acted more decisively, it is doubtful if the Astaire-Rogers partnership would ever have materialized. He had spotted Ginger's potential talent in some of her earlier undistinguished films and was about to offer her a long-term contract. Unfortunately for him, he made the mistake of getting her to do a test first before deciding finally, and then killed his own chances of signing her by showing the results at his home in front of his friendly rival from RKO, Merian Cooper. Cooper hadn't been at RKO long having been brought in by David Selznick. When the latter left RKO, Cooper took over. Ginger's test was poor, but Cooper was impressed by her basic talent and promise and wanted her for RKO. While the unsuspecting Harry Cohn took his time in deciding what to do, Cooper, applying the principle of 'all is fair in love and war' to the business of movie-making, got on to Ginger's mother Lela, who looked after her daughter's business affairs, and fixed a meeting. His casual, low-key approach didn't entirely deceive the shrewd, hard-bargaining Lela. She could tell he was keen to sign Ginger but after a certain amount of negotiation, terms were finally agreed. Harry Cohn found himself out-manoeuvred, and by the time Astaire moved on to the set of *Flying Down to Rio,* Ginger could already count herself a success in Hollywood, comfortably secure with an important seven-year contract in her handbag.

She had, in fact, made her first feature film in 1930, appearing with Claudette Colbert and Charles Ruggles in a Paramount offering called *Young Man of Manhattan.* Three more films in 1930, another three in 1931, five in 1932 and, before *Flying Down to Rio,* no fewer than eight films in 1933, had given her a wealth of experience. But thin plots, poor scripts and low budgets too often combined to prevent her from developing her ambitions to be a good dramatic film actress.

Ginger Rogers, almost twelve years younger than Astaire, was born on 16 July 1911, in Independence, Missouri, and christened Virginia Katherine McMath. 'Ginger' came affectionately from a cousin and 'Rogers' from her mother's second marriage. Lela Rogers was a particularly doting and obsessive mother with a raging ambition to see her attractive daughter a success in show business. She started early by getting Ginger, then only five, in some local nondescript advertising films. At fourteen, displaying some of the early dance potential which was eventually to take her to Astaire, Ginger became the Charleston Champion of Texas. She later went on tour with her Charleston presentation and when this had run its course, Lela brought two other redheads into the act, pepped up the routines and as 'Ginger Rogers and the Redheads', the new group enjoyed plenty of dates and a fair measure of success. Her debut with a song-and-dance solo act was at Memphis and after touring around the country she got a useful break when she was seventeen, appearing with comedian Willie Howard in an act which played for eighteen weeks in Chicago. This led directly to an engagement at the Paramount Theatre on Broadway.

Lela Rogers was disciplined, hard-working and shrewd, and she not only championed Ginger in front of booking agents and producers, but was an astute manager, an understanding general assistant and helper, and dutiful chaperone. Before she was nineteen, Ginger Rogers was spotted in vaudeville by Charles Morrison, boss of Hollywood's Mocambo Club, and when later he was talking to Bert Kalmar and Harry Ruby, who were looking for a lively soubrette for their new musical comedy *Top Speed,* mentioned her name. She was cast in the second female lead and made her first appearance on Broadway in the show, at the 46th Street Theatre, where it ran for 102 performances. It hardly made history, but Ginger did well with a song called 'Hot and Bothered' and caught the attention of a couple of critics.

At this time, and shortly after, Ginger's career was influenced by some people who were also to be influential in Astaire's career, though it was still four years before the two were to come together in *Flying Down to Rio*. Hidden away in the chorus of *Top Speed,* for instance, was a young man called Hermes Pan. It wasn't to be long, either, before George and Ira Gershwin crossed careers with Ginger to influence her professional life. Ginger then moved into a show called *Girl Crazy,* which was produced by two other familiar 'Astaire' names — none other than Alex Aarons and Vinton Freedley. The Wall Street Crash of 1929, bringing with it the macabre spectacle of ruined investors flinging themselves off skyscraper roofs and worthless money being torn up in the streets, still hung heavily on American life. It is difficult to see how, in such circumstances, even a really good show — which *Girl Crazy* was not — could be successful. It ran for only a few months and was undoubtedly saved from an earlier grave by a particularly tuneful score by George Gershwin, with lyrics by brother Ira. Ginger and the Gershwins became firm friends and her big hit in *Girl Crazy* was a beautiful song which was to become an all-time standard — called 'Embraceable You'. In the cast of *Girl Crazy,* incidentally, was another potential star enjoying her first big break on Broadway, Ethel Merman.

Ginger Rogers inherited her mother's capacity for hard work. This, combined with a professional discipline, attractive looks, a smoothly shaped figure, a pleasant if undistinguished singing voice and the capacity to dance and to be happy and bubbly on film, gave her a head start in the jungle that was Hollywood in the 1930s and '40s. When she first went to Hollywood in 1931 she had no real trouble breaking into films, having already appeared in five films made in New York for Paramount in a stamina-sapping schedule which saw her appearing in, first, *Top Speed,* and, later, *Girl Crazy* in the evenings, and filming most of the day. When *Girl Crazy* ended its run she was offered a Hollywood contract to make three movies, starting off at 1,000 dollars a week. She took it. Although she had appeared in two Broadway shows and had toured the United States extensively in vaudeville, it is true to say that as a stage performer she never reached the heights of Astaire, when he appeared with sister Adele.

Significantly, it was 'Embraceable You' which Ginger Rogers did in the New York show *Girl Crazy* which led to her first experience of working with Astaire. The man who brought them together was Alex Aarons, who had produced Fred and Adele's earlier stage successes, *For Goodness Sake, Lady, Be Good!* and *Funny Face.* Astaire was in New York with the ill-fated Ziegfeld flop, *Smiles,* and one day received a telephone call from Aarons, who was then working with the nineteen-year-old Ginger Rogers on George Gershwin's *Girl Crazy* and about to stage a song-and-dance routine to Gershwin's superb melody. Could Fred give a hand? Astaire went next day to the Alvin Theatre and there met Ginger. Together they worked on the number in the foyer of the theatre and a friendship developed. After that they went out from time to time to see a movie or to dinner. In *Steps in Time* Fred explains: 'Our favorite spot was the Casino in Central Park, which had been converted into a flashy night spot featuring Eddie Duchin and his orchestra. We danced now and then for fun, with no plans whatsoever of working together.'

Fred got to know Lela Rogers well and on visits to the Rogers' apartment Fred would sit with Ginger and her mother discussing the future, the professional ambitions of himself and Ginger and how their careers might develop. Never for a moment did either of them consider that their futures would be remotely interwoven. Nor did their friendship develop into any kind of romance. It was to be three more years before Fred married Phyllis and at the time of her meeting with Astaire, Ginger had already experienced one failed marriage. They simply enjoyed each other's company and had a pleasant time together, but when Ginger left to pursue her career in Hollywood, Fred had no expectation of working with her, or perhaps even seeing her again.

The first faintly discernible moves which were to pull them together again professionally can, with hindsight, now be identified. Ginger, though kept very busy in Hollywood, was not exactly creating an enormous impact, and her flurry of films for all kinds of studios, including Pathe, First National, Monogram, Twentieth Century Fox, Warners, Universal, Paramount and even RKO, were not making her into a major star. But as Fred followed her to Hollywood just two years later to appear in *Dancing Lady* and *Flying Down to Rio,* Ginger's career was blown off its mundane course with what turned out to be significant offers by Warner Brothers. In 1933 they pointed her towards what was destined to become a sparkling if, for her millions of admirers, a disappointingly short career in screen musicals.

The key was finally turned by Mervyn Le Roy — the same who tried desperately but unsuccessfully a few years before to get studio boss Jack Warner interested in a film version of Astaire's stage success *Gay Divorce.* He was at this time seeing a lot of Ginger and it was he who urged her to take the chance of appearing in a new Warner Brothers musical called *Forty Second Street* directed by Lloyd Bacon. The man had earlier made movie history by making the very first film ever with dialogue, the Al Jolson epic, *The Singing Fool.* With amazing and eccentric sets by Busby Berkeley, *Forty Second Street* turned out to be a significant movie, recreating a public interest in screen musicals. With a cluster of memorable songs, *Forty Second Street* brought Ginger some of her best co-stars for a couple of years, including Warner Baxter, Bebe Daniels, George Brent, Ruby Keeler, Dick Powell, Una Merkel and Guy Kibbee. As a hard-boiled chorus girl, her performance wasn't outstanding but it was enough to get her cast in a Warner Brothers follow-up called *Gold Diggers of 1933,* with Joan Blondell, Ruby Keeler and Dick Powell. Four films of indifferent quality followed and then after making *Sitting Pretty* for Paramount, she returned to RKO for *Chance at Heaven* with Joel McCrea and Andy Devine.

This was almost the last piece in the jigsaw for it meant that Ginger just happened to be around when they were looking to cast *Flying Down to Rio* and her recent work in *Forty Second Street* and *Gold Diggers of 1933* was remembered. Being available completed the puzzle. Much later one writer uncharitably pronounced that no one at the time thought Ginger Rogers to be a great dancer — or a great anything. 'But she was available and thus easy to team with Astaire.' And so she was and that, really, is all that mattered. As casually as that the greatest screen song-and-dance partnership of all time came into being.

After *Roberta,* their third successful film together, Astaire and Rogers were now set for top billing and this came for the first time in what was arguably their best movie of all, *Top Hat.* It also turned out to be the most profitable movie they were to do together. Released in 1935, it was adapted by Dwight Taylor and Allan Scott from the play *The Girl Who Dared* by Alexander Farago and Aladar Laszlo. The plot, typically lightweight, was comparatively unimportant and featured Astaire as an American dancer who falls in love with Rogers, following her to romantic Venice and rescuing her from a rebound marriage. Astaire objected to the screenplay in its original form so much that his own part particularly, which he felt portrayed him too much as an unsympathetic and downright objectionable character, was rewritten so that in the end his 'Jerry Travers' was charming, pleasant, witty, appealing and thoroughly likeable. It proved his instinctive feel for what he was doing, for this portrayal, plonked down into different situations, was carried forward virtually unchanged to his remaining films with Rogers.

Top Hat was also special because it marked, for the first time, the ascendancy of the partnership over the screenplay in terms of public recognition and importance. *Flying Down to Rio* had given them a featured spot in a perfectly ordinary film. Though retrospectively important, they were nonetheless, when the movie was planned, subordinate to the story and, indeed of course, to the film's main stars. This didn't change entirely in either *The Gay Divorcee* or *Roberta.* But in *Top Hat* we saw for the first time a film created from start to finish to exploit the talents of Fred Astaire and Ginger Rogers. There were no compromises and the timing was perfect. The couple had emerged from their screen apprenticeship together with the highest possible marks; the film musical was back in favour with the public (helped already by Fred and Ginger); and *Top Hat* was therefore, and not surprisingly, an unashamed attempt to showcase the charm, the appeal, the talent and the extraordinary screen magic of the Astaire-Rogers partnership. It did so impeccably.

The film successfully reunited Fred and Ginger with Mark Sandrich, who had directed *The Gay Divorcee,* and with Pandro Berman in charge of production, an impressive array of background talent was assembled. These included Hermes Pan as dance director, those supremely sophisticated masters of screen farce, Eric Blore, Edward Everett Horton, Alice Brady, Helen Broderick and, to complete the team, Erik Rhodes, and most significantly of all perhaps, Irving Berlin, who produced scintillating music and adorable lyrics specially for the film. His magnificent score for *Top Hat,* almost a complete package, was quickly to lodge itself into the archives of film music.

The genius of Berlin had long since been recognized through masterly compositions like 'Alexander's Ragtime Band' and 'Everybody's Doin' It', which seemed almost uncannily to encompass what has been so appropriately pin-pointed as the 'Americanization of the popular song'. Credit for recruiting Berlin to the *Top Hat* team goes to the astute Mr Pandro Berman, contributing yet another monumentally important step in the phenomenal career of Fred and Ginger. He knew Berlin could be difficult to work with, but guessed if anyone could handle him, Astaire could. Fred had enormous respect for Berlin and as early as 1914 he and Adele had bought an Irving Berlin number called 'I Love to Quarrel With You' for their vaudeville act, although they did not meet him at the time. In *Top Hat,* and indeed in subsequent films they did together, Astaire and Berlin's ability to work successfully together was uncanny. They quickly developed a keen respect for one another's talents. Berlin said later, according to Michael Freedland: 'You can't work with Fred without knowing you're working for him. He's a real inspiration for a writer.' Such did that respect and admiration grow over the years that it is said that Berlin only decided to work on the 1942 movie, *Holiday Inn,* after knowing that Astaire was in the picture. 'I'd rather have Astaire introduce my songs than any other performer,' he said.

The story of *Top Hat* concerns Broadway dancer Jerry Travers (Fred Astaire) who goes to London for the British production of his latest American success and stays with his old friend and producer, Horace Hardwick (Edward Everett Horton), in his hotel suite. Hotels, incidentally, were often effective backgrounds to Astaire-Rogers movies. Matchmaker Madge Hardwick, Horace's wife (played by Helen Broderick) sets about finding a suitable wife for Jerry, who doesn't really want a wife. Jerry expresses his feelings in the song 'No Strings' and the dance routine which ends the musical sequence rouses Dale Tremont (Ginger Rogers), who was sleeping in the room below. Annoyed at the disturbance, she goes upstairs to complain, and Jerry, falling for her instantly, apologizes. To make the point, he sprinkles sand on the floor of his hotel-room and dances again, but softly this time, in a cheeky, amusing attempt to lull her to sleep. Dale's anger eases, but is aroused again during the following days when she discovers that Jerry is pursuing her. He catches up with her when she is forced to shelter from a thunderstorm in a bandstand while out riding in the park. She finds herself softening towards him as he sings 'Isn't This a Lovely Day to be Caught in the Rain' and they dance together. At this point the film could be within a stone's throw of ending, as the attraction of Dale for Jerry and of Jerry for Dale is established, but then an elaborate series of romantic misunderstandings before the final reconciliation is enough to take the movie through to its full 101 minutes' running time.

It starts when the scheming Madge sends Dale a message saying that her husband, whom Dale has never met, is staying at the same hotel, but will soon be joining her at the Lido in Venice, and Madge invites Dale to go along too. Intrigued to know what Madge's husband looks like, Dale is unable to control her curiosity until Venice, checks the suite number of Madge's husband and, of course, finds it to be that of Jerry, whose name incidentally she still doesn't know. She draws the wrong conclusion, thinks that Jerry is Madge's husband, and saddened and angry, storms off to the Venice Lido with her business associate and would-be wooer, Alberto Beddini (Erik Rhodes). Incredible complications follow rapidly one after another, punctuated without too long an interval to make the entertainment tedious, by those wonderful Irving Berlin melodies. Astaire sings 'Top Hat, White Tie and Tails', and dances with a male chorus. In a brief magical moment when Ginger, in the film, relaxes her guard and softens somewhat towards Astaire's attempts to win her back, Fred sings and dances the evergreen 'Cheek to Cheek'; and amid the excitement of carnival night at the Lido, Fred and Ginger dance 'The Piccolino' with the chorus, Ginger on this occasion providing the words. Quickly, in the end, all misunderstandings are sorted out and everybody lives happily ever after.

Top Hat firmly established Astaire's debonair, charming, man-about-town image, and he and Ginger performed Berlin's brilliant score with an almost unbelievable style, presence, verve and sensitive appreciation which was sheer perfection. Every one of Berlin's five songs for the film became major hits and three — 'Isn't This a Lovely Day', 'Top Hat, White Tie and Tails', and 'Cheek to Cheek' became popular music standards to be forever indivisible from Astaire. 'The Piccolino', obviously intended to follow the blockbusting traditions of 'The Carioca' and 'The Continental', was lavish and exhilarating and a worthy successor. It was staged at a fiesta at the Lido in Venice and, as noted by Dick Richards, 'then danced in stylish ballroom fashion by Ginger and Fred, with the former singing the song at the beginning of the dance in wooing, caressing tones'. *Top Hat* was a popular film with

Astaire. He considered it a good, ageless kind of picture, a kind of standard. 'I've always loved that movie,' he said many years later. *Top Hat* is also remembered for Ginger's dress of feathers and the bother it caused. The sequence was 'Cheek to Cheek' and Astaire had worked out a particularly smooth choreography to fit the mood of the dance, all romantic and flowing. There was no trouble in rehearsal because Ginger normally worked out in trousers, but because Fred knew from bitter experience how critical Ginger's dress could be in the sometimes close and vigorous nature of their duets, he had made it a rule to do at least one rehearsal in costume. It would be too late once shooting had begun to discover that Ginger's dress would become entangled around Fred's legs or feet.

This time, when he called for Ginger to wear the dress, a particularly attractive style with ostrich feathers sewn on, it wasn't ready so she wasn't able to wear it until the day of shooting. All was well during the song, but once they started to dance together, the feathers, literally, began to fly. They simply dropped off and settled all over — on the floor mainly, but also on Astaire's suit, on his hair and eyelids, up his nose even. Perfectionist Astaire blew his top, and Hermes Pan said it was one of the few times he saw Fred irritated. 'He was calling that dress all kinds of names,' he said. There were so many feathers they had to be swept up. It was impossible at first to get a satisfactory take, but in the end, with most of the loose feathers having already fallen off, it was decided the number would have to be photographed, feathers or no feathers. Amazingly, in the end it worked out all right, thanks to a background which was almost entirely white, but it is said that if you look really intently during this scene in the film, it is possible to pick out one or two flecks of white against the black and white floor. Next day, when Astaire had cooled off, he and Hermes Pan worked out new words to the chorus of 'Cheek to Cheek'. For amusement only . . . *Feathers — I have feathers; And I hate them so that I can hardly speak. And I never find the happiness I seek, With those chicken feathers dancing, Cheek to Cheek.*

If this is the most amusing behind-the-scenes incident in *Top Hat,* the most brilliantly inventive and amazingly articulate front-of-camera dance sequence must surely be Astaire's solo offering in which he uses his cane as a gun to shoot down the top hatted and elegantly attired members of the male chorus. The origins of this impressive and creative sequence went back to an early morning spark of inspiration when Astaire was planning and rehearsing for the stage show *Smiles,* which included a number called 'Young Man of Manhattan'. He was sharing an apartment with his sister

71

and his mother at 875 Park Avenue, New York, at the time and as he lay awake in bed at about 4.00 a.m. the idea came to him: the male chorus in one long line and dressed in full evening dress, each man with a cane, and as the number developed, Astaire would simulate a gun with his own cane, shooting the chorus line down, one at a time, each one falling precisely as he strongly 'tapped' out the sound. Then he would mow them all down, using the cane like a machine gun. Fred said he jumped out of bed immediately, grabbed an umbrella from the corner of the room and, while humming the tune, performed the first crude run-through of the routine which was to become one of his most famous. Included in its early form in the disastrous *Smiles,* it never made an impact, but when the ideas were being sorted out for *Top Hat,* Astaire talked to Irving Berlin about it, who wrote *Top Hat* specially for the number and, of course, it was also the inspiration for the film's title.

One of Astaire's favourite stories from *Top Hat* is about the cane number and the day his old friend, the great Jimmy Cagney, turned up on the set. Cagney was a deceptively versatile performer, despite his more remembered reputation as one of the screen's classic 'tough guys'. His first work in show business in the early 1920s was as a dancer — in drag! He was an unabashed Astaire fan and followed his career closely. Among Fred's most prized possessions are the telegrams of congratulations he received from Cagney. Fred always hated rehearsing in front of anyone so when Cagney dropped into the studio when the crew were actually shooting the cane scene, he admitted to being unusually nervous. Fred insisted on ad libbing one sequence to reach the degree of spontaneity he wanted and after about the third take of this difficult and tricky manoeuvre, Cagney whispered to him: 'Don't shoot it again, kid — you've got it on the second take.' Being Astaire, he did it one more time for good measure, but Cagney was right. The second take was the one used in the film.

Top Hat succeeded lavishly. When the picture was first shown in New York's Radio City Music Hall, it smashed all previous attendance records. Out on world release it was soon turning in spectacular business. It became the most financially successful movie for RKO during the whole of the 1930s. By the end of 1935 Fred Astaire and Ginger Rogers were ranked fourth top attraction among all the movie stars — an enormous achievement for a song-and-dance partnership so recently established. Astaire had become one of Hollywood's top superstars and an outstanding box-office hit the world over. He had moved out of one successful career into an even more successful new one and his losses, resulting from the

Depression, were forgotten. He was well on his way to amassing a huge fortune — *and all in just two years. Top Hat* cost 650,000 dollars to make, but long, *long* before it was financially spent, it grossed more than three million dollars in film rentals. It is difficult even to make a guess at what *Top Hat* alone was ultimately worth to Astaire, but it is said that Pandro Berman arranged for Astaire, Berlin and himself each to receive ten per cent of the gross take. In his autobiography, Fred admitted to contractual problems with RKO at about this time. It had something to do with his basic contract, which apparently hadn't been updated to reflect his star status and which allowed for 1,500 dollars a week for a guaranteed three-week period with options for four years at annual increases of 500 dollars a week while making a picture.

The arguments with RKO weren't to be settled easily. The situation was further complicated because neither Fred nor Ginger had the heart for becoming a permanent partnership. Fred particularly was against it because he was beginning to feel the strain of thinking up fresh ideas for every new picture. He also didn't want to go on long enough for audiences to start complaining that they had seen it all before. It was Fred's policy with each film he did with Ginger never to repeat a dance step. He also wanted to spend more time with Phyllis and his family.

It was a messy and unsatisfactory argument and while Astaire's lawyer was sorting out the problem with the studio, RKO became sufficiently antagonized, when another lawyer appeared on the scene supposedly working for Astaire, that they were said to be close to letting him find some other studio with which to continue his career. Hardly any controversy invaded Astaire's many years in the entertainment business and this situation worried and upset him. In the end a settlement was reached, though the terms of Fred's new contract were never officially disclosed. He claimed, however, that he finally got everything he was supposed to get.

As RKO rushed to team Astaire and Rogers yet again, *Top Hat* was playing to packed cinemas all over the world. In the end, when the partnership had run its course and film historians could judge with the objectivity of hindsight, *Top Hat* emerges as perhaps the movie which simply *was* Astaire and Rogers. It said everything. All the essential ingredients were there in just the right measure at exactly the right time and the whole package somehow managed to climb that fraction higher, reach that shade deeper and sparkle just that much brighter to make it a perfect gem of its kind — the yardstick for all other screen musicals. Not everyone agreed. Critics must stick out their necks, jump in with two feet, and almost before the reel has stopped spinning, come forward with a judgement which, though created in an instant, can label them for all time. Two, who in the light of cinema-goers' response to *Top Hat* can hardly claim to have represented the public viewpoint, were distinguished reviewers Grahame Greene and Alistair Cooke. Irving Berlin's music hung heavily it seemed with Greene, who likened Astaire to a human Mickey Mouse. Cooke, too, saw Astaire as a human Mickey Mouse who, once all the nonsense with Ginger Rogers came to an end, could do no better than make another series of musicals with, in Cooke's own words, 'his first and oldest flame, Miss Minnie Mouse'.

But among the millions of paying customers and most critics and reviewers, Greene and Cooke were lonely voices in the wilderness. *Top Hat* was like all the Astaire-Rogers musicals: sheer entertainment. Even if at times the plots were bewildering and almost always bordering on the banal, it didn't matter. To look for more was to miss the very essence of their appeal. You could relax and be whisked away on a magic carpet ride to a wonderland of lilting, rhythmic melodies and exciting dancing. There was no sinister plot, no hidden message. An Astaire-Rogers movie didn't change your views about anything. It merchandized happiness and enjoyment and you simply sat back in your seat and marvelled at the sheer artistry of those dancing feet. The extravagant offerings of Busby Berkeley had whetted the public's appetite for musicals again, but they were pure celluloid, featuring an endless succession of cardboard cut-outs. Their charm was in the enormous sets, scores of beautiful girls, the intricate patterns, distant camera shots and a kind of untouchable larger-than-life implausibility. Nobody remotely imagined they had anything at all to do with real life. With Astaire and Rogers it was different. *Top Hat* and the others were still fairy stories, but they were touchable and had an intimacy. Where Busby created fantasy, Fred and Ginger were in the business of romance. And *Top Hat* had the bonus of Irving Berlin.

He, it appears, was not always easy to get along with. He drove a hard bargain, professionally, dictating his own terms to Hollywood. Arthur Freed once said that it took longer to write one of Berlin's contracts than a whole script. He always insisted on a stake in the movie's profits. Nor would he allow anyone to tamper with his compositions. There was never any cutting, changes or re-arrangements once filming had started. All this was written into his contracts. But once the contract was settled to his satisfaction, he quickly got down to produce some of the finest screen music ever written.

At the time Pandro Berman signed him for *Top Hat,* Irving Berlin was trying to recreate some of his triumphs of the 1920s. He succeeded superlatively with his score for *Top Hat*. Even if 'The Piccolino' struggled a bit to climb alongside 'The Carioca' and 'The Continental', the rest of his work was generally considered to be sheer genius. 'Cheek to Cheek' was nominated for an Oscar, along with Jerome Kern's and Dorothy Field's 'Lovely to Look At', from the Astaire-Rogers movie *Roberta*. His attention to detail and his obsession with perfection struck a recognizable chord with Astaire and their close collaboration and meticulous standards of creativity and professionalism had a lot to do with the success of *Top Hat*. In the end, though it failed to claim an Oscar, *Top Hat* was nominated for five top awards that year. Against powerful dramas like *The Informer* with Victor McLaglen, and MGM's *Mutiny on the Bounty,* a song-and-dance film was never going to stand much chance, but *Top Hat* was nonetheless nominated for the Best Picture of the Year, Best Art Direction (Van Nest Polglase and Carroll Clark), Best Dance Director for 'The Piccolino' (Hermes Pan) and was also specially honoured by the American publication, *Film Daily*. And while talking about honours for Astaire-Rogers pictures, *The Gay Divorcee,* in a quieter way perhaps, also won critical acclaim, being nominated for Best Picture, Best Art Direction (Van Nest Polglase and Carroll Clark), Best Scoring (RKO Music Department), Best Sound Recording (Carl Dreher) and Best Song ('The Continental', by Con Conrad and Herb Magidson).

Writers over the years have struggled to find the formula for the Astaire-Rogers success. They have plotted, analyzed, observed all the elements in depth, and from time to time put forward finely drawn, scientifically calculated and often scholarly assessments. But much of the time they have perhaps tried too hard to be objective and to pin-point and pigeon-hole. Their precisely logical findings seem disappointing and against the very spirit of the partnership, which was soft, rounded, flexible, extremely human and therefore fallible. You need only read Hermes Pan's description of the shooting of the 'Cheek to Cheek' number to put things into perspective, for it was he, and not Ginger, who made those precise and punchy dance steps. It was all to do with what is known as 'post film synchronizing', as Pan explained. 'I would have a pair of earphones and Fred would have a pair, too. I would do Ginger's taps and Fred would work on his. You stood on the wood flooring and watched the film and heard the music on the earphones; you then followed the action on the screen and just synchronized together.' Pan said they had to do it over and over again to get it right and it had to be split up into sections as it would have been virtually impossible to go through the whole routine with perfect timing. Fred himself was never pretentious about the magic of his dancing with Ginger. He much preferred, if you could get him to react at all, to smile disarmingly and suggest that they . . . *just danced.*

But it was never as easy or simple as he made out and opinions too cursorily formed and casually expressed do gross injustice to their boundless talent and uncanny feel for song and dance on film. It must begin with attitude. Astaire was a perfectionist. His demands on others were excessive, but he worked himself even harder. It is well known that for the 'Top Hat, White Tie and Tails' number he rehearsed for almost two months to reach the perfection which created one of the all-time music and dance classics on film.

He pushed himself so hard on *Holiday Inn* with Bing Crosby some years later that his body weight dropped fourteen pounds. For just one dance shot in *Roberta* it is said that he rehearsed every day for nine weeks, Sundays and holidays included. Often in life hard work has to make up for lack of vision or limited basic talent, but not with Astaire. Add his extraordinary application to brilliant tap technique and a sharp creative sense and the image begins to materialize. He was fortunate, too, in working so much with Hermes Pan, a kindred soul. They talked the same language, reached for similar objectives. Pan would see what Fred was getting at when he worked out his dance routines, and would dance Ginger's part with Fred in early run-throughs, offering suggestions and ideas. They were a superb partnership.

Also important was the way Astaire cleverly combined tap technique with flowing stage movement and even ballroom steps, to create mood and feeling, though he confessed to being a pitiful ballroom-dancer. In the early days tap-dancing on film was little advanced on dance class exercises. You hardly moved from one spot. It was a demonstration of technique and syncopation, clever and rhythmic, but hardly more than a demonstration nonetheless. Later, some dancers like the Nicholas Brothers for instance, would go to the other extreme, bounding from one side of the stage to the other in exceptionally active, athletic and clever routines. George Murphy and Dan Dailey adopted a similar approach to Astaire, but were too often solo dancers and they never captured the flair and sense of style which put Astaire into a class of his own. As an exponent of the dance, the one single quality of Astaire was the expressive way he danced with his whole body. The changing body movements, arms, shoulders, head, hands and fingers, even the face and eyes were all made to contribute to the mood and the expression of the routine. Not even Gene Kelly did this to the same extent, and his more muscular and less compact physique meant he was never able to project the sense of compactness, lightness and sheer grace of movement which was an Astaire hallmark.

He was alone in the skilful way he maintained interest and attention through even the longest routine with a rapid change of pace or direction. From an effortless glide he would move instantly into an incisive spin which in turn would be followed by two rapid and defiantly loud tap beats held back until the last fraction of a second. He was a master of the pause and no one matched him for creating light and shade.

The magic potion is now almost complete, but it still lacks two essential ingredients, plus, if you like, a bonus vitamin. One: in Ginger Rogers he found, or created, the perfect partner. Two: he was supported by some of the finest composers and lyricists of the day. The bonus was his deceptive ability to sing — and 'sell' a song. Ginger was a capable but not brilliant dancer. She was vivacious and charming and had a lovely figure; and she was a beautiful mover, particularly in the arms of Astaire. The merging of the two of them into a romantic dance partnership, however, was essentially due to Astaire. The choreography and its interpretation on the set was due substantially to the vision and feeling for a mood or situation which with Astaire was impeccable. Ginger's contribution, and it should not be underrated, was in creating the perfect foil. Other partners in later years never managed to fit quite so snugly into Fred's arms, nor were able so completely to suggest that special togetherness which Ginger found with Fred. By 1980s standard their dancing was sexless, yet in the twirling movements, the angle of the body, the juxtaposition of the two dancers and often by the sheer energy, vitality and excitement of their movements, there existed a distinct, if clean, kind of sensuality. It was compelling the way he made demands on her through the dance, often with movements which gradually gained speed and rhythm. Ginger, almost hypnotically responded to his lead and always it seemed, if the dance called for it, with just a shade of discomfort and difficulty. In its way this was supremely artistic. The sensuality would have been destroyed had Ginger matched Fred's demands with a frolicking ease and a big smile on her face. This was a new kind of screen love-play where, as writer Benny Green so aptly explained, 'consummation lies in the touch of a hand.'

Then there were the songwriters. Astaire attracted all the giants. They jumped at the chance of working with him, among them

George Gershwin, Cole Porter, Jerome Kern, Irving Berlin and the much underrated, in terms of popular recognition, song-and-words team of Jerry and Dorothy Fields. Their 'The Way You Look Tonight', which they wrote for *Swing Time,* embodies the very essence of that relaxed charm and romance of the Astaire-Rogers partnership. All these composers and lyricists had a profound effect on Astaire's career. That being so, then we come back to the genius of Pandro S. Berman, for not only did he 'discover' Fred Astaire for the movies, but it was he who hired Gershwin, Berlin and the others in one picture after another. As producer of eight of the ten Astaire-Rogers RKO musicals, his career flourished along with theirs. Though he had been with RKO since the company was formed in 1928, he maintained an element of independence for many years, sometimes, as with *The Gay Divorcee,* taking up ideas which RKO didn't want. His father Harry M. Berman had much earlier 'bought into' the small company which over five or six years was developed and, with the coming of the talkies, expanded into RKO. Almost from the start, it lacked corporate policy. Changes at the top occurred frequently and, in consequence, changes in ideas, direction and priorities. Within this unsettled and loose framework, whoever was in charge at any given time had the latitude to run the studios as he thought fit and make the films he wanted. In this way, it benefited from a young production genius called David O. Selznick who, though arrogant and tough, upgraded the studios' artistic reputation and was also responsible for recruiting Pandro Berman.

Berman's reputation rose along with the success of the Astaire-Rogers partnership, but shortly after producing Fred and Ginger in *The Story of Vernon and Irene Castle* in 1939, he left for MGM, discontented with the policies of RKO's new corporate president George Schaefer, Berman, above all others, recognized the importance of good music to the success of the Astaire-Rogers movie partnership, and acknowledged his good fortune in being able to attract the best composers to write for his films. Until then he reckoned nobody had done as much as he had in engaging the greatest song-writing talents of the day for one picture after another.

The bonus attached to the Astaire-Rogers movies was Fred's singing voice. To be fair, no one at the time thought it was very good. His voice, like his physical appearance, defied the accepted standards of the day. It was too thin and not sufficiently rounded and that's why, it is almost certain, he never made much of an impact on record. He said later he was disappointed about this. 'It would have been kinda fun to have had half a dozen smash records, but I never had anything like that.' But he had a pleasant enough voice which was not bad to listen to if there were other things going on. His 'discovery' as a singer was made years later, when commentators, writers and film historians who should know about such things started coming out enthusiastically about the way he 'sold a song'. Nobody interprets a lyric like Fred Astaire, they said, and they praised his phrasing. If you don't rate his singing any higher, it is difficult not to concede that the casual, disarming style and the sometimes almost frail intonation, added to the amalgam that was Astaire and Rogers. In some measure, it was his dancing brilliance and the movie magic he made with Ginger which left his voice with less than a sporting chance of making its mark. It was also perhaps slightly out of its time, trying to be heard in an era when the full-bodied tones of Crosby and others held sway.

Fred's own attitude to his singing voice was typically carefree. Critics may later have felt it chic to commend it, but Fred never reckoned he had much of a voice, or that he could sing well. The way he sang seemed to blend with the dance routines and the light-hearted storylines of his films, and that was all there was to it. He was as disarming and self-effacing about his singing ability as he was about his dancing success and his place as one of the giants of the movie business.

And so to the final garnishings. There were two. First, the talent of art director Van Nest Polglase, who seems to have fared less well than he might have expected at the hands of Astaire-Rogers buffs. Pandro Berman and directors Mark Sandrich and George Stevens, who between them worked on seven of the Astaire-Rogers movies, and even musical director Max Steiner, are documented in most accounts of the Fred Astaire-Ginger Rogers partnership. Polglase, however, receives little attention, though undoubtedly his skilful and imaginative sets, including particularly those false perspectives and effective backcloths in *Top Hat,* made an important contribution to the impact and success of the films. The second garnishing must surely be that certain, inexplicable, indefinable special something which Fred and Ginger seemed to find when they worked together on film. All the elements came together abundantly in *Top Hat* which for many remains the definitive Astaire-Rogers movie.

After filming ended, Fred took Phyllis on a short holiday to Europe. In just three years Astaire had climbed from being a film unknown to one of the biggest stars in Hollywood. There was little time to relax. RKO rushed through arrangements for his next film with Ginger, an adaptation by Dwight Taylor and Allan Scott of the play *Shore Leave* by Hubert Osborne, and he signed to do his first radio work, being featured as a kind of entertaining master of ceremonies for the Lucky Strike Hit Parade, to be beamed from New York. Fred, disarming as ever, wondered why, as principally a dancer, he had been chosen for radio. 'Not the best way to exploit my specialities', is how he put it. But he sang plenty of Irving Berlin's songs from *Top Hat* and enjoyed the experience.

Before that, however, he and Phyllis enjoyed that holiday in Europe. They went first to Ireland and to the beautiful Lismore Castle, where Adele was enjoying a blissful marriage with Charles. The good news was that she was expecting another baby in a few months' time. Then he and Phyllis moved on to London and it was while they were in Britain that Phyllis broke the news that she, too, was pregnant. They celebrated quietly in their hotel with a half bottle of champagne. A few days later they were back in New York where Fred prepared for his radio show. After being put together there for a couple of weeks, the whole thing moved with Fred to California so he could begin rehearsals for *Follow the Fleet*. For a while life was particularly hectic as he attended the film set every day and prepared for his weekly radio show at night. He wasn't sorry when the radio commitment came to an end. Despite his success, he continued to live modestly, much preferring to stay home in the evenings with Phyllis than go out on the town. He seemed unimpressed by his new-found stardom and his values remained the same. He was devoted to his mother, retained strong and affectionate links with sister Adele, and most of all his life with Phyllis was idyllic.

It is hardly surprising, therefore, that the news that Adele had lost twin boys in birth shattered and saddened him greatly.

SEVEN

Just one darn film after another

Six pictures in the next four years — five of them with Ginger Rogers — was to be Fred Astaire's busy programme. Pandro Berman was a sound businessman as well as being a successful producer of films, though it did not take a genius to see that casting Astaire once more with Rogers was the only sensible move to make. The objective and challenge now was how best to repeat the successful formula. Like most people in the risk business, Berman did not shorten his odds unnecessarily. So he stuck with the elements which were to make *Top Hat* a smash hit. He kept Mark Sandrich as director, had Max Steiner once more direct the music, and re-engaged writers Dwight Taylor and Allan Scott. Dance director and art director respectively were, of course, Hermes Pan and Van Nest Polglase. Irving Berlin was the natural choice for both music and lyrics.

Berman didn't wait for shooting to end on *Top Hat* before fixing up the next film. *Shore Leave* had been a silent movie back in 1925 and although RKO had made a successful musical version of this Hubert Osborne play in 1930, called *Hit the Deck* starring Jack Oakie, Berman wasn't put off. As *Follow the Fleet,* the new story was based more on the original play than the movie. It featured Fred as a dancer turned sailor and Ginger as a dance-hall girl and former partner who together put on a show to help raise funds to salvage a ship. It was a trite little tale which did nobody any harm except perhaps Randolph Scott. Loaned from Paramount, he took the romantic lead opposite Harriet Hilliard in a secondary plot and, although he had done well in *Roberta,* he looked somewhat out of place and uncomfortable in this latest Astaire-Rogers offering. Early in the 1930s he had appeared in a series of Zane Grey-inspired westerns and later went on to become the archetypal film cowboy. Lucille Ball, Betty Grable and Tony Martin were cast in minor parts.

While Berman made plans and Fred and Phyllis snatched their brief holiday in Europe, Ginger slotted in another inconsequential

81

movie called *In Person,* with George Brent. She had enjoyed *Top Hat* and was later to claim it as her favourite of all the seventy-plus films she made. So after *In Person* she was more than ready to return to Astaire for *Follow the Fleet.* Astaire swopped his top hat, white tie and tails for a sailor suit, but the throwaway style, the casual manner, the intriguing singing voice and, most of all, the perfection of his dancing were still there in abundance. Ginger's partnering was as charming as ever. The film followed the pattern of previous Astaire-Rogers movies by finishing with a show-stopper. This time it was the magical 'Let's Face the Music and Dance' for which Fred reverts to tails, and Ginger appears in a fur-collared full evening-gown. It was timed as a four-minute sequence to be shot complete without a break, but Ginger's dress again caused problems. It was quite heavy with beaded sleeves which hung loose at the wrists and Fred had his doubts about its suitability during rehearsal. In the middle of a dance those sleeves could inflict a nasty blow and Fred knew he must be careful to keep out of their way. The easy-going Ginger said it would be all right and Fred, without thinking too much about it, didn't object. Early on in the actual shooting Ginger spun quickly and her sleeve clouted Fred in the face. He reckoned it dazed him so much he couldn't remember much about the rest of the take. Although it looked okay to the crew, they shot it again just in case, but it didn't flow well. They worked all day on the sequence, right through until eight o'clock in the evening. They'd done some twenty takes by the time they crawled home, and still weren't sure that they wouldn't have to continue the agony next morning. But when they saw the rushes they found that the very first take was fine and it was the one which was used in the picture.

Irving Berlin's score for *Follow the Fleet* was well up to the standard of *Top Hat* and Astaire did it justice by following his policy of not repeating anything he had done before in his dance sequences with Ginger. His originality in 'I'd Rather Lead a Band' is impressive and exciting as he leads his fellow sailors through a fascinating and extremely precise close-order tap drill. The plot, simpler than the *Top Hat* story, has Fred taking the part of Bake Baker who, as the film opens, is featured in a breezy 'on deck' ensemble number while mockingly singing about the benefits of being in the United States Navy in 'We Saw the Sea'. Later, visiting the Paradise Ballroom in San Francisco with his buddies, he meets his former dancing partner, Sherry Martin, played by Ginger, where she is a featured singer. Sherry loses her job after she and Bake win a dance contest and he promises to help her find something else. Before he can do anything, his ship leaves port for distant parts, but when he gets back to San Francisco he does find her work, but foolishly if innocently, ruins her chances almost immediately. To make amends he offers to put on a benefit show to help Sherry's sister, Connie (Harriet Hilliard) raise money to recondition a dilapidated ship left to her by her father. Because of Bake and Sherry's final number, the show is an outstanding success and the ship is saved.

The dancing of Fred Astaire and Ginger Rogers was the spectacular success of *Follow the Fleet,* though Berlin's outstanding score included such memorable songs as 'I'm Putting All My Eggs in One Basket', 'Let's Face the Music and Dance', 'Let Yourself Go', and a number which went high in the Hit Parade in 1936, 'We Saw the Sea'. The way Astaire and Pan worked together to keep dance routines fresh and stimulating is well demonstrated in *Follow the Fleet.* As a dance develops, Ginger gets stuck in a step and stays frozen until Fred comes back and nudges her out of it. She quickly catches up with him and along they go together again until Ginger gets stuck yet again and once more Fred comes back and nudges her. It was imaginative and novel, and once Astaire and Pan had stumbled on the gimmick it would have been easy for them to wring it dry. But in the context of the entire routine it was used cleverly and with discretion and was a joy to watch; a fine example of Astaire and Pan's subtlety and style. In 'Let Yourself Go' the sparkling exuberance of Fred and Ginger sends a tingle up your spine as they out-dance all the other couples to win the contest. For sheer energy, vitality, pace and style — not to say technique, the number lingers with many Astaire buffs as still one of the best of its kind. Ginger, clad in exotic bell-bottom satin trousers and shimmering blouse, and Fred in his Jack Tar uniform, build up the rhythm and excitement in a formidable routine which for pure 'swinging' appeal matched anything they had done before.

Stripping Fred of his formal dress and giving him a sailor's uniform to wear worked well and complemented his easy charm and perky style. It perhaps invests Berman and/or the writers with too much skill and guile to suggest that the story was chosen intentionally for that reason, but supposing it was, then it was even more astute of them to put him back into evening dress for the final number. The successful and profitable image of Astaire was as the debonair man-about-town and that is the picture which, in potential cash terms, audiences must be left with, primed for the next offering. For whatever reason, however, 'Let's Face the Music and Dance' was honourably justified. The melody is haunting, the song original and the dancing supremely matched to the mood of the occasion, and executed, one is left to conclude, as only Astaire and Rogers could.

As shooting continued on *Follow the Fleet, Top Hat* marched on in triumph, eventually taking up what seemed likely to become an unassailable position at the head of Astaire-Rogers movies. *Follow the Fleet* didn't really have much of a chance of catching *Top Hat* in commercial terms, but it fared well; very well in fact. By now it was almost impossible to stop the treadmill of Astaire-Rogers musicals and while *Follow the Fleet* was still in production, Pandro Berman sorted out details for their next film together, to be called *Swing Time*. Both went out on release in 1936 and contributed substantially to the two and a half million dollars of profit made that year by RKO. The two Astaire-Rogers films topped the studio's revenue chart for 1936, being placed well ahead of all the other thirty-seven films released by RKO that year.

It is doubtful if Fred himself knew how much he was worth once the Astaire-Rogers bandwagon began to roll — but he must have been among the richest men in America. Certainly he figured among the 'best paid' Hollywood stars in 1935 with reputed earnings of almost 128,000 dollars for the year.

Despite their phenomenal success together, Astaire managed to convey a feeling of unease about the partnership when considering this period years later. It is difficult not to conclude that he tolerated it only with some difficulty and that he would not be too disturbed if circumstances should somehow dictate a change of course. In his autobiography he uses tell-tale phrases like 'the old cycle kept rolling on' and 'there seemed to be no sign of a let up in interest for these musicals and it was difficult for any of us to make a decision about breaking up the format'. Astaire must have been an extremely rich man, but it's hard to believe that this could have been the reason for his indifference. It is more likely that he was simply becoming tired of the stereotyped format of his films with Ginger and was looking for something fresh. He had never favoured being cast continually with the same partner and seemed less irritated years later when his co-stars changed with virtually every new film. It is hardly likely that at this stage he was seriously keen to act. That didn't happen for another twenty-three years with the widely acclaimed *On the Beach*. These instincts were always stronger and keener in Ginger who, while never seeing herself as a great dramatic actress, always looked for suitable straight roles. At about this time John Ford was casting for a new film about Queen Elizabeth of England and Ginger did an 'anonymous' test. But after such enormous success with Fred as his singing-and-dancing girlfriend in so many hit pictures, it was hard for any director to see her as anything else and the part went to Katherine Hepburn.

Meantime, Pandro Berman's concern was to get the next picture rolling as soon as possible and he once again assembled most of the regular members of the package for *Swing Time.* However, George Stevens came in for Mark Sandrich as director, and Jerome Kern, not Irving Berlin, was hired to do the musical score. Dorothy Fields provided the lyrics. Only the year before, of course, Kern had worked with Astaire on *Roberta,* but all except two songs had been lifted from the Harbach-Kern Broadway original. 'I Won't Dance' and 'Lovely to Look At' were Kern's new compositions and, with lyrics supplied by Dorothy Fields, they had been brilliantly successful. So Kern and Fields were brought together again for *Swing Time* to provide a complete new song package, and their work was sensational. Two numbers became all-time Astaire classics — 'The Way You Look Tonight', which won an Academy Award in the best song category, and 'A Fine Romance' — and the show-stopping 'Bojangles of Harlem', with Fred dancing with shadows, made many fans and critics rate *Swing Time* the best Astaire-Rogers film yet, even ahead of *Top Hat.* It also provided a welcome return of a recognizable comedy element in the form of Helen ·Broderick and Eric Blore.

For the first time, New York was chosen as the background to the film with Fred playing Lucky Garnett, leader of a team of vaudeville dancers and on the verge of marrying his hometown sweetheart, played by Betty Furness. In New York he falls in love with dancing instructor Penny Carrol (Ginger Rogers). The plot followed the well established pattern of misunderstandings, complications and true love almost lost, before the final reconciliation of Fred and Ginger. Howard Lindsay, who incidentally had directed *Gay Divorce* on stage, and Allan Scott, who had worked on the scripts of *Roberta, Top Hat* and *Follow the Fleet,* adapted Erwin Gelsey's original *Portrait of John Garnett,* and as usual left ample room to include the reason for it all: those extraordinary songs and dances from Fred and Ginger.

'Pick Yourself Up' was notable for being danced on the bare boards of a practice room and without accompaniment. It was one of the most athletic routines they had done. To cope with the pace and movement of the finale, Ginger's dress had to be extra generously cut. 'The Way You Look Tonight' comes at a point in the film where Ginger is furious with Fred for not showing up for an important night club audition because he doesn't have any evening clothes. It is vintage Astaire in what had become by now a vintage

Astaire-Rogers romantic situation, Fred charming Ginger and easing her out of her anger through dance and song. Jerome Kern's ballad and Dorothy Field's impeccable words matched the mood superbly and there was so much inherent quality and taste about the song that it is not surprising it won an Academy Award. In sharp contrast was the exuberant 'Waltz in Swing Time' which in the film Fred and Ginger use as an audition number. For graceful control and sustained timing it is sheer perfection, lasting some two and a half minutes and shot in one continuous take. Ginger's radiance in long white, fluffy gown contrasts delightfully with Fred's, as usual, impeccable dress-clothes.

Of the six numbers written by Jerome Kern and Dorothy Fields specially for *Swing Time,* 'A Fine Romance' has perhaps lasted best of all in its close association with Astaire. No one made songs more his own than he did and no one song fuses with his image so completely as 'A Fine Romance'. In dance terms, however, the sensation of the film was a number called 'Bojangles of Harlem', devised by Hermes Pan as a tribute to the father of American screen tap-dancing, Bill 'Bojangles' Robinson. The sequence was inspired. Fred dances the number first with the girls of the chorus and then, once the set is cleared, by himself. Black-faced and dressed in jazzy jacket, side-striped trousers, jaunty hat and white gloves, he is alone against the white backcloth. As he moves once more to the music, three enormous shadows of himself materialize on the backcloth and begin to dance in perfect unison with his own movements. That in itself was an outstanding idea, full of impact, but the way Astaire and Pan developed the theme was little short of screen genius. Fred gradually builds up the pace and complexity of his dancing. His shadows have difficulty staying with him and in the end they lose the beat, admit defeat and storm off the backcloth in disgust.

Hermes Pan later described how he got the idea: 'I was on the rehearsal stage one morning and there were top lights on the stage which were casting shadows on the floor from different angles, so if you moved around you would see a shadow here and a shadow there. So when Fred came in I told him this was an interesting effect for a dance. And from that evolved the Bojangles number.' Dorothy Fields mentioned the lengths Fred went to to impress upon Jerome Kern the need to capture in the number, not jazz exactly, but more of a hot beat. He apparently went over to Kern's house one morning and danced all over the place — living-room, upstairs, alongside the pool — demonstrating how he felt it should be done. It was an exciting number, outstanding in a film which fully maintained the standards set by previous Astaire-Rogers musicals. It came as no surprise to anyone when Hermes Pan was nominated for an Academy Award in the best dance direction category for the Bojangles number, for it was a delightful example of screen imagery.

'Never Gonna Dance' was another masterpiece. The dance comes towards the end of the movie where Fred and Ginger take an anguished musical farewell before the final joyous and ultimate reunion. For a musical film it was quite an emotional moment with Ginger about to go off into the night never, it seems, to see Fred again. But, of course, everyone knew differently. The dancing starts quietly with Fred luring Ginger into the movements. The excitement develops as the sequence gains pace and then the movements ease down again as Ginger takes her wistful parting. It was beautifully done, but the final movie-screening gives no hint of the punishing hard work and infinite patience required to get it right. Pan reckoned it took well over forty takes to get the last sixteen bars as they wanted it and Ginger, never complaining, literally had raw and bleeding feet at the end.

A lot has been written about the heavy demands made by Fred on Ginger in the cause of dance perfection, less about Ginger's attitude. Most of the time she was responsive, co-operative and didn't get angry, though during the shooting of *Swing Time* she was said to have become difficult to work with — brought on largely perhaps through her frustration at being partnered repeatedly with Fred in song-and-dance films when she really wanted to carry out a dramatic career for herself; less so at having to play second fiddle to Fred so often.

Swing Time opened in New York to full houses. Once more it seemed that the Astaire-Rogers bandwagon had rolled on to another smash hit. It registered huge business once released nationwide. Fred and Ginger were now rated third in a major motion picture poll of top box-office stars, only Shirley Temple and Clark Gable were ahead. But for all the promise, Astaire wasn't convinced that the public was not beginning to tire of the familiar routine. The warning signs were beginning to show, for it was now obvious that *Follow the Fleet,* for all its initial impact, was not going to be as good box-office as *Top Hat.* Time would prove that *Swing Time,* again despite its promising start, would begin to dip even sooner and gross even less; but Fred really was too busy to analyze the situation too much. *Shall We Dance,* a follow-up to *Swing Time* and again with Ginger, had already been slotted into the RKO studio programme and he was now also busy in radio and record deals. Against his better judgement and Phyllis's advice, for he knew it would mean a cripplingly heavy schedule, he signed to do thirty-nine weeks with the Packard Motor Car Company as master of ceremonies for their hour-long weekly radio show. He would do a number of songs, some dancing, and take part in a few comedy sketches. He was well into this routine when shooting began on *Shall We Dance*. Although Astaire's recording career had begun in London as early as 1923, he didn't really get into his stride in the United States until 1935, but from then until 1938, he made a total of thirty recordings for the Brunswick label, all featuring the hits from his own movies.

So life was even busier than usual and, typically, Fred worried about fitting everything in and particularly about not having enough time to plan his radio commitments properly. But Packard were delighted and in the end the professional satisfaction Fred enjoyed from widening his activities more than made up for his anxieties, certainly for the time being. Filming, of course, continued to be his main activity, and Pandro Berman had yet again marshalled a formidable and well-tried tour-de-force for *Shall We Dance*. The lovely Harriet Hoctor, with whom Fred dances a ballet-type number, was in this one, along with Eric Blore, who had been in *Swing Time*. The film also benefited from the return of that superb professional, Edward Everett Horton, who had last appeared with Fred and Ginger in *Top Hat* and had really been missed since then. Berman continued as producer, Mark Sandrich was back as director, who else could be dance and art director respectively but Hermes Pan and Van Nest Polglase, and George and Ira Gershwin were brought in to supply the music and lyrics.

This time Astaire is a ballet-dancer, with more than a little twinkle in his toes, and Ginger is a musical comedy star. Fred pursues Ginger in time-honoured tradition, but complications arise when, through a misunderstanding, it is generally assumed that they are already married. Ginger's manager, played with finesse by Jerome Cowan, encourages the belief to prevent her from marrying and retiring from the stage. The usual complications and diversions follow until Fred and Ginger agree that the only way to convince everyone that they are not married, is to get married; then they can divorce immediately after. The ceremony takes place, they go on a short honeymoon, but soon realize that they really are in love and dance out of the film together.

Shall We Dance, though enjoyable and commendable, was to become a turning point in the Astaire-Rogers partnership. By the time shooting ended, box-office returns from *Swing Time* were giving more than a hint that perhaps at last the formula was losing its magic spell. The signs were unmistakable, though neither film was remotely a failure. *Swing Time,* as already mentioned, contributed handsomely to RKO profits for 1936 and *Shall We Dance* was to make well over 400,000 dollars profit for the studio. But the decline was enough for Astaire to suggest a temporary break from Ginger. She agreed totally, for despite their overwhelming success together, both had seemed impatient from quite an early stage to move on to other things. Ginger's ambition to do some straight acting was well known and although Fred had been unsettled by the way the partnership continued with no discernible end, there were also rumours of rows and disagreements in the same way that there had been gossip and speculation about off-screen romance in the early days. None of it was true. The split was by general consensus and it was not decided at that time to make it permanent. Indeed, while Ginger went off to do *Stage Door* with Katherine Hepburn and Adolphe Menjou, Pandro Berman had already fixed up for Fred to star in *A Damsel in Distress* and, more significantly, had also schemed into his 1938 calendar the return of the Astaire-Rogers partnership in a film to be called *Carefree*.

The Gershwin score for *Shall We Dance* was sparkling. Although in some ways dancing took a back seat, there were many memorable moments and of the six musical numbers created for the film, three were quickly to establish themselves as Astaire exclusives. The most talked about was the sensational dance on roller-skates to Gershwin's 'Let's Call the Whole Thing Off'. It took up only two and a half minutes of film time yet four whole days were spent in shooting the sequence and Fred and Ginger were said to have covered an estimated eighty miles in doing it. Fred and Ginger meet in Central Park to avoid reporters and the novel twist which made it such a talking point comes when they see a roller-skating rink and decide to have a go. Developed out of a basic idea of Hermes Pan, it took around 150 separate takes to get it right, but some reviewers said it was unnecessary and pretentious. But for all that the dancing is still impressive and the execution immaculate — the result of Fred and Ginger spending three whole days getting the feel of moving on skates.

Another Astaire standard was born on a New Jersey to Manhattan ferryboat at night and amid the plaintiveness of the fog swirling around the water as Fred sings to Ginger: 'They Can't Take That Away From Me'. *Shall We Dance* is also remembered for 'They All Laughed' and perhaps marginally less so, for 'Slap That Bass'. In the latter, Astaire displays his virtuosity in an imaginative setting in which he sings and dances against the syncopation of a ship's machinery. The former had all those indefinable qualities which made it an Astaire 'natural' from the outset. The number starts with Ginger singing, after being called up front at a nightclub where she is dining with Fred. At the end of the song, and to her discomfort, the bandleader announces that her partner is also present and invites Fred to join Ginger to dance. His balletic leaps leave Ginger at a loss, but after the fun he soon eases into a fine tap routine, with Ginger joining in. The sequence ends in spectacular fashion with a giant leap on to a piano. It was vintage Astaire-Rogers and as charming, dazzling and captivating as anything done before. Visually, however, the most fascinating sequence was towards the end of the movie. Astaire gives director Mark Sandrich credit for the idea which had him dancing with a whole chorus of Ginger Rogers look-alikes. The number — 'Shall We Dance' — has all fourteen girls wearing face masks, the real Ginger revealing herself towards the end of the sequence.

The temporary break-up of the Astaire-Rogers partnership proved to be a happier interlude professionally for Ginger than for Fred, fuelling niggling doubts among some observers that Astaire couldn't survive commercially on his own. *Stage Door* gave Ginger one of her best straight parts till then and her first-class portrayal of a materialistic, sarcastic broad won her good notices, despite the proximity of Oscar-winning Katherine Hepburn. One critic said she was a 'brilliant individual comedienne'. Another praised her performance above that of Hepburn. The film was widely recognized as being the best of the year from RKO. It received four Oscar nominations, even if it didn't rate too highly in profit terms.

Fred's *Damsel in Distress,* meantime, turned out to be a sad experience because of the incomprehensible casting of Joan Fontaine opposite Astaire. Ruby Keeler was tipped for the part, so was Jessie Matthews, but it went finally to the up-and-coming Fontaine, recently signed by RKO. Theoretically, the film had everything to make it a winner — sound production and direction by Pandro Berman and George Stevens, immaculate dance and art direction from Hermes Pan and Van Nest Polglase, and also superb music and lyrics by George and Ira Gershwin. But the sad reality was that Joan Fontaine was not a singer, nor a dancer, and didn't possess the ability or experience at that time to showcase, as Ginger did, Astaire's polished talent. They had only one dance number but Miss Fontaine's inability to complement Fred's artistry was painfully and embarrassingly obvious, despite valiant 'paste-over' efforts by director George Stevens. It had its good points — a more soundly based P.G. Wodehouse script, effortless comedy performances from

George Burns and Gracie Allen, and an Oscar went to dance director Hermes Pan — but this surely was one film which Astaire-Rogers fans might have wanted to forget — except for that superlative Gershwin music. 'Nice Work If You Can Get It' quickly became an Astaire special and 'A Foggy Day' was destined to become one of the greatest popular music standards of all time.

Fred made light of the film's shortcomings, concentrating more on the relief he had experienced resulting from the break in his partnership with Ginger. 'This was my second professional separation, of course, and I felt certain about never wanting to get into that sort of predicament again,' he revealed in *Steps in Time.* Of the picture itself, he thought it was a 'goodish picture' though not a 'strong picture', but it's true to say that his comment that Joan had handled their one dance together 'beautifully' was an opinion not shared by many people. It is difficult to pin-point Astaire's ingratiating attitude towards his partnership with Ginger; not to Ginger, for whom he has always appeared to have had the greatest respect, but the partnership. Was it simply the routine of it all? Was it that the demands of the partnership and its astonishing success prevented him from performing in ways which were more attractive to him? The latter hardly seems to have been the case because when he finally shook himself clear of Ginger he continued to make films which were fundamentally the same — but with different co-stars. Not until 1959, by which time he was over sixty, did he emerge as a totally different kind of entertainer — an actor — and a fine one at that in his own right. Nor does the former emerge clearly as the reason, for when the partnership was virtually at an end at the conclusion of shooting on *Carefree,* he was negative and uncertain about the future and even, by his own admission, thinking about the possibility of retirement.

With the end of production on *Shall We Dance,* Astaire took the chance to ease back on his work schedule and pulled out of his radio commitments. The Packard Hour radio show was a commercial success and the sponsors were disappointed and reluctant to let Fred go. He enjoyed radio and said later that he never really felt that he had made the most of the radio opportunities open to him. But at the time the burden of filming, combined with a weekly radio show commitment, was just too great. When he insisted he was serious in wanting to leave, arrangements were made for him to be released from his forthcoming options. He was disappointed to sever relations with Johnny Green. Both professionally and as a colleague he had got on well with the talented bandleader and composer and during their thirty-nine show stint, they had worked out many interesting numbers together.

Fred was stunned and saddened soon after by the shock death of George Gershwin. He had seldom been ill, but while working on *A Damsel in Distress,* he had suffered severe headaches. These led on one occasion to temporary paralysis of the hands, so he could not play the piano. He died at the tragically early age of thirty-nine shortly after an operation and before *Damsel* was released.

Some of Astaire's success was undoubtedly due to his close liaison with the most talented popular music composers of the day, the inspired works of people like Jerome Kern, Irving Berlin and George Gershwin making a substantial contribution to the immortality of his work. The wonderful vision of those sparkling films with Ginger would fade with the passing of time, but those haunting melodies would, as surely as the song predicted, 'linger on'. Fred, as mentioned earlier, had known Gershwin from the days when they were both struggling unknowns and living on dreams. George had fantasized about writing a major hit musical for Fred and Adele. The breaks came earlier for the Astaires, but in 1924 Gershwin's dream became fact when he and brother Ira wrote the music and lyrics for their first major Broadway musical, *Lady, Be Good!,* and, appropriately, Fred and Adele were the stars. The association was revived again on Broadway in *Funny Face,* but looking back on their successes together — although Astaire and Rogers made seven successful musical films in the five years 1933-1937 — regrettably, only for *Shall We Dance* (and *A Damsel in Distress,* featuring Fred without Ginger), did Gershwin write the music. It is sad also, in view of their close friendship, that Gershwin had not felt completely satisfied with his work on *Shall We Dance.*

Pandro Berman pulled the old team together once more for *Carefree.* Ginger was pleased to be back with Fred. After the successful *Stage Door,* two more RKO films, *Having Wonderful Time* with Douglas Fairbanks Junior, and *Vivacious Lady* with James Stewart, had done little to further her career as a dramatic screen actress. Fred, too, for all his earlier protestations, admitted that he liked the idea of resuming the partnership for a couple more films. No one closely associated with the making of these Astaire-Rogers movies was now harbouring any real delusions that the best times were over. *Carefree* was to be the test, for after the self-imposed break, it would show if their massive box-office following could be recaptured. One more film had already been scheduled to follow *Carefree* — out of tune in some respects with the light, romantic, fictional offerings of their 'series' films. In contrast, *The Story of Vernon and Irene Castle,* was to be based on the succcessful partnership of real-life ballroom-dancers. It would end the Fred Astaire-Ginger Rogers association for a decade.

Carefree had a stronger plot than many of Astaire's earlier films with Rogers and included his most memorable and sensational dance routine. Irving Berlin did a wonderful job with original music and lyrics. It is a pity, therefore, that it came towards the end of the Astaire-Rogers cycle for in all it was a better film than some which scored more heavily. *Carefree,* unfairly, was the first Fred-and-Ginger film to lose money at the box-office. It proved that the public appetite had been satisfied and that nothing, even in the magic world of films, lasts for ever. In this movie, Fred is a psychiatrist who agrees to psychoanalyze Ginger to find out why she keeps breaking off her engagement. Ginger falls for Fred, but in a determined effort to remain true to her fiancé, forces him to hypnotize her to impress on her subconscious that she hates Fred and loves her fiancé. But the whole thing is satisfactorily unravelled before the end of the film, with Fred and Ginger happily together. *Carefree* gave Ginger the opportunity to show just what a good comedienne she was. The film was also special because it was the first time in all their films together that Fred was called on to play anything other than a dancer or musician. But most of all, *Carefree* became a popular Astaire-Rogers legend because in this, their eighth film together, Fred kissed Ginger for the very first time. Astaire never saw himself as a popular hero and probably because of this, discouraged any talk of romantic scenes in his early movies with Ginger. All the flirtation and love was subtly expressed in song-and-dance, so director Mark Sandrich went along with the idea. As most films then had what Fred described as 'mushy love scenes' or 'sticky clinches', their absence in Astaire-Rogers films was different, a novelty, almost a gimmick. Certainly, the idea seemed to be an asset early on, but as one film led to another, with still no kissing, the fan magazines took up the theme that it was really because Fred's wife Phyllis objected to the idea and had forbidden him to kiss his co-star. Even Ginger reckoned that the reason she and Fred didn't kiss was because Phyllis wouldn't have liked it, or that Fred thought she wouldn't approve.

Fred reckoned by this time that the speculation had gone far enough and decided in *Carefree* to turn it to advantage and gain additional publicity for the film. Courteously, he asked Ginger if she would mind if he, as he put it, 'gave her the kiss of the century so that they might end this international crisis'. Responding in the spirit of the occasion she joked: 'Oh, all right — but you'll have to speak to my agent.' The momentous moment came at the end of a dream dance sequence to Irving Berlin's 'I used to be Colour Blind'. The slow-motion ending was novel and was also judged as an ideal slot for the kiss. To create the desired effect, a special camera was used. The scene dissolved with Fred and Ginger holding the kiss, but Sandrich let the special camera run on. There was great fun next morning at the rushes. Fred had invited Phyllis to come and see this landmark in his career and the slow-motion dance went through beautifully. Then came the kiss and, because of Mark Sandrich's fooling during shooting, the kiss was held on screen for all of four minutes. The place was in uproar with Phyllis laughing more than anyone. In the film, of course, it lasted only four or five seconds.

Berlin's score for *Carefree* included a particularly exciting dance number for Fred and Ginger called 'The Yam'. Popular show business writer, the late Dick Richards, described it as 'almost an anthology of the Astaire-Rogers technique, with dash, movement, pauses, timing, elan and dramatic lifts'. In fact, lifts and jumps are what Astaire did perhaps more than any other dancer. This he felt would be a problem for him when he first went into radio, for his dancing was restricted to a small square close to the microphone. 'There wasn't much I could do in the way of steps, because my regular style was to cover ground and also get off the floor and up in the air a lot,' he once said. 'Change Partners' was another Berlin number composed especially for *Carefree* and which quickly became an Astaire special. Like so many of the songs featured first in Astaire-Rogers movies, it was still being played forty years later. In this sequence Ginger pretended to be hypnotized, leaving Fred free to take her through a delightful and graceful dance routine to Berlin's captivating melody.

Ralph Bellamy was also in *Carefree,* playing Ginger's fiancé, along with Jack Carson and delightful Franklin Pangborn, Luella Gear and Clarence Kolb. The impeccable sets and imaginative dance direction were once more triumphs for Van Nest Polglase and Hermes Pan. The song 'Since They Turned Loch Lomond Into Swing' was soon forgotten, but Astaire's dance sequence to it was brilliant, spectacular and one of the most remarkable dance routines ever committed to film. One report described it as 'dazzling almost beyond belief'. The basis of the routine is simplicity itself. There is a line of golf balls. Fred swings a golf club at each ball in quick successsion, but the whole extraordinary sequence is wrapped round some extremely nifty foot movements. No one has described it better than Philip Jenkinson: 'The finale, when he drives five balls down the fairway in perfect syncopation with his tapping feet and the quickening beat, ranks among the great virtuoso numbers of all time.' His control was extraordinary. The routine was unbelievably difficult, demanding the most precise timing. It was Astaire's own idea. Golf was his favourite game and he had planned a golf sequence some years before, but didn't get a chance to slot it into one of his movies. He got the feel of the idea on the Bel Air Golf Course, found it worked and convinced Mark Sandrich that it should be written into *Carefree*. For two solid weeks he practised on an improvised driving range on the set, using buckets and 300 golf balls. The result was staggering. It became, along with 'Change Partners', one of his favourite numbers.

Carefree was only short, lasting just 83 minutes against 100 minutes for *A Damsel in Distress* and 116 minutes for *Shall We Dance,* but it was good value for money. Fred and Ginger were to do two more films together, but *Carefree* was effectively the end of those lighthearted, romantic offerings in song and dance which had so captivated cinema audiences for the past six years.

Work on *The Story of Vernon and Irene Castle* began about September 1938. Rumblings of war were being heard across Europe, times were changing, and the world was becoming a different place. Even Astaire and Rogers were to part! The news that *The Castles* would be their last movie together was received with dismay by their devoted fans. Though the audience for film musicals was shrinking, seeing Fred Astaire and Ginger Rogers in their romantic offerings had become for many a way of life, seeing them through the aftermath years of the Depression and remaining as fairy tale havens in the troubled times that followed. Fans wrote letters of protest. Newspapers and fan magazines gave plenty of space to the news. On the film set, however, nothing much happened. There was no major farewell party, no sad lingering departure scenes, not even when *The Castles* had finished shooting and everyone went their separate ways.

If *The Story of Vernon and Irene Castle* was untypical of Astaire-Rogers musicals, it at least brought them together again for one more time. The Castles had been a phenomenally successful husband-and-wife ballroom-dancing partnership in the years before the First World War, but the famous partnership ended with the death of Vernon in a training accident just before he was due to be released from the service. Based on Irene Castle's real-life story, the film was a major departure for Fred and Ginger. For the first time when co-starring together they played real people, playing out a dramatized version of a real story. Instead of new songs from a contemporary composer which could quickly become identified with Astaire and Rogers, there were well-known numbers from the years covered by the picture such as 'The Maxixe', 'The Tango' and 'The Texas Tommy'. Whatever the film's critical assessment, it lost 50,000 dollars at the box-office. Many would have preferred the sequence of Astaire-Rogers musicals to have ended with a film more typical of their greatest successes, and with an outstanding triumph, but there were consolations in *The Story of Vernon and Irene Castle*. The film did justice to the memory of The Castles and it included over sixty old songs including favourites like 'When You Wore a Tulip', 'Robert E. Lee', 'Little Brown Jug', 'By the Light of the Silvery Moon' and 'Hello, Frisco, Hello'.

It also brought to an end a special period of movie history. Had it not been for the sensational and massive commercial success of Astaire and Rogers dancing and singing together, RKO would undoubtedly have gone out of business. The partnership had also nurtured the delectable skills of Hermes Pan and Van Nest Polglase. Without being heard by so many people in Astaire-Rogers musicals, it is doubtful if those gloriously abiding melodies of George Gershwin, Jerome Kern, Cole Porter and Irving Berlin would have been able to lodge themselves quite so deeply into the hearts of nations? Indeed, would they have been written at all? Tap-dancing itself, as a popular art-form, owes almost everything to those Astaire-Rogers films. But now it was over. For the time being, the public had grown tired of screen musicals, and, even, it seemed of two performers who together had virtually created the popular form.

So an epoch ended. Pandro S. Berman, the dynamic film executive whose vision had spotted the potential in teaming Astaire with Rogers in the first place and had astutely chaperoned the development of the partnership with his choice of film material and composers, was about to cut away from RKO. *The Story of Vernon and Irene Castle,* for which he was executive producer, was his last film for the studio. He resigned as head of production and departed at the end of the year for the mighty MGM. He and Astaire did not work together again. Ironically, while the last in the sequence of Astaire-Rogers films was not a financial success, two pictures which Ginger made on her own in 1939 — *Bachelor Mother* with David Niven and *Fifth Avenue Girl* — were among the most profitable RKO released that year.

As Europe went to war and the world faced momentous change, the partnership of Fred Astaire and Ginger Rogers which had glistened and glowed through nine magical movies, faded from view. Members of the team whose lives had been governed for seven

Pandro Berman, genius at RKO who recognized the potential in pairing Fred Astaire and Ginger Rogers. He produced all their most successful films together.

Fred and Phyllis arrive in Ireland to be greeted by their brother-in-law, Lord Charles Cavendish, in 1939. The Astaires stayed at Adele and Charles's home at Lismore Castle in County Waterford.

A new partner for Fred Astaire. In *Broadway Melody of 1940* he successfully teamed with Eleanor Powell, one of the greatest female dancers of all time, and George Murphy.

Much of Fred's successful radio work was with bandleader conductor Johnny Green. The pair are seen working with an obvious degree of informality on the script for Fred's Packard Hour, put out by the NBC Red Network each Tuesday evening at 9.30.

Fred worked with some of the loveliest girls in Hollywood. In *Second Chorus* (1940) his co-star was Paulette Goddard. Band-leader clarinetist Artie Shaw was also in the film, along with Burgess Meredith.

Fred said he danced a lot of th
time off the ground, and prove
it with Rita Hayworth in this
still from *You'll Never Get
Rich*. He held a particular
affection for Miss Hayworth,
with whom he starred again in
You Were Never Lovelier.

Joan Leslie was seventeen,
Fred approaching forty-four,
when they appeared together in
The Sky's the Limit, but when
they danced the age difference
didn't seem to matter.

Lady Adele Cavendish arrives back in the United States for the first time in ten years, landing a La Guardia Airfield, New York, in 1945. She visited friends on the East Coast before moving to California to see Fred and Phyllis.

he two Freds share a joke. staire, with Fred Junior, njoys a relaxing moment on e set of *Easter Parade* in 948.

The great Ann Miller. An outstanding dancer whom Fre[d] admired enormously. They appeared together in *Easter Parade*.

Fred's love of racing brought him much enjoyment over many years and he owned a number of horses. This shot was taken from *Easter Parade*.

The inspired pairing of Fred Astaire with Judy Garland was never more successful than in the remarkable tramps number from *Easter parade*. No elegance or sophistication for the normally man-about-town Mr Astaire in this outstanding sequence.

Time out. Fred relaxing with co-stars Ann Miller and Peter Lawford, with composer and lyricist Irving Berlin knocking out the tunes.

Together again! Judy Garland should have been Fred's co-star in *The Barkleys of Broadway* in 1949 but when she became ill, somebody hit on the idea of bringing in Ginger. It was their first movie together for ten years.

One of the most dynamic and exciting partnerships on film. Astaire, with the stunning Cyd Charisse, in *The Band Wagon* in 1953.

long and busy years by the phenomenal success of the partnership, split to find professional expression elsewhere. Astaire took Phyllis on holiday to Europe, visiting Ireland and London, where he found intense preparations for war being made. He renewed acquaintances and had luncheon with the Duke and Duchess of Kent, talking over old and less threatening times. Sadly, it was Astaire's last meeting with the Duke, who was killed in an air accident during the forthcoming war.

Back in Hollywood, Fred moved to the MGM studios. In 1940 his second film for MGM was released, *Broadway Melody of 1940* with Eleanor Powell, George Murphy, Frank Morgan and Ian Hunter. Then came the Paramount picture *Second Chorus* with Paulette Goddard, Artie Shaw, Burgess Meredith and Charles Butterworth. Astaire was free at last of the Rogers partnership syndrome. It's hard to understand why he looked forward to it so much, because his films afterwards weren't all that different. The plots were still largely trivial, the backgrounds and general atmosphere and approach hadn't substantially altered, the films continued to stand or fall on their sense of rhythm, the music, singing and, most of all, the dancing. Only his partner changed. But after *Second Chorus,* changing partners may well have lost, if only temporarily, some of its attraction for Fred. With America moving closer to war, the dark clouds had already appeared over his own head. For the first time since he moved to Hollywood seven years before, he found himself in the astonishing position of having completed a picture, and having no follow-up picture scheduled, not even for the distant future. Big budget musicals were too risky for such unsettled times and Astaire was left with nothing to do but kick his heels . . . and go off and play golf.

EIGHT

Change Partners

The 1940s brought a shift in the pattern of Astaire's career. His partnership with Ginger ended. So did his association with RKO. The Second World War, which the United States entered in December 1941 following the attack on Pearl Harbour, added its own complications. More personal to Fred was the reluctance for the time being of studios to spend lavishly on spectacular musicals. Once or twice during the decade it meant that Astaire was not offered film work of any kind.

The changes, even collectively, were not all that dramatic, but to Astaire, who had dedicated the previous seven years to making major musicals with Ginger Rogers, almost without a pause, they were a shock to the system. After all, since *Flying Down to Rio* in 1933 he had co-starred with only one other partner. In seven crowded years he and Ginger did nine movies together — singing and dancing their way through more than 900 minutes of big-screen time. Professionally they knew each other almost as well as they knew themselves. In contrast, the seven years from 1940 would see Fred starring in nine more musicals, but almost always with a different partner — Eleanor Powell, Paulette Goddard, Rita Hayworth, Marjorie Reynolds, Joan Leslie, Lucille Ball and Joan Caulfield. Judy Garland and Ann Miller were added to the list in 1948, before his reunion with Ginger for *The Barkleys of Broadway* in 1949.

Then there was his break with RKO. Not once in the seven years he was there, was he left to wonder where his next film was coming from. Pandro Berman lined them up in quick succession — shooting one; negotiating another; a third already in mind. When he moved to MGM it was for one film only. Not until 1945, when his former associate Arthur Freed was there, did they put him under contract. Even then, it seemed, they didn't always know how best to use him.

It is hard to assess how Astaire was affected by all this. He said plainly that his schedule at RKO had been heavy and that in future he didn't want to make more than one picture a year. On the other hand, he was plainly upset when nobody offered him work — and he had nothing planned — even for a week or two. He would go on holiday with Phyllis, play golf or give more time to his racing interests, but he found it hard to accept not being automatically in demand all the time, as he had been in the Thirties. Over the next fifteen years he would hint and threaten retirement when work dried up and when studios didn't call him, but compared with some stars he was never 'resting' for long and overall he endured much longer than most.

The first enforced pause in his screen career came after *Second Chorus,* his second film after leaving RKO. For the first time since moving to Hollywood more than seven years before, he found himself with no film planned. He had offers to go back on the stage and to do radio work, but he wanted to stay in films. Later, when an idea for a movie with Columbia didn't seem to be getting anywhere, he became depressed. He went off, as he put it, 'to sweat out this blank future of mine on the golf course', adding afterwards, 'My career began to bother me mentally.' But he had no cause to worry. Several weeks later Columbia not only came up with a film with Rita Hayworth, but made plans for a second film, again with Hayworth. Paramount also wanted him for a major movie with Bing Crosby.

His co-stars in the 1940s were inevitably compared with Ginger Rogers. Some were much better, technically, but none perhaps seemed so 'right' for him. The public certainly retained a soft spot for Ginger, though her successors hardly had the chance to establish a partnership in the way Ginger had. Not once afterwards, right up to the end of his dancing career some twenty years on, did he appear with the same girl more than twice. Mostly, his partner changed with every new film.

Astaire in public never criticised any of his partners. He made them work hard and never compromised the high standards he set with Ginger. While the less talented of dancers might well have found working with him an arduous and at times difficult experience, they all seemed to respect him greatly, both as a person and as a dancer. Two who were able to respond fully to his exceptional technique were Eleanor Powell and Rita Hayworth. He seemed to have a special affection for them, particularly Hayworth, who was the daughter of an old music-hall friend. Some years later he also especially admired the talent of Cyd Charisse, whose formal ballet training at first left him not a little overawed and nervous. His youngest co-star was the delightful Joan Leslie in RKO's *The Sky's*

The Limit. Not given to thinking about advancing age, he nonetheless inwardly questioned whether the generation gap might not make it hard for the public to accept them as co-stars. Joan was then barely seventeen and was still governed by laws relating to juveniles in films, which meant she had to break from shooting to have her school lessons and could only work by law for a set number of hours a day. Fred was forty-four at the time!

One of the hallmarks of an Astaire movie continued to be those outstanding musical scores from some of the greatest popular composers and lyricists of the day. Cole Porter, Irving Berlin, Jerome Kern, Johnny Mercer, Harold Arlen, Harry Warren, Arthur Freed, Frank Loesser, Burton Lane, Alan Jay Lerner, Howard Dietz and Arthur Schwartz all produced unforgettable melodies and words for almost twenty musical films in which Astaire starred during the 1940s and 1950s. One of the remarkable features of Astaire was his close identification with a whole collection of songs. You could take them completely out of film context, but still identify an Astaire song instantly. 'A Fine Romance', for instance, could that song even remotely belong to any other performer? The same question applies to 'They Can't Take That Away From Me'.

A particular joy for Astaire in the 1940s was his reunion with Arthur Freed. They had first met as kids in vaudeville and he stepped back into Astaire's life when, once again, he had run out of films. Freed offered him a contract and in the second half of the 1940s they did four movies together. Freed also helped Astaire achieve an ambition — to appear in a technicolour film. Fred had hoped as far back as 1938 that *Carefree* would be in colour. He was disappointed again when *The Story of Vernon and Irene Castle* a year later, originally scheduled to be shot in colour, was switched back to black and white because of the need to restrict budgets in such unsettled times. It is interesting to contemplate whether the addition of technicolour to those later Astaire-Rogers movies would have provided the boost necessary to preserve their partnership at the box-office for a few more years. And how magnificent some of those earlier films would have been in glorious technicolour.

Despite the occasional month or two when he found himself out of work; his good intention to do no more than one film a year, and the periodic hints he dropped about retirement, Astaire managed to keep very busy during the war years. Between 1941, when America entered the war, and 1946, he had seven films released — two each by Columbia, Paramount and MGM, and one by RKO. Much to his satisfaction he also did some tours to help the war effort. The first was a whirlwind whistle-stop journey round Ohio in 1942 with Ilona

Massey and comedian Hugh Herbert, promoting the sale of war bonds. For two weeks he appeared as many as twenty or thirty times in a day. In Cleveland a pair of Astaire's tap shoes raised 100,000 dollars in war bonds and his laces alone brought in 16,000 dollars. Later he joined a whole bunch of established Hollywood stars in a blockbuster of a tour. In the party were top-liners like Judy Garland and Mickey Rooney, Betty Hutton, Kathryn Grayson, Dick Powell, Lucille Ball and James Cagney, but to see them you had to buy a war bond. Such tours raised enormous amounts for the war effort. One show at Madison Square Garden in New York which featured Fred Astaire raised an astronomical eighty-six million dollars in bonds in one evening alone.

Eventually, he realized his ambition to make an overseas tour, travelling first to England and then on to the continent. In London he performed at the famous wartime venue, Rainbow Corner, in Shaftesbury Avenue, along with some members of the famous Glenn Miller band, virtually on the eve of the tragic Paris-bound flight on which Miller disappeared. He then went to France, Belgium and Holland, appearing sometimes with Bing Crosby. They had great fun together, Fred always making a point of dancing in GI combat boots. It was a hectic tour, but he found it a memorable experience. Astaire was always typically reticent about the tougher moments of his wartime entertaining in Europe, but others have testified to his courage and almost total disregard for his own safety. He would perform as often and wherever he was required — to groups of hundreds and thousands, or to a handful of troops in a forward casualty station. He came under fire, but never said much about it himself, and would go anywhere the troops wanted to see and hear him.

The war apart, Astaire's film career in the 1940s and '50s was fragmented and less definable. Even in the 1980s the public retain a crystal-clear image of the Fred Astaire-Ginger Rogers era. Their whole screen persona fitted perfectly into those pre-war years and the repetition of their simple formula for success in one film after another led to easy, deeply established points of identification and recognition. Afterwards it was different. The mould was broken and nothing quite as tangible or lasting emerged to take its place. It is not surprising in the circumstances, therefore, that as a period of his career, the post-Ginger Rogers years are looked back on with slightly less affection. Some writers criticize the films he did with other co-stars as being 'indifferent'. It has been said that they didn't project him any better or progress his screen image any more successfully than his famous films with Ginger — which were made ten and even fifteen years before. 'And at least you knew where you stood with an Astaire-Rogers film — you could depend on them even if they were predictable,' complained one established fan.

The comparisons, if understandable, were surely not wholly true. It could well be argued that some of Astaire's most famous dance sequences came in those later films — 'The Girl Hunt' from *The Band Wagon,* for instance — and that some of the songs for which he is best remembered ('They Can't Take That Away From Me', though admittedly with Ginger, and 'I Guess I'll Have To Change My Plan') came from his 1940s and 1950s musicals. Certainly, while the choice of some of his co-stars was difficult to understand, others couldn't be improved on for dancing ability. Moreover, the storylines, however thin and inconsequential, could hardly have been more banal than some of the Astaire-Rogers offerings. There is general agreement on one point, however: that the monumental talent of Astaire continued to shine through all those later films.

This second major period in Astaire's screen career had an unfortunate start. The first Broadway Melody film, titled simply *The Broadway Melody,* had been put out by MGM in 1929 as their first sound film and gave golden opportunities to lyricist Arthur Freed and composer Nacio Herb Brown. It was an enormous success, being what many see as the first real musical ever filmed, and won the 'Best Picture' Academy Award for that year. Follow-up movies — *Broadway Melody of 1936* and *Broadway Melody of 1938,* both starring dancer Eleanor Powell (the latter also starred a fifteen-year-old prodigy called Judy Garland), were enormously successful too, but by 1940, when Powell and Astaire were brought together for *Broadway Melody of 1940,* the idea was unfortunately beginning to run out of steam. It turned out to be the last of the hit musicals with the famous title.

The other disappointment was that it was shot in black and white and not colour, as originally intended, though Fred's reaction was tempered by the opportunity to dance with Eleanor Powell, who was from about the mid-1930s to 1943 one of MGM's greatest musical stars and generally considered at that time to be the best girl tap-dancer in the world. Thirteen years younger than Astaire, Eleanor Powell danced on the stage in revue before making her film debut in 1935 as a guest in the Twentieth Century Fox musical *George White's Scandals.* She was spotted by MGM and featured in a number of spectacular musicals including the Broadway Melody films, *Born to Dance* and *Rosalie.* Her abilities as an actress were limited, but as a solo dancer, she was unequalled — long-legged, with a whirlwind, vigorous style which, it has to be said, was best exploited when dancing on her own. She didn't blend with Astaire as well as Ginger had done, but their major number together, Cole Porter's 'Begin the Beguine', where they tap-danced spectacularly on a mirrored floor, was a magical moment worthy of remembrance among the best. George Murphy also starred in *Broadway Melody of 1940*. His and Astaire's song-and-dance number, 'Please Don't Monkey With Broadway', was a lot of fun and other good tunes included 'I've Got My Eyes on You' — but overall the film wasn't such a big success that MGM kept the title going. Fred paid handsome tribute to Eleanor Powell's dancing: 'she "put 'em down like a man" and really knocked out a tap-dance in a class by herself.' 'I Concentrate on You' was probably the choicest tune in the film.

After *Broadway Melody of 1940*, MGM, it seemed, had nothing for Astaire, so he moved to Paramount for *Second Chorus* with Paulette Goddard, Artie Shaw and his orchestra, Burgess Meredith and Charles Butterworth. Astaire took the part of a jazz trumpeter who competes with Meredith for a job in the Shaw band and for the love of Paulette Goddard. Although she had earlier featured as a Ziegfeld girl and Goldwyn girl, Paulette Goddard was known more as an actress than as a dancer and for her starring role in *Modern Times* in 1936 with Charlie Chaplin, whom she married. 'Dig it' was the Astaire-Goddard dance number in which, as one commentator put it, 'Paulette did her best to keep up with him', but the film generally was more exciting to big band enthusiasts than devoted followers of Astaire, and included the trumpet playing of the legendary Billy Butterfield and Bobby Hackett.

For the next five years, until Arthur Freed brought him back to MGM for *Yolanda and the Thief,* released in 1945, Astaire faltered in a kind of no man's land. His career, as Benny Green, precise as always, put it in *Fred Astaire,* published by Hamlyn, was 'a somewhat disjointed cavalcade punctuated by more of those amazing moments where for a split second popular art seems to pause and contemplate itself through Astaire's dancing and singing.' After *Second Chorus* Astaire had no film scheduled, but then came two contracts with Columbia, which boosted his hesitant screen progress and one for Paramount. *You'll Never Get Rich,* with Rita Hayworth, was released in 1941 and *Holiday Inn,* with Bing Crosby, and *You Were Never Lovelier,* again with Rita Hayworth, came out in 1942. Rita Hayworth was a much happier choice of co-star and, on the whole, more successful. She was an accomplished dancer, could act well and, for the first time since the break with

Ginger Rogers, Fred seemed to have found a co-star whose dancing was talented but which didn't impose itself too strongly on the partnership. He seemed to find the idea of co-starring with the daughter of his old vaudeville friend, Eduardo Cansino (Rita's real name was Margarita Carmen Cansino), a trifle embarrassing at first, but it was obvious he enjoyed making the two films and had a great affection for her. Fred and Adele had worked with Rita's parents — Eduardo and Elisa Cansino — in the old days in vaudeville when they topped the bill as exciting and colourful Spanish dancers and Fred and Adele were struggling to make a name for themselves at the bottom of the bill. Fred's embarrassment at co-starring with Rita, ill-founded as it turned out, came solely from their different ages. She was barely twenty-two. At forty-one, he wondered if the age gap might not be too great, but the years were of no importance when they danced together. They made an inspired team and better, claimed some observers, than even Fred and Ginger. Rita had been dancing for almost as long as she could walk and had gone through the formal grind of years at dance school. Her Hollywood debut was in 1935 in an obscure offering called *Under the Pampas Moon. Only Angels Have Wings* in 1939 and *Blood and Sand* with the top-ranking Tyrone Power in 1941, were important stepping stones, but she was still finding her way through the Hollywood jungle when the chance came for her to star with Astaire.

According to Rita, it was Astaire's own idea to cast her in the film. He'd heard that a daughter of his old vaudeville buddy Eduardo Cansino was under contract at Columbia and, knowing that any child of Cansino was sure to have been trained properly, suggested her as co-star. Another version credits Columbia boss Harry Cohn with bringing them together. He'd got Fred interested in doing a film at Columbia and, looking around for a possible partner, had remembered seeing Rita dancing in an earlier film. One thing is certain however, for both Fred and Rita, the pairing was opportune. Astaire hadn't made a film for a year and, in a sense, was ready to live down the fairly mediocre *Broadway Melody of 1940,* and, certainly, *Second Chorus.* Rita might have remained a struggling dramatic actress had it not been for her sparkling performances in the two films she did with Astaire. She became a leading pin-up of the Second World War and one of the most beautiful and glamorous of film stars during Hollywood's golden years.

In *You'll Never Get Rich,* Astaire was a Second World War soldier who had been a dance director before joining up, and Rita was a chorus girl with whom he falls in love. Curiously, although Cole Porter wrote the music and lyrics for a variety of numbers for the film, none was to become an Astaire trade mark, though a radio network strike which kept the songs off the air for some time, cannot have helped their chances to become big hits. Their second film together — *You Were Never Lovelier* — is generally considered to be better, this time with music by Jerome Kern and lyrics from Johnny Mercer. This movie also starred Adolphe Menjou and Xavier Cugat and cast Fred as a likeable dancer-gambler who loves and wins Rita, the daughter of an Argentinian hotel-owner. Kern and Mercer did a magnificent job on the score and three or four numbers became all-time standards, including the title song, in which Fred and Rita dance romantically; 'I'm Old Fashioned' and 'Dearly Beloved'. 'Shorty George' was reckoned by many Astaire buffs to be the best dance number he and Rita did together, and another extraordinary dance sequence used trick photography cleverly and had Astaire dancing around an office on top of a desk, periodically beating the rhythm with a cane on the head of Adolphe Menjou, who was supposedly sitting behind the desk. Hayworth blended well with Astaire. She had a particularly fluent, easy and confident style and never showed a trace of the insistent demands which dancing with Fred entailed. The smile was relaxed and her dancing was always exciting, even in slower, more sensitive interpretations. Astaire said she was delightful to work with and he obviously enjoyed the experience very much. Too much of a gentleman to nominate favourites, it is not difficult to see from comments Fred has made, however, that he not only admired the dancing talent of Rita Hayworth, but felt she fitted in to his style of choreography perhaps more easily and successfully than some of his other partners.

Mind you, when they first met, he immediately had doubts. Always worried in case his partners were going to be too big for him, one of the first questions he asked her was: 'How tall are you?' Ideally, Fred at 5 feet 9¾ inches liked his partners to be no more than 5 feet 6 inches because if they then danced in high heels there might be little difference in their heights. Rita was about 5 feet 6 inches and happily agreed not to wear very high heels opposite Fred. The two films she made with Astaire helped Rita Hayworth get noticed and, although they were a talented and successful combination, they did not appear together in another film. While others often felt that Fred was being over-fussy about the height of his partners, it obviously worried him a lot and there is the delightful story which concerns Eleanor Powell, when MGM considered bringing them together for *Broadway Melody of 1940*. No less a figure than Louis B. Mayer himself took a personal hand in trying to assure Astaire that Powell would not be too tall. He got them both in his office and by a complicated plan finally had them stand back to back. Eleanor was shorter than Fred by about 2½ inches and he reckoned that would not be too much of a problem. But before finally deciding, he took her away so the two of them could go through some dance routines together in front of mirrors.

Between the two movies he did with Rita Hayworth, Astaire managed to crowd in the Paramount film *Holiday Inn* with Bing Crosby, Marjorie Reynolds and Virginia Dale. Mark Sandrich, from Astaire's earlier RKO days, directed, and Irving Berlin provided the music and lyrics, a number of which he wrote specially for the film. The novelty element of casting two relatively unknown girls to partner Fred and Bing proved successful and both did well in numbers with Astaire. He did 'Easy to Dance With' with Virginia Dale; 'Be Careful, It's My Heart' and 'I Can't Tell a Lie' with Marjorie Reynolds. He also did a jitterbug dance with Reynolds in which he, having had more than enough to drink, brought the sequence to an end by falling flat on his face. This along with the solo 'firecracker' number in which, to quote Fred, 'I threw torpedoes to explode in a rhythmic conglomeration with my feet', were the most spectacular. As the years rolled by, the film became famous for Bing's introduction of the most famous seasonal popular song of all time — 'White Christmas'. It was the first time Astaire had worked with Bing in a film and for the casual Crosby, Fred's absolute dedication to perfection was a revelation. It was the film in which Astaire's weight dropped from 140 pounds to 126 pounds, and he did one routine thirty-eight times before he was happy with the result. Bing said that Astaire danced himself so thin he could almost spit through him and didn't advise anyone appearing in a film with Fred to do any more dancing than was necessary. 'He's so quick-footed and so light that it's impossible not to look like a hay-digger compared with him,' said Bing. *Holiday Inn* was Astaire's most successful film, financially, since his break with Ginger, though he modestly put that down mostly to Bing's vast following. He enjoyed making it and sounded only one real regret; he wished yet again that it had been made in colour.

By 1943 the film industry was booming, war-slanted musicals helping to make vast profits for the studios. In that year alone, RKO made almost seven million dollars, and it was in 1943, too, that Astaire went back to his former studio to make *The Sky's the Limit'* with the delectable Joan Leslie. Fred was not over-keen to re-join RKO, especially as at first they were talking about reuniting him with Ginger Rogers. In the meantime, he had offers to return to Broadway, but even Irving Berlin, and the prospect of an exciting new show, couldn't tempt him. As Berlin went off to do other things, RKO finally enticed Fred back for the film with Joan Leslie. Composer Harold Arlen (famous for 'Over the Rainbow') and lyricist Johnny Mercer were among those recruited. Arlen hadn't written for Astaire before. Among the best remembered songs were 'One For My Baby and One More For The Road' and 'My Shining Hour'. The film was never considered one of Fred's best, but it is significant for one technical point: it was the only film where Astaire received a formal credit as dance director. The storyline was wafer-thin and cast Fred as a Flying Tiger pilot who shuns a hero's reception in Manhattan, preferring to pose as a civilian loafer. He meets Joan Leslie, a photographer for a picture magazine and patriotically anxious to do what she can to help the war effort. She is therefore unimpressed by Astaire's seeming desire to idle the war away, but Fred finally captures her heart. Miss Leslie, despite her youth, had already appeared with Gary Cooper in *Sergeant York* and with James Cagney in *Yankee Doodle Dandy,* and was seen as having such potential star talent that RKO had traded the rights of a couple of what were to emerge as blockbusting films to persuade Warner Brothers to release her, and the laconic John Garfield, for the Astaire film and *The Fallen Sparrow* respectively. Despite her charm and obvious ability, and the film's nomination for an Academy Award in the best song category ('My Shining Hour'), *The Sky's the Limit* was never highly thought of, coming to sparkling life only during the song-and-dance sequences. It was heavily criticized, but it made money for RKO. Also in the film were Eric Blore and Peter Lawford, and music fans could enthuse over Freddie Slack's Orchestra and the band singing of Ella Mae Morse, who dubbed for Joan Leslie. Though not considered one of Astaire's best films at the time it went out on general release in the 1940s, it stands up remarkably well to television showings more than forty years later, being quite entertaining, and not as dated or slow-moving as might have been imagined.

Once more Astaire had no follow-up films scheduled. RKO offered him nothing and he was beginning to wonder if he should think about an overseas USO tour, when his agent called to say MGM were interested in offering a number of movies within a term contract. Arthur Freed, the genius producer of musical films, was central to MGM's phenomenal success with song-and-dance productions around this time and he was to be responsible for eight

Astaire films between 1945 and his last real musical film, *Silk Stockings,* in 1957. Freed had served a long and detailed apprenticeship, having worked as a song-plugger, vaudevillian and lyricist before producing his first musical for MGM in 1939. This was the outstanding Judy Garland-Mickey Rooney film *Babes in Arms,* which started a cycle of such films dealing with talented youngsters putting on a show and included *Strike Up The Band* and *Babes on Broadway.* The first film Freed had in mind for Astaire was *Ziegfeld Follies,* planned as a multi-star revue and featuring Lucille Ball, Lena Horne, Esther Williams, William Powell, Judy Garland, Kathryn Grayson, Red Skelton, Virginia O'Brian, Cyd Charisse (tucked away in the chorus) and Gene Kelly. This 110-minute tribute to Florenz Ziegfeld was the third movie to use the master showman's name, with permission of his widow Billie Burke, and was a lavish production directed with notable flair by Vincente Minnelli and choreographed by Robert Alton. Being a revue, Astaire had comparatively little to do in *Ziegfeld Follies,* but what he did, he enjoyed. He had wanted for some time to stage a number to the famous 'Limehouse Blues' and was delighted when Freed gave him the go-ahead to work out some dances, at the same time instructing Vincente Minnelli and Bob Alton to work on a production idea for the number. Fred disarmingly described the result as an 'intricate dramatic ballet pantomime combination'. Others considered it 'brilliant'. Astaire's new partner for this, and the superbly staged 'This Heart of Mine', was the beautiful Lucille Bremer, who had gained her reputation as a dancer at New York's Silver Slipper Club. An attractive redhead, Miss Bremer had been 'discovered' by Arthur Freed who was grooming her for stardom. They were predicting a big future for her in films and, although she undoubtedly had talent, and was cast opposite Astaire again in *Yolanda and the Thief,* the partnership never lived up to Freed's expectations and she soon retired. Movie history incidentally was made in *Ziegfeld Follies,* the world's two most popular screen dancers — Fred Astaire and Gene Kelly — appearing in the only film they made together. Their duet was 'The Babbit and the Bromide' — an old George Gershwin number which Fred and Adele had originally introduced in 1927 in their Broadway show *Funny Face.* It was a fun thing really, of no intrinsic significance in terms of film dance, but both men seemed to have enjoyed the experience. They had first met when Kelly visited the Paramount studios while Bing and Fred were working on *Holiday Inn.* Kelly was younger by some thirteen years and had grown up with Astaire as his inspiration. In the 1930s he had been a fan of Fred's and was excited to meet him. They became good friends over the years, but on the set of *Ziegfeld Follies* their relationship, according to Clive Hirschhorn's biography of Gene Kelly, was polite but guarded and cautious. Virtually all Fred said about it was that they both had fun doing 'The Babbit and the Bromide' together.

It took MGM almost two years to get *Ziegfeld Follies* out on release, but it eventually emerged to do very good business. The studio was so long making revisions and deletions that *Yolanda and the Thief,* with Fred appearing once more with Lucille Bremer, came out ahead of it. Miss Bremer showed what a graceful dancer she was — some critics rating her as one of Astaire's best partners; but the film was never able to rise above its stodgy, uninspired plot. The music by Harry Warren, with lyrics by Arthur Freed, was soon forgotten, as was the movie, but Astaire's dancing with Lucille Bremer was delightful and staged with imagination by Eugene Loring. Fred reckoned it was too much of a fantasy to score heavily with the public and, although everyone seemed to work particularly hard to make it a success, it made little lasting impact.

So far, Astaire's most recent work for MGM had not been altogether distinguished. While he had enjoyed making *Ziegfeld Follies,* the revue format had given him comparatively little to do. Nor could it be claimed that *Yolanda and the Thief* had been an outstanding success. He was desperately in need of a big-hit musical, but he didn't see it being *Belle of New York,* the next film MGM had scheduled for him, with shooting to start in just a few months. Already there were problems with the script, but as Fred and Phyllis went off to relax and forget about it, he had an instinctive feeling that it just wasn't right for him. Typically, in Astaire's career, the decision was virtually made for him. Paramount wanted to team him again with Bing Crosby in *Blue Skies* and to Fred this looked a much better proposition. The holiday was cut short as the two studios got together to fix Fred's loan to Paramount. MGM resisted at first because they had already planned some of the early work on *Belle of New York,* but Fred finally got Leland Hayward to release him. From the start, Astaire was much happier with *Blue Skies.* He welcomed working with Bing again and the film looked to have all the ingredients to make it a box-office hit. His old chum Hermes Pan was hired to do the choreography, and Irving Berlin was in charge of the words and music. Also in the cast were Joan Caulfield, Billy De Wolfe, and Olga San Juan. It turned out to be a successful movie and Fred enjoyed doing it. He had been toying with the idea of retirement for some time, but wanted to go with just one more box-office hit under his belt. Even during the shooting of *Blue Skies,* he knew this would be the film, and announced his intentions. His fans were in uproar. There was much public attention because a petition was started to keep Fred in films. Some letters were hostile, others expressed disappointment and regret. There were a few fans who were convinced he was ill and was keeping some dreadful disease a close secret. Just a few genuinely seemed to understand that what Fred had said about his impending retirement was true; that after making twenty movies in thirteen years and having spent over forty of his forty-seven years as a professional dancer, he'd gone about as far as he could and that there was nothing more to do. He was genuinely flattered that so many people were interested in his retirement, even if some of them felt it was just a gimmick and that he wouldn't go through with it.

In a way they weren't too far short of the mark but at the time Astaire was totally serious about retirement and he fully expected *Blue Skies* to be his final film. 'A Pretty Girl is Like a Melody' is perhaps the most remembered tune from the film, but Fred scored in a cute number with Bing called 'A Couple of Song and Dance Men'. He demonstrated his more sophisticated smooth style with sultry Olga San Juan and in 'Heat Wave', he also showed his acrobatic qualities as a dancer, falling from a bridge. The dance routine to capture public attention, however, was 'Putting on the Ritz'. It included a clever trick solo which Astaire explained was done 'with a series of split screens to produce the effect of me dancing in front of a chorus of eight images of myself'. But it was also publicized as Fred Astaire's 'last dance' and the media specialists made the most of that, gaining worldwide coverage with a series of still pictures.

Even as Fred settled down at the end of *Blue Skies* to a private life devoted to his family, his new ranch, his racing stables and the setting up of his dancing schools, circumstances were already conspiring to bring him back into public view. Fred was back in front of the cameras within a couple of years in a film called *Easter Parade,* which seemed dogged by ill-luck at the start. Arthur Freed had lined up Gene Kelly, Judy Garland, Peter Lawford and Cyd Charisse, but Cyd Charisse went out first after breaking a leg and, after shooting had begun, Gene Kelly broke an ankle. The delectable and extremely talented Ann Miller stepped in for Cyd Charisse and Fred came out of retirement to fill Gene's role. Popular versions of the incident suggest that Fred was lured out of retirement when Louis B. Mayer, beside himself without a replacement for the injured Kelly, telephoned Astaire to ask him if he would take over from Gene. It's true, in some measure. Mayer certainly did telephone Fred, at the suggestion of Gene Kelly himself it should be stressed, but Astaire needed little real persuading to pull on the old dancing-shoes. He had been hectically busy in retirement, giving a lot of time to establishing his chain of dance schools and personally training well over a hundred teachers, but the urge to get back into films was strong. In his own words: 'There I was, full of ideas and ambition again, but no picture to do, and it would take at least a year to plan and get one ready, if I did tell Metro that I wanted to come back. I also was not sure the movies would want me back.'

Astaire's comeback could hardly have been more successful. *Easter Parade* was an outstanding hit, with good reason. Fans rushed to see Fred in action again, Judy Garland was at the peak of her career and an outstanding draw and, for extra measure, there was the vivacious Ann Miller, the British actor Peter Lawford, and no fewer than seventeen Irving Berlin songs. And the film was in technicolour. Proving that the best ideas cannot always be produced to order, producer Arthur Freed had a flash of inspiration after production on the film had begun. He suggested the introduction of a tramps number and the result was the outstanding duet which quickly became a classic for Fred and Judy, 'We're a Couple of Swells', with the normally immaculate Astaire in tattered clothes, a heavy growth of beard, totally unkempt and, wait for it, a blacked-out tooth and the most battered top hat you ever did see. Judy was dressed in similar fashion. Fred played a tap dancer who, after being deserted by his partner (Ann Miller), made a star of an unsuccessful chorus girl (Judy Garland), falling in love with her in the process. Apart from the tramps number, the movie was packed with memorable songs including 'I Love a Piano', 'Waiting for the Robert E. Lee' and 'Easter Parade' (all with Judy) and 'It Only Happens When I Dance With You', 'Steppin' Out With My Baby' and 'When the Midnight Choo-Choo Leaves for Alabam'. Astaire was indeed back with a vengeance. He loved working in front of the cameras again and was thrilled with the talents of both Judy Garland and Ann Miller. There was a feast of dancing for Astaire — three with Judy, three with Ann Miller and two on his own. He said later that working with Judy was one of the highspots of his career and he found her uncanny knowledge of showmanship exceptional. Ann Miller he considered 'a terrific performer'. Producer Arthur Freed soon had *Easter Parade* marked down as a winner and before shooting finished he lined up *The Barkleys of Broadway,* as an immediate follow-up for Fred and Judy. Once again, an extraordinary quirk of fate took a hand. Judy, who had been under psychiatric care before making *Easter Parade,* wasn't showing any sign of improvement prior to *The Barkleys of Broadway.* She started to put on weight, was ill and depressed, and was suffering badly from nervous exhaustion. The studio waited as long as possible in the hope that she would recover and be well enough to begin work, but in the end a replacement had to be found. The major problem was solved when someone came up with the brilliant idea of getting Fred and Ginger together again. It seemed a perfect solution and the additional publicity resulting from the pairing, after Fred and Ginger had been apart for almost ten years, would focus box-office attention on the film. Knowing how much Astaire loathed his repeated partnerships with Ginger in the 1930s, MGM might have expected to overcome some dour resistance to the re-matching. By this time, too, Ginger had established herself as a capable dramatic actress. Her part in *Kitty Royle* as long ago as 1940 gained her an Oscar. Whether another song-and-dance role would be to her liking, theoretically at least, must have been doubtful.

In the event, it couldn't have been easier. Ginger agreed almost immediately to the idea of taking over from Garland and told director Chuck Walters and Fred, 'I think it will turn out to be fun.' If Fred was dismayed at the prospect of working with Ginger again, he certainly didn't show it. Typically, he didn't say much, but later revealed that he and Gin, as he affectionately called her, had often discussed the idea of getting together again for a film. Any suggestion that it might be for anything more than just one movie, however, might have prompted a far different reaction. Some hasty re-writing by Betty Comden and Adolph Green was required, Harry Warren provided the music, Ira Gershwin and Arthur Freed the lyrics, and on most of the dance numbers Astaire worked with dance director Bob Alton, though Hermes Pan worked on the sensational 'Shoes With Wings On'. It was the first film to show the immaculate pairing of Fred and Ginger in technicolour and it did moderately well at the box-office.

The story of this backstage musical is of a married couple who have a successful double act, but who run into problems when the wife, Dinah Barkley (played by Ginger) wants to leave musicals for straight drama. The plot was a poor second to the song-and-dance routines, even if it did in parts offer more than a passing glance to the Astaire and Rogers real-life partnership. Supporting stars Oscar Levant and Billie Burke gave good and witty performances and tuneful melodies abounded, though some were destined to be lost forever in the mists of time. Still remembered, however, is 'My One and Only Highland Fling' with Fred and Ginger bedecked in traditional Scottish gear. This was probably intended as a follow-up to the successful 'Swells' number with which Fred and Judy scored so heavily in *Easter Parade,* but, although Fred counted it as one of his favourites from the film, it was not generally considered to be the best. On the other hand, 'Shoes With Wings On' was in a class of its own and showed Astaire's typical inventiveness and technique in a brilliant and dazzling solo. The conception, a dream-fantasy idea by Astaire and Hermes Pan, was original and novel and had Astaire in a shoe-repair shop with hundreds of pairs of shoes which come to life and dance around him. It was a masterful piece of inspired cinema dance, in which Astaire and Pan called up all the support of trick photography to provide what many regard as one of the most sensational cinema dance sequences of all time. Shoes jumped off the shelves and danced with Astaire in a variety of extraordinary ways and Pan said later that it was a very difficult thing to photograph. Fred's routine was done separately from the choreography of the shoes, and the trick photography was used to merge the two sequences. Astaire's great problem was in visualizing where the shoes would be at any particular time. As Hermes Pan explained, if he was chasing them with a broom, for instance, he would have to work out their positions.

The song itself, by Harry Warren with lyrics by Arthur Freed, was typical Astaire and his interpretation was, as always in his heyday, impeccable. The Gershwin brothers number 'They Can't Take That Away From Me', lifted from the earlier *Shall We Dance,* was probably the best song from *The Barkleys of Broadway,* but the most historic was certainly 'Manhattan Downbeat', in which Astaire sang with the chorus and then, still with a chorus background, danced with Ginger. Largely forgotten as a dance routine, it was nonetheless staged as a spectacular finale to the film, with Fred and Ginger dancing together on a packed, colourful stage, the screen alive with movement in traditional style. As the picture faded and 'The End' told patrons it was time to go home, it really was the end for this phenomenal partnership because *The Barkleys of Broadway* was the last time Astaire and Rogers danced together on the silver screen. In the style of their earlier films, which featured 'The Carioca', 'The Continental', 'The Yam' and 'The Piccolino', *The Barkleys of Broadway* came up with the latest Astaire-Rogers popular dance offering, called the 'Swing Trot'. The 'Swing Trot' was supposed to have been 'dreamed up' by Astaire shortly after he made one of his rare ventures into a nightclub one evening. According to an issue of the monthly publication *Danceland* in 1949: 'He noted that the modernly-minded dancers were crying for a dance they could swing to on a typically small floor, in the midst of a typically overflow crowd. "As it was, all they could do was stand up and sway in a monotonous rhythmn with the music, or without it," he recalls. So Astaire figured out a solution. When he and Miss Rogers were reunited as partners for *The Barkleys of Broadway,* they decided to let the public in on his answers to the agonies of 'undanceable' floors'.

A more commercial explanation might well have been that by this time there were some thirty-odd Fred Astaire Dance Studios established and the 'Swing Trot' became a popular part of the course offered to students at the studios.

In the late 1940s and early 1950s Fred Astaire was a happy and contented man. His sheet anchor was still his devotion to his wife Phyllis and their blissful marriage together. They shunned the bright lights of Hollywood, went to few parties, and kept their private life extremely private. Unlike the 1930s when he was first establishing his movie career and then, with Ginger, consolidating it, he now had more time to enjoy life in his own way. He'd tried conventional retirement, meaning no more film work, and found he didn't enjoy it, but there was not now the same intensity about his career that there had been. He had time to take breaks away from home with Phyllis, develop his racing interests, see his own horses competing, have a round of golf or a quiet game of pool. They had two children together, Fred junior and Ava, to whom he was devoted, and his stepson, Pete, was also a happy member of the close-knit family. Although film studios' insistent urge to promote and project him as RKO had done in the 1930s had relaxed a little, there was no real shortage of work and he was to make five more films between 1950 and 1953. He was teamed with Betty Hutton and Jane Powell (once) and Vera-Ellen (twice), before starring with Cyd Charisse in the 1953 production of *The Band Wagon,* by far the best of this crop of Astaire films and the start of his final quartet of musicals before scoring his first dramatic success in *On the Beach.*

It's hard to be precise about Astaire's own view of his career at this stage. In some measure he was preoccupied in establishing his chain of dance schools, but after completing *The Barkleys of Broadway* he planned some time away from the film studios when a movie he said he would do for Paramount with Betty Hutton became delayed because the script wasn't completed. Instead — and despite his holiday plans — he jumped at the chance to play

Bert Kalmar, a real-life former vaudeville dancing star, when MGM's Jack Cummings gave him the script to read. Astaire had known Kalmar and his partner, Harry Ruby, from his own vaudeville days and had followed their careers as a successful songwriting team. For this biopic tribute MGM chose one of the team's greatest musical hits for the title of the film — *Three Little Words*. George Wells produced a commendable script, a young man called André Previn was the musical director and once more Hermes Pan was in charge of the dance direction. Red Skelton was cast as Harry Ruby, Vera-Ellen as Mrs Kalmar, Fred's screen wife; Arlene Dahl was Harry Ruby's wife, the former silent movie star Eileen Percy; and a minor role was played by a young potential star called Debbie Reynolds. The title song apart, the film's best known songs were 'I Wanna Be Loved by You', 'Who's Sorry Now?', 'You Are My Lucky Star' and the delightful 'Nevertheless', which Astaire sang as a duet with Vera-Ellen, her voice being dubbed by the superb Anita Ellis. The best dance Fred had with Vera-Ellen was probably the exuberant 'Mr and Mrs Hoofer at Home'. Astaire later labelled *Three Little Words* as one of the top favourite films in which he appeared and described it as outstanding. A favourite of his it might well have been, but you would have to go a long way to find a showbiz critic who shared his enthusiasm for the film's merit.

Three Little Words was released in July 1950, but it barely did justice to a dancing-man whose phenomenal movie career, just three months earlier, had been honoured with the presentation of a special Academy Award for his contribution to musicals. However, as much as Astaire enjoyed making those early 1950s musicals, they certainly can't be listed among his best, for a variety of reasons. Benny Green might have been a trifle harsh and unfeeling when he later wrote about 'a long succession of indifferent Astaire movies saved from catastrophe only by Fred's own performance', but he certainly wasn't far from the objective truth. The choice of partner for Astaire, by design or in one case by default, was hardly inspiring. The screenplays were largely trivial and the determination by studios to make richly orchestrated musicals was beginning to crumble. During the decade they disintegrated entirely as television rose above the movies as the most powerful influence of mass communication. Even so, Arthur Freed had *Royal Wedding* lined up for Fred and the petite June Allyson, and announced it even before work began on the delayed Paramount picture, *Let's Dance* with Betty Hutton. Miss Hutton was an outstanding performer with enormous enthusiasm and a zappy personality, and Astaire enjoyed making the film with her. But in spite of showing quite a lot of promise in the first few weeks after its release, *Let's Dance* was never a big hit. Adapted by Allan Scott and Dane Lussier from the story *Little Boy Blue* by Maurice Zolotow, Astaire plays the former partner of Betty Hutton and helps her when her mother-in-law threatens to take her son away. There was a string of original songs and lyrics by Frank Loesser, none of which made a lasting impression, and Hermes Pan was yet again the dance director. 'Why Fight the Feeling' was probably the best song. 'Oh, Them Dudes', with Astaire and Hutton pairing well as cowhands was a not-quite-successful effort to duplicate the 'Swells' number but this, together with Fred's 'Piano Dance' solo in which he dances all over a grand piano, were the remembered dance sequences.

For *Royal Wedding* (named *Wedding Bells* in Britain), Astaire returned to MGM and at the start the film showed outstanding promise. Arthur Freed was in charge of production, Chuck Walters was directing, and Alan Jay Lerner had produced a novel screenplay which seemed as though it might just capture public imagination. Astaire and June Allyson were an American brother and sister dance act who visit London, fall in love with respective partners and marry on the same day as Princess Elizabeth and Prince Philip. It was partly based on the career of Fred and Adele and their experiences. Hardly had June Allyson started rehearsals when she had to quit through pregnancy. MGM, despite their earlier problems with Judy Garland, offered her the part. Director Chuck Walters then quit, officially to move to another film, but unofficially because it was said he couldn't face the prospect of working with Judy again. Stanley Donen, who had earlier worked with Gene Kelly, took over. Fred must have been doubtful also. He admired Judy's extraordinary talent immensely, but he knew well enough that she was by no means the easiest co-star to work with. In box-office terms, of course, Judy's inclusion could only have enhanced the film's chances of success. In the end it didn't work out. Judy, sadly, was far from well and began turning up late for rehearsals. Sometimes she wasn't even there at all which proved difficult for work to continue on the set. Finally MGM sent her a telegram dismissing her from the picture. Her place was taken by Jane Powell, a first class singer but by no means an accepted dancer. She was personable, attractive, sang well and, in fact, surprised the crew with the competent way she handled the dance routines. But the film was not a hit. Burton Lane's music, with lyrics by Alan Jay Lerner, included the lovely ballad 'Too Late Now' for Miss Powell and that long, l-o-n-g song title 'How Could You Believe Me When I Said I Loved You When

You Know I've Been a Liar All My Life?', which made a good comic dance number for Astaire and Powell. Although the film was set in London and included some newsreel footage from the Royal Wedding, Astaire's inventiveness and ingenuity, not to say his sheer dexterity and dancing skills, gave the movie its real meaning and once again he used trick photography in the memorable sequence when he danced up the wall, across the ceiling and down the other side. This was another of Fred's ideas which came to him as he lay awake in bed in the early hours.

Even when you're as big a star as Astaire you can't side-step the inevitable, it seems, for the movie he had avoided doing by going into retirement six years before — *Belle of New York* — was now brought up again by Arthur Freed and Fred was co-starred with the delectable Vera-Ellen once more. It had all the makings of a good picture. It had plenty of financial backing, Charles Walters took care with the direction, Harry Warren wrote a good score and Johnny Mercer worked out some excellent lyrics; but it never really took off. This time the elements of fantasy were carried too far as Fred danced on air and twirled and swayed Vera-Ellen away into a large starlit sky to end the film. It was all just a bit too much for the public to take. 'I Wanna Be a Dancin' Man', though not destined to gain immortality as an Astaire standard, was nonetheless a catchy tune and ideal for Fred's lighthearted vocal treatment. Nearly thirty years later it still sounds good and perhaps less dated than one or two other numbers which became traditional Astaire classics.

Astaire had one more picture to do to complete his contract with MGM and, despite his disappointment with *Belle of New York,* Arthur Freed quickly had it scheduled. He took for his inspiration the music of Arthur Schwartz and Howard Dietz from *The Band Wagon,* which Fred and Adele had starred in on Broadway back in 1931 and which had prompted Twentieth Century Fox to make *Dancing in the Dark* in 1949. MGM bought the rights to the title and music and introduced a completely new storyline by Adolph Green and Betty Comden, which was much better than the original. They got Vincente Minnelli to direct, and paired the leggy and luscious Cyd Charisse with Astaire, and also recruited the English dancer-actor, Jack Buchanan, to play an important supporting role when Clifton Webb turned it down. The film sparkled with witty dialogue, ageless songs, exciting, graceful, immaculate and inspired dancing, and there were excellent supporting performances from Oscar Levant and Nanette Fabray as two fast-talking, joking show writers. The barely moderate success of Astaire's recent films was forgotten as *The Band Wagon* was acclaimed by the critics and enthusiastically received at the box-office. For many, Cyd Charisse was arguably the best partner Astaire ever had, including Ginger. Her physique, dancing technique, interpretative flair and sheer style were a joy to watch and seemed to bring the very best from Fred. She matched him, move for move, and produced outstanding grace, fun and sensuality to order. Astaire's own dancing was surely never more eloquent than in *The Band Wagon*. The couple had both been in *Ziegfeld Follies* back in 1946 when Charisse was such an unknown that she appeared far down the cast list, lower even than Bunin's Puppets! In the intervening seven years though, she had appeared in *Singing in the Rain,* the famous Gene Kelly film of 1952, in which she was provocatively sensational as a gangster's moll. Her star talent had been recognized as early as 1948 when, after being cast in the Ann Miller role in *Easter Parade,* a broken leg kept her out of the final production, and in 1951 she had to turn down a part in Vincente Minnelli's important *An American in Paris* with Gene Kelly because she was pregnant. Tall, supremely elegant and statuesque, Cyd Charisse was born in Texas as Tula Ellice Finklea. She married her ballet teacher, who helped her get into pictures. After touring with the Ballet Russe she made her film debut in 1943, when she was twenty-two, in *Mission to Moscow,* after which under contract to MGM she had small-part dancing roles in pictures like *The Harvey Girls* and *Three Wise Fools.* In 1946 she was in *Till the Clouds Roll By,* a big box-office hit based on the life of Jerome Kern, and in 1948 in *Words and Music,* the film biography of Rodgers and Hart. Her dancing with Astaire in *The Band Wagon* was electrifying and moved some writers to claim her as the screen's finest female dancer with the most gorgeous legs in films. They were seen to shimmering advantage in the Mickey Spillane sequence from *The Band Wagon* — the immortal 'The Girl Hunt Ballet' — filmed as an outrageous parody of the popular writer's gangster novels. Charisse, excitingly seductive, danced with enormous feeling and sensuality, both in this now famous number and in the calmer, more melting moments of her duet with Astaire 'Dancing in the Dark'. Seldom if ever has a film duet been danced with such razor-sharp feeling and finesse.

In *The Band Wagon* Fred takes the part of an ageing song-and-dance man who, after a successful Hollywood career, becomes part of a dismal stage musical which flops because of its stilted, 'out of touch' presentation. When all seems lost after a disastrous provincial try out, he inspires the cast to continue, leading them into a much sharper and popular re-hash of the show, which then becomes a smash-hit on Broadway. Taken at face value, *The Band*

Wagon was a meritorious and delightfully satisfying movie. It was also fascinating in the skilful way screenwriters Betty Comden and Adolph Green patchworked a fictional tale with snippets from their own careers and Astaire's — the whole concept owing more than a passing glance to the latter. An allusion would occasionally be so subtle that you needed to be 'in the know' to recognize it — as, for instance, when Fred in the film arrives back in New York and is staggered by the degenerate changes on Broadway since he was last there. 'Where's the New Amsterdam?' he enquires. 'I had one of my biggest successes there.' And so he did, with Adele in 1931 and 1932 in their stage version of, of course, *The Band Wagon*.

The film also represents, symbolically, a last defiant gesture of the movie musical before it, and the big screen generally, were to be stripped of their traditional power and glory by the inevitable onset of television. In the film Charisse plays the young ballet-dancer who partners Astaire in the new Broadway musical, and other superb performances come from Oscar Levant, Nanette Fabray and the debonair Jack Buchanan, whose delightful duet with Astaire in 'I Guess I'll Have to Change My Plan' remains a treasured moment. Many of the musical numbers were taken from the old stage version and from various other revues from the same period, including the typical Astaire number, 'A Shine on My Shoes', and 'By Myself'. 'That's Entertainment', written specially for the new film version, became a stupendous hit and has long since become the archetypal showbiz song. It combines a witty and interesting lyric with the rallying overtones which are part of almost all symbolic songs. The music for 'The Girl Hunt Ballet', narrated in the film by Astaire, was written by Arthur Schwartz, with words by Alan Jay Lerner. This jazz ballad of the underworld is a perfect setting for Astaire, as Raymond Chandler's private-eye 'hero', and Charisse, first as a sultry and sexy brunette, then as a slinky and equally sexy blonde, to present a show-stopping performance, brilliantly spoofed with clichés in almost every other phrase or movement. 'You and the Night and the Music', 'Louisiana Hayride', the funny 'Triplets' number featuring Fred with Nanette Fabray and Jack Buchanan, and 'Something to Remember You By' all contributed to a song-studded movie which concluded Astaire's contract with MGM on a positive note.

However, Astaire's film career at this point faltered perceptibly. With his MGM contract ended, and with no other studio coming forward with an offer, he thought again about retiring, but with no announcement this time. In his own words: 'I would just fade gently out of action for a while, return minus the old dancing shoes and possibly go into producing when I got the urge'. But it was at Belmont Park race meeting in the summer of 1953 that the first symptoms of a much graver situation presented themselves when Phyllis felt faint and dizzy and asked that they leave early. There were similar attacks over the next few months, the last one leading to hospital tests which showed the urgent need for major surgery. The first operation (on Good Friday, 1954) was successful but an unexpected relapse while she was still recovering meant more surgery. This time Fred was warned that her chances of survival were slim. Within three months she was home again, but later that year she went into hospital once more for further major surgery. Although she was able to return home afterwards she never recovered and died from the effects of a brain tumour during the morning of 13 September 1954.

NINE

The Band Wagon

The formula for a Fred Astaire musical was simple yet effective. It had to be kept light, with plenty of superficial dialogue. It might help if the storyline developed into the staging of a show. Never, under any circumstances, should anything obstruct those jewelled sequences, spread through the film with at times outrageous predictability, where Fred, on his own or with a beautiful partner, would sway or glide into a dance or swing into a song.

The construction was straightforward. Only the situation, location and characters changed. Nobody cared about the plot anyway. It was only a framework, something on which to peg the musical numbers. The reason for it was the music, singing, dancing and the sheer delight of it all.

The Band Wagon was as representative as any of Astaire's films. It opens with a kind of overture being played behind the titles and, to make sure that nobody is in any doubt about what is in store, the familiar top hat and stick are shown on film as the cast list unfolds.

Fred plays Tony Hunter, a singing and dancing man who was at his peak ten years before and hasn't made a picture in three years. He's seen on a train heading for New York. He steps onto the platform to a group of waiting reporters. Surprised at the reception, he begins to respond, only to find that they are waiting for 'Miss Gardner'. When she steps down from the train the reporters cluster round her and Fred is left on his own.

Cue for song. The film has been rolling less than five minutes and Astaire is launched into a two minute song sequence. Strolling jauntily down the platform, wearing a straw hat but no cane this time, he is into 'I'll Go My Way By Myself'. It's an ideal start for a Fred Astaire musical and it is sheer magic, but it doesn't last long enough. Astaire always seems to leave you wanting more. He is met by his old show-writer buddies, played by Oscar Levant and Nanette Fabray. There is a lot of nonsense chatter, but the upshot of it all is that the two writers have a show in prospect for them all which also involves director producer Geoff Kordover, played by

Jack Buchanan. When they part, Fred makes his way to Forty-second Street and with a carefully designed set including amusement machines, a fortune-telling stall, distorting mirrors and a hot dog stand, he is soon leading gently into his first dance routine. With a shoeshine stand as its axis, Fred uses all the props with telling effect as the dance builds up into a big musical number. He taps while perched high on the shoeshine stand and more traditionally on the sidewalk, leaps into the air, then he's down almost on his knees. He dances solo and at times with coloured shoeshine dancer, LeRoy Daniels. The number? What else but 'A Shine on Your Shoes'. It's a great fun thing, well in the Fred Astaire tradition.

The film then cuts to the new show in rehearsal, but under Buchanan's direction it's ponderous, slow-moving, corny, far too theatrical and totally lacking in a popular musical concept. His idea of making it the story of Faust in a modern setting is doomed from the start. It is during rehearsals that the familiar pattern between Astaire and his co-star, Gabrielle Gerrard (played by Cyd Charisse) develops. The formula is standard, used with various modifications in most of Astaire's musical movies. At first they don't get on, the atmosphere is decidedly frosty and friction develops. Fred dislikes her for being, basically, a ballet-dancer ('I haven't done ballet since I was a kid,' says he) and because her boyfriend is the show's choreographer. Fred, you see, is instantly captivated by Cyd's elegant beauty and distant sensuality and even at this early stage it's not hard to see that the choreographer boyfriend, though he's a nice, genuine guy, isn't really going to stand a chance in the romance stakes now Fred has moved in on the scene.

Mind you, there is some way to go yet and in the meantime, rehearsals are becoming a shambles. In the midst of all the confusion, however, the main purpose of it all is not forgotten, and there are some good and enjoyable sequences of 'That's Entertainment' and 'You and the Night and the Music'.

After three weeks of solid rehearsal the show doesn't look in any better shape. Numbers are cut out, parts are changed, Fred and Cyd can't get on and in the end Fred temporarily quits. Now begins the softening process. Cyd goes to Fred apologizing for her behaviour. Fred insists it is he who should apologize, going on to admit, 'I've been scared to death of you'.

'Can you and I really dance together,' says Cyd sympathetically. Astaire buffs can recognize the signs that another musical number is on the way. Fred confirms it with 'Let's Find Out'. They take a buggy ride, then walk casually through the park. The occasional dance step is inserted into the walk and our patience is finally

rewarded as Fred and Cyd move gently into a most delightful interpretation of 'Dancing in the Dark', beautifully choreographed. For
this sequence alone it is worth seeing the movie time and time
again. The elegance is perfection, four solid minutes of artistry
with not a word spoken or sung. Everything is conveyed in the light
and shade of the dance, the slow sweeping movements, the fast but
elegant spins, the perfectly held pauses. It is faultless and, even
thirty years later, unbeatable. All too soon the dancing melts away
and it is all over.

Meanwhile, rehearsals continue in chaos and to the point of
tedium, but relief comes with musical interjects, like 'You and the
Night and the Music'. Even Jack Buchanan has to admit, finally,
'It seems to be a little too much, doesn't it?' Opening night is a
disaster and the backers pull out. Fred forlornly goes to the
scheduled after-show party, entering the room to the strains of
'Give Me Something to Remember You By', but there is nobody
there and Fred departs. In the hallway he hears noises from another
room and finds the remainder of the cast assembled, depressed by
the show's failure, and enjoying a 'good old fashioned wake'. But
the scene is set and gradually builds up into a superbly rousing
chorus number, 'I Love Louisa'. It's exciting and energetic, with
Fred singing (in a just passable German dialect, but it doesn't really
matter), backed by the chorus, dancing, leaping onto a chair, dancing with Nanette Fabray and Oscar Levant. The whole cast joins in
and with good orchestral backing, it makes a great number.

More significantly, in terms of plot development, it gives Fred
the idea that, with all this talent, they ought to be able to put on a
show which is successful. We're not closing the show, he announces, but we'll re-do it from top to bottom. But with no backers, can
the show be a realistic possibility? Fred tentatively approaches Jack
Buchanan and suggests that his ideas for a heavy interpretation
must be abandoned in favour of an out-and-out, all-singing, all-
dancing musically happy show which will provide enjoyment for
the public. Buchanan accepts the reasoning and plays his part by
using his influence to get financial backing for the new show.

Another niggling problem is conveniently solved when Cyd
Charisse's choreographer boyfriend doesn't want her to do the
show — but by now she is too much a member of the team and
stimulated by the challenge of it all, not to say her growing fascination and love for Fred, to depart. She stays — which neatly clears
the way for Fred, though he has yet one more doubting moment to
live through.

But now we're building up to an outstanding finale, musically speaking. The show opens, playing various towns in the United States before finally moving to New York. An old cinema ploy is now used successfully. The cast travel from town to town by train. The screen is filled with the train hurtling along, but then town names, growing in size, break into the picture, before dissolving completely into a show number. At the end of the musical sequence, the film cuts back to the train and the whole thing is repeated, but this time with a different town name.

This technique then leads into a sequence of superb numbers — 'See a New Sun' from Cyd Charisse, and 'I Guess I'll Have to Change My Plan', with Fred and Jack Buchanan in top hat, white tie, tails and with a cane, singing and dancing softly, with a captivating syncopated rhythm. Then Nanette Fabray leads the chorus into 'Louisiana Hayride', a colourful, energetic number with plenty of singing and movement. This is followed by the famous 'Triplets' number with Fred, Jack and Nanette dressed up in baby bonnets in a novelty piece which, if it doesn't improve with age, certainly had the distinction of being unusual if not unique at the time of its creation.

The best is left for the end and as the train steams into New York and the cast face the biggest test, the scene dissolves into the now legendary 'The Girl Hunt Ballet'. Fred narrates and the cliché-ridden Mickey Spillane sequence is full of 'hammy' lines, the best of which are probably 'Somebody was trying to tell me something', 'I was playing a hunch' and, surely, the unbeatable, 'She came at me in sections, with more curves than a scenic railway'.

That last line was provoked by Cyd Charisse whose dancing, both as a brunette in a glittering black dress and then in a shimmering orange gown with long black evening gloves and orange shoes, and again as a provocative blonde, was alone worth the admission price to the cinema. The dance in the salon is excitingly rhythmic and incredibly atmospheric and Fred and Cyd's performance is surely one of the best dance sequences ever committed to film.

All the pieces are now beginning to drop into place as the movie approaches its end. The show is obviously an enormous success and only confirmation that Fred and Cyd are together remains to tie up all the ends. Fred is in his dressing-room at the end of the show and there are no scenes of celebration, as one would have considered theatrical tradition demanded. As a member of the cast puts his head into the room to wish Fred goodnight and to say 'See you tomorrow', Fred is obviously disappointed and asks dejectedly: 'What's the matter ... doesn't anyone celebrate after a show anymore?' Then he wonders about Cyd and enquires, 'Did Gabby go out with Paul (the former boyfriend choreographer)?'

Fearing that she has left the theatre with him, he leaves the dressing-room on his own, singing 'By Myself' ... As he moves into the theatre on his way out there is an enormous surprise waiting for him. The entire cast is assembled. He is astonished and lost for words as they break into 'For He's a Jolly Good Fellow'. Cyd steps forward to express their gratitude, admiration and 'our love' and the scene dissolves into the finale and 'That's Entertainment'.

It's all over.

Particularly interesting in *The Band Wagon* were the little digs and the cheeky yet subtle references which Fred was able to make against himself. For instance, his reference to the New Amsterdam Theatre was described in the previous chapter. Another was when Fred sees Cyd for the first time and is struck by her beauty. 'Fabulous, sensational, the loveliest thing I've ever seen', but then ... 'she's a little tall, isn't she?' Nanette Fabray responds, 'Stage illusion'. When they meet on the stairs you can see Fred quietly trying to assess her height against his own and then, 'Pretty shoes,' he remarks, 'Do you always wear high heels?' Nice little touches, these.

In fact Cyd Charisse *was* a little tall for Fred and it is interesting in 'The Girl Hunt Ballet' scene to see the way she cleverly hides the fact. Often she is draped around Fred, bringing her lower, and in the movements she is often on bent legs — not easy, but exceptionally well done.

125

TEN

Getting to know the man

Fred was devastated by Phyllis's death. He adored her all their married life and for a long time was unable to come to terms with her passing. Rehearsals for his next film — *Daddy Long Legs* with Leslie Caron — had begun just a couple of months before, but as Phyllis's condition became critical he had to leave the set. Fortunately Twentieth Century Fox, rather than replace him, said they would wait until he felt ready to continue. This was the best thing that could have happened. The last thing Fred wanted to do was to carry on with the film after Phyllis's death and had they let him off the contract it is doubtful if he would ever have made another film. As it was, feeling under an obligation to return as soon as possible and not let anyone down, he was back on the set early in October. The studio was understanding, easing him gently into the picture again as he struggled to pick up the threads of his now empty life.

Astaire had always been essentially a private man and while he dedicated himself completely to his film work *while he was working,* his home, family and private life meant a great deal to him. Indeed, he said that after his marriage, it always came first. Family ties were always close. He had loved his parents, was devoted to his sister Adele, and many times, to friends and in public, he said how fortunate he was to be married to Phyllis; and he adored his children, Fred junior (born in 1941) and Ava (born in 1942). His other interests were limited — racing of course, playing cards, golf and pool — and his few friends he chose carefully and valued the pleasure of visiting their houses for an informal dinner party or having them round for a quiet family gathering.

One of his special friends was David Niven. They first met in 1935, indirectly through Astaire's interest in racing. Niven, not long in Hollywood, had a letter of introduction from English bookmaker Lord Tommy Graves, a friend of Astaire's, and presented himself with it at the Astaire home one evening after playing a hectic game of tennis. The only problem was, he forgot to put his shirt back on before ringing the doorbell. When Phyllis

126

opened the door she was taken aback and called to Fred with some apprehension and hesitation. Niven, it should be remembered, was unknown in 1935. He was only twenty-five then and didn't make his film debut until later that year, when he appeared as an extra in *Mutiny on the Bounty.* But it was from this unlikely doorstep encounter that, as Niven explained in *Bring on the Empty Horses,* 'a friendship grew which perhaps meant more to me than any other in Hollywood'. Niven said that Fred and Phyllis together were 'a joy to behold'.

Although from the start Fred and Phyllis's relationship was totally harmonious, it is doubtful if a marriage bureau would have picked them out to share a life together. She had no interest in the theatre, and as a society New Yorker, knew no one in show business. She seemed hardly the natural choice for a vaudeville hoofer, the son of an Austrian immigrant who had spent all his life in show business. Phyllis was short-tongued which gave her a captivating lisp and although Fred fell for her immediately, she held back for a while. Presumably she was unsure about the kind of life she might find herself in if married to a man whose vaudeville days were over and with no film career yet to take its place. But that side of life quickly sorted itself out as Astaire became a Hollywood star within a couple of years. They were a sane, sensible couple, unaffected by the excesses and freakish behaviour of much of Hollywood in its golden years. While Fred made a fortune dancing from one film success to another, Phyllis stayed quietly in the background, carefully working out the finances and investing astutely. She deftly handed-off professional business managers with their exciting 'get rich quick' schemes, preferring instead to seek the advice of known friends in New York.

She had a keen and instinctive eye for business affairs. Soon after moving into their first Hollywood home in North Canon Drive, Phyllis was busy planning their next move. She acquired a four-acre package on choice Summit Drive in Beverly Hills from John Boles. It was too big for their needs, but Phyllis insisted it was a good investment. So it was. She arranged for their new home to be built on a two acre plot and included in the plans a swimming-pool and tennis courts, despite Fred's protestations that he didn't play tennis. Phyllis said it would be useful if the children wanted to learn to play and in any event, was useful for resale value. 'Out here nobody wants a house without a tennis court,' she said, sensibly. Later Phyllis arranged for another house to be built on the remaining two acres, bigger and better than the first, and she and Fred moved in, selling the original house to famous film director

William Wyler. Her wisdom in selecting choice real estate in one of the most glittering parts of Beverly Hills, among the lush orange groves which separated the plot from other houses about a quarter of a mile away, only then became obvious to Astaire in business terms. He was even more impressed when he discoverd that Phyllis had from the start intended to build two houses on the large plot so they could sell the first house a few years later at a handsome profit. Fred never bothered his head about business matters. He would worry all night about getting a dance routine exactly right, but he left the business side of his career entirely to Phyllis. She loved it, was good at it, and she invested sensibly and wisely.

When working on a picture Fred would seldom have time to relax, getting to the studios early in the morning and often working until late in the evening. He dedicated himself to polishing and perfecting his dance routines and would go over them again and again, extracting that extra fraction of performance. The picture filled his time, but at weekends when there was a pause in the hectic schedule, he and Phyllis would take off for their beloved Blue Valley Ranch, which they established in 1950. When a picture was done, the two of them would relax for two or three months, playing golf, going to see Phyllis's family and friends, enjoying a holiday in the States or abroad. Although Phyllis seldom visited the studios, they were always together when work was done. These spells between pictures were gems in Astaire's life. His film work satisfied him professionally and he found it fulfilling, but it is significant that he most frequently made reference to his contentment, pleasure and sheer happiness in life when referring to the times he was able to put the studios behind him and go off and relax with Phyllis.

He enjoyed golf, pool and cards, but most of all his sport was racing. He was fascinated by it during those early London shows when Sir Alfred Butt invited him to several of the important meetings. He has written so enthusiastically about George, his London valet from those days, that it is difficult to decide whether he admired him more for his passion for racing than his valeting prowess. George, in fact, was not a betting man, but according to Fred he certainly had a knack for picking a winner. During the London run of *Lady, Be Good!* in 1926, Astaire got to know British jockey Jack Leach, and after winning a few bets began to take a real interest in the prospect of owning a horse himself. He later bought a half share in a mediocre runner called Dolomite for £500 and although it was never a winner, Fred was able to make a good profit when he sold the horse to a foreign buyer. Sidney, another

Astaire, with co-star Jack Buchanan, during their superb syncopated tap routine from *The Band Wagon*, 'I Guess I'll Have To Change My Plan'.

he world's greatest song-and-ance man relaxes between kes of *The Band Wagon*.

Surely one of the most eloquent and fluent dance sequences ever screened was 'Dancing in the Dark' in *The Band Wagon*. The easy grace and sheer perfection was breathtaking. Fred and Cyd Charisse.

Benefactor and Beau—that was Fred in *Daddy Long Legs*, a captivating tale and an enjoyable film in which Astaire appeared with the elfin-like French actress and dancer Leslie Caron.

Fred in flight. He was the most relaxed and elegant of dancers, but when needed no one could generate more excitement, energy or sheer exuberance.

Proud father. Fred escorts his beautiful seventeen-year-old daughter Ava to the annual debutantes ball in Los Angeles. The columnists predicted a movie career for Ava, but she wasn't interested.

Fred relaxes with co-star Audrey Hepburn during the shooting of *Funny Face* in 1957. He was so thrilled at the prospect of working with Miss Hepburn that he kept his professional diary free until she was available.

In 1957, *Silk Stockings* brought Fred together once more with the leggy Cyd Charisse. Cole Porter provided the music and the lyrics. Arthur Freed produced and Hermes Pan was one of the dance directors.

Cyd Charisse mid-way in the metamorphosis process from stiff, tunic dressed Russian to the frilly 'decadence' of the West in *Silk Stockings*.

Nevil Shute's dramatic story of the last days of the world after a nuclear disaster—*On The Beach* from United Artists in 1959—gave Astaire his first non-musical role.

In *The Midas Run* (*A Run on Gold* in UK) in 1969 Astaire played a Secret Service agent and co-starred with Anne Heywood and Sir Ralph Richardson.

Touch of the old days as Fred dances (though ballroom style) with Jennifer Jones in the 1975 Oscar-winning disaster movie, *The Towering Inferno*.

Fred and Adele Astaire photographed in New York in 1972. They had a great affection for each other. Adele died in 1981, aged eighty-four, in hospital in Arizona, where she was being treated for a stroke.

Fred Astaire at seventy-seven years of age, Hollywood legend and the cinema's greatest ever song-and-dance man.

How's this for a famous chorus line? Fred links arms with Cyd Charisse, Leslie Caron and Gene Kelly in the Embankment Gardens of London's Savoy Hotel in 1976 for the reception for the Gala Première of the film *That's Entertainment Part 2*.

Astaire and his new bride Robyn Smith pictured soon after their marriage at their Beverly Hills home. Fred, 81, and Robyn, 35, were married in June 1980.

horse in which Astaire also had a half share, *did* win, however, and as Fred himself remarked, 'There's nothing like a winner of your own to give you that certain feeling.' He bought a few more and later started breeding, but for a long time he was never present to see one of his horses win. It happened for the first time in 1945, around the time Astaire was making his 'retirement' film, *Blue Skies.*

His interest in racing had been revived about a year before, after a number of years when he didn't own any horses, when he decided to get his old trainer friend, Clyde Phillips, to look for a couple of racers for him. One filly Phillips *almost* acquired for Astaire became something of a champion, winning a lot of money, but he did eventually buy what turned out to be a three-year-old colt named Triplicate for six thousand dollars. Fred was thrilled when Triplicate started winning, and he was even happier when he saw his horse in action for the first time at a meeting at Belmont Park, finishing fourth. When Fred retired after *Blue Skies,* he spent a lot of time watching Triplicate race. The horse continued to improve and Fred had a wonderful day when the horse won the San Juan Capistrano by five lengths and before 60,000 people. Said Fred: 'As I fought my way to the winner's circle I got slapped on the back so many times that I was more beat than the horse. What a day!' Another proud racing moment for Astaire was when he received the Hollywood Gold Cup, thanks again to Triplicate. Altogether Triplicate won about a quarter of a million dollars.

A particular racing thrill was when Astaire and daughter Ava were on their way to Europe to spend a few days in Paris and stopped over in England to see Fred's horse Rainbow Tie run at Goodwood. It was a royal occasion and Queen Elizabeth sent a message inviting Astaire and Ava to join the royal box. Fred had met the Queen many years before, when she was a diminutive Princess Elizabeth, and was able to chat happily about the film world and racing. Fred tells a lovely story about their conversation. When he mentioned that he had danced with the Queen's mother (who later became the Queen Mother) some years before, said Fred: 'With her fascinating smile she topped me with "You mean she danced with you!".'

Astaire's mother once told Jack Leach that no one in the family had been interested in racing. Yet when Fred and Adele first arrived in New York, and Fred's interest in the horses was developing, he would often be missing in the afternoons, spending an hour or so at Belmont Park. Leach said that Astaire's knowledge about the game became remarkable and in England he got to know practically every jockey, trainer and owner in the country, and at one time had all the British form books stretching back to the early 1920s. A nice anecdote which Leach recalled to demonstrate Astaire's fascination with racing was the time Fred arrived in England and, facing a barrage of reporters, held up their questions by asking them, 'When is the next race meeting and where is it?'

After racing, golf was probably Fred's next favourite sporting interest. Phyllis could beat him at tennis and was herself no mean golfer, being a particularly long hitter for her height and weight. The two would often relax together on those exotic American courses like Palm Springs and Bel-Air. It was a fine way to unwind — and, of course, Fred never forgot that it was golf which in a way brought them together all those years before.

The love he had for his own mother, father and sister, was carried forward to his own family. Peter, Phyllis's son from her previous marriage, was always one of the family and a great deal of affection and respect developed between them. Fred was overjoyed when first his son Fred and then his daughter Ava were born. He had an adjoining room in the Good Samaritan Hospital in Los Angeles for a week, staying close to Phyllis, after Fred was born.

During that time, at Phyllis's insistence, he spent a few afternoons following the races at nearby Santa Anita, and song-writer Irving Berlin, a great chum of the Astaires, would come down in the evening and play gin rummy with Fred for hours — though it seems that Berlin's mind was seldom far away from the business of song-writing. And when later Ava was born in the same hospital, Fred says he remembers thinking to himself that he must be about the happiest fellow in the world.

Fred never ceased to be thankful for what he often called the extraordinary luck and good fortune which enable him to be so blissfully happy and contented with life. Events always seemed to have a happy knack of working out to his advantage. If you consider his career in detail, there are few times when he was forced into making a really conscious decision which had serious implications for the outcome of his career. Much more often events took over to guide him along certain paths. One of the strongest convictions of his entire life, however, was to marry Phyllis and he never stopped being grateful that their life together with their three children was so idyllic.

Of course, there were sad times in his life — when his father died for instance, and later when Adele, after her retirement from the famous brother-and-sister stage act, lost children in childbirth; and yet again when her husband died. Though for much of their life, after Fred settled in California, they were separated by huge distances, Fred and Phyllis would make special efforts to see Adele and Charles at their home in Ireland and, even later, when she was working in London. Fred and Adele were always close and it was heartbreaking for him when she first lost a daughter in premature birth and then twin boys, also at birth. During the Second World War Charles and Adele opened their home at Lismore Castle to air-force men needing to convalesce and recuperate from battle fatigue. Charles had not been well and was desperately disappointed that he was denied a more active role in the war. Later Adele joined the American Red Cross and, working in London, wrote letters home for active service personnel, linking them with families, wives and sweethearts. The close affinity with Adele he again felt deeply when, during rehearsal for *Ziegfeld Follies,* he received a cable from his mother, who had been living at Lismore permanently to take care of the ailing Charles Cavendish, to say that he had died. 'The news saddened me a great deal,' he said. He must have felt particularly sorry for Adele who was, at the time, in London serving with the American Red Cross and unable to go home to Ireland to share Charles's final days because of a travel embargo imposed by the authorities due to the proximity of D-Day.

This great friendship and love for each other was despite their very different attitudes towards life. Adele was extrovert, fun-loving, with an effervescent personality. Fred was quieter with a deeper sense of responsibility. It was not unusual for him when he was filming to excuse himself from whatever company he was with in the early evening so he could get to bed at a reasonable hour, ready for a prompt start at the studios next day. Astaire didn't usually make deep lasting friendships instantly. He'd take his time getting to know people. That well-known British author, broadcaster and entertainer, the late Alan Melville, put it well when he said: 'Fred was a terribly cosy man once he'd decided you were a chum. He loved his home, his glass of Scotch and a chat with his friends. He wasn't a party boy at all and, even socially, was always very professional.' Fred and Adele remained close after her second marriage and he retained a close brotherly affection for his sister. Her death in 1981, when she was eighty-four, hit him hard.

Never far from Astaire, either physically or mentally, was his mother. For many years she lived with him, but it was still a wrench when she died at ninety-six and her passing depressed him.

Astaire never cultivated a public image. He has always positively disliked interviews, and when he is pressed into them doesn't really have all that much to say and is inclined to close the proceedings when he feels he has said enough. For journalists looking for a good quote or a strong angle he has been irritatingly obscure and matter-of-fact, with no really positive views about anything, least of all dancing and his own career. Yet his legs were said to have been insured by RKO for one million dollars back in the late 1930s and early 1940s when he had Ginger Rogers as his partner and his major films for the same studio reputedly grossed in excess of 200 million dollars.

He is as adroit at avoiding pointed questions as his feet were nimble in those all-singing, all-dancing 1930s and 1940s films. As recently as 1981, the celebrated British showbiz writer and London *Daily Mail* columnist David Lewin managed to trap him in his lair in Los Angeles. However, in the end he didn't really make all that much progress with the cleverly evasive Astaire. Lewin asked him what sort of memorial he wanted to leave. Said Fred, quoted Lewin: 'I want no memorials. I am not an image or an idol or a great success. I just don't think that way.' The questioner tried again, asking him how he would like to be remembered. 'It doesn't matter. Either I will be or I won't. I cannot influence the way others will think of me.' He added, parrying the question nicely, that he started to dance because his sister Adele did. 'I followed in her footsteps, literally. Adele had the talent. I just went along for the ride.' He certainly doesn't give the impression of being proud of what he has done, the success he has made of his life, of what he has accomplished. In a wry sort of way it seems to please him more that he has been able to make a few bucks.

If you can get him to talk about success — and that's an achievement in itself — he has no secrets to impart, no magic formula to reveal. Instead he mentions comparatively boring things like luck, determination and perseverance. In working out his famous dance routines he says he came up with ideas which pleased him, rather than what he felt might be good box-office. He realized, he said once, that audiences must also like what he did and that he tried to put himself in their place. 'But I do nothing that I don't like, such as inventing 'up' to the arty or 'down' to the corny.' He has been accused among reporters of being stubborn, churlish and uncooperative. He has admitted to being bad-tempered, impatient, hard to please and critical; and that he didn't like top hats, white ties and tails. He claimed that some of his most interesting and memorable moments were on an empty stage in an empty theatre, by himself, running through some of his steps. He told David Lewin that he had no fear or worry of death, no boredom, no sense of the past. 'I have no regrets in my life. Everything that happened has been accidental anyway. I am not concerned with messages in my films

— I never was.'

One of his most astonishing and surprising admissions was perhaps when he told Lewin that he didn't watch any of his old films. He once told Brian Vine in New York: 'Sometimes I see a bit of one of my pictures on TV and I can't even figure which film it is until I look at the TV guide.' He said to another reporter that he had never been as impressed with what he had done professionally as much as people thought he should have been. 'I never took my dancing as seriously as everyone else did,' he claimed. The fact that he is a legend seems to have passed him entirely. He just doesn't accept or even think about his own greatness in the world of film entertainment. And the most astonishing part of him is that all this modesty, in so great an entertainer, is genuine and honest. He *really* doesn't want to talk about the past. He *really* doesn't think he has done anything particularly remarkable. He *really* cannot see what all the fuss is about and *really* would much prefer to be left alone to live the remainder of his life quietly, enjoying his simple pleasures.

Basic to everything Astaire has done has been his love for Phyllis and, particularly in the early years when his career was at its height, his devotion to his family. To the outsider, his relationship with Ginger Rogers has always been a fascination, yet in truth there was little fascination about it. It was simply extraordinarily *ordinary*. Despite spending so long together professionally — often eighteen long hours a day at the studio — they hardly ever mixed socially and usually only when they happened to meet by chance at friends' houses.

Their friendship was essentially platonic and although they were friends, not even a close friendship developed. Some years later, in a magazine article, Ginger admitted that they didn't see each other very often. Yet she said that she felt there would in some way always be a firm friendship between them. Astaire himself appreciated Ginger's contribution to the success of their partnership and has said that she was brilliantly effective, and deserves much of the credit for their success. Talking at one time about his brilliant craftsmanship, she said she respected him and found him helpful and unselfish. She claimed they never had quarrels, only strong arguments and differences of opinon. 'But we never had harsh words,' she claimed. Once, when they differed bitterly over something on the set, they just didn't speak to each other until the tension eased.

Yet Astaire would be the first to admit that he wasn't always tolerant of his partners and his demands were often excessive in his constant desire for perfection. Only one of his partners — and she wasn't really a partner in the strictest sense — seems not to have enjoyed too much the experience of working with Astaire. Nanette Fabray has been reported as saying that while working on *The Band Wagon* she found him insensitive to her problems, abrupt and indifferent and that when work was over for the day he would just disappear. The explanation must have been his terrible worry over his wife's illness, a situation which Miss Fabray later appreciated, though it certainly made life, and the making of *The Band Wagon,* at that stage, extremely difficult and cast a shadow over the proceedings.

For someone who felt it unfair that when so many people were slaving away at jobs they didn't particularly like, he was able to enjoy his work such a lot; and for someone who honestly felt himself to be the luckiest person in the world because of his love and affection for Phyllis and his children, the blow that struck Astaire in those dark, dark days of 1954, was savage and grievous. Basically a religious man, he found solace for a time in a conviction that she was bound to pull through. A fatal illness was a catastrophe which for Phyllis he simply had never contemplated. Almost to the very end he felt no need to consider the worst possible consequences of her illness. Even after major surgery when shortly afterward she was once more rushed to hospital, Astaire remained optimistic. Home again, but unable to regain any strength and with her condition deteriorating, Fred was still hopeful — even when, yet again in hospital, she slipped into a deep coma. The shock was all the more numbing when the end came.

ELEVEN

The march of time

Despite the trauma of Phyllis's death, Astaire managed to pick up his film career again. Working on *Daddy Long Legs* he admired the professionalism of beautiful French star Leslie Caron, who would go to endless pains to get her dance sequences right and would only let the cameras roll once she was confident of her work. She was a little nervous perhaps at working with the man who had been her inspiration when she was going through dance school back in France. Her big success before *Daddy Long Legs* was in 1951 when she starred with Gene Kelly in *An American in Paris*. Even so she was some thirty-odd years younger than Astaire and, with a classical ballet background, was a trifle overawed by his monumental reputation. Fred, however, thought she was delightful and a fine artist. He was also pleased that he had asked popular composer and lyric-writer Johnny Mercer to do the music. Some excellent material emerged and Astaire fulfilled an ambition he had cherished for some time. He loved Mercer's 'Dream' and was convinced that this popular tune would make an excellent theme for a romantic dance. *Daddy Long Legs* gave him the chance to prove it and he was happy with the result.

Altogether, the film was highly favoured by Astaire, in spite of his sorrow at the time. He considered the film script one of the best he had ever worked on, and Johnny Mercer had produced a completely original score. He enjoyed the atmosphere of the Twentieth Century Fox studios and admired their film music department, headed by Al Newman, whom he knew from earlier days. The powerful Darryl Zanuck was still running Fox at the time and his influence, and the way the studio worked, was much to Fred's liking. He was keen to do another film there and the studio talked a lot about a follow-up, but the ideas which came up didn't particularly attract Astaire, and *Daddy Long Legs,* somewhat disappointingly, remains the only musical Fred Astaire did for Twentieth Century Fox. This is all the more surprising when considered against the film's good record in the United States and its even greater popularity abroad, where it was in the top ten most successful foreign films to be released that year.

Leslie Caron's girlish awkwardness was captivating as she played an orphan college girl whose education is financed by a wealthy, but anonymous, businessman. Her gratitude builds into a fantasized romance and the situation becomes complicated when she meets someone and falls in love. At first she has no idea that her unknown benefactor and her real-life boyfriend are the same — Fred Astaire. Included in the musical numbers are Johnny Mercer's phenomenally successful 'Something's Gotta Give'. 'History of the Beat' was a good rhythmic sequence with Astaire, tie loosened and prop pipe in mouth, blasting away behind a drum-kit. But generally acknowledged to have the edge was 'Sluefoot', though the film has long since faded for all except Astaire's and Mercer's most devoted fans and that particular sequence is not now considered one of Fred's best.

Astaire was fifty-six by the time *Daddy Long Legs* went out on release and already his enormous talent had outlived the natural life-span of the film musical. Just two films remained for him, before it could legitimately be claimed that his career as a movie song-and-dance man was ended. *Funny Face,* with Audrey Hepburn, and *Silk Stockings,* with him teamed once more with Cyd Charisse, were yet to come, but for a while after *Daddy Long Legs,* there was nothing.

It was perhaps the most difficult time in Astaire's life. He found for a long time that life without Phyllis was hardly bearable, but his loneliness drew him even closer to his mother, Fred junior and Ava. His ranch was now a thing of the past. He and Phyllis had spent so many idyllic times together there, but he couldn't bear to go back without her. He drew enormous comfort from his family and spent a lot of time with Ava, now thirteen, taking her all over. An early event after *Daddy Long Legs* was a trip to Europe with Ava and his mother, though he preferred to remain quietly and contemplatively in Lismore Castle while Ava went on to Dublin and then to London. Once he was back in California there still seemed no great rush to get him on a film set again, though Fox continued to discuss various projects, all of which came to nothing. There were rumours that he was retiring and that he didn't want to face films, or the world, without Phyllis. But in fact he felt the need to keep busy and didn't enjoy the enforced lull. Paramount had an idea which disappointingly didn't work out. There was a film in the offing which would have brought Astaire and the incredibly talented Sammy Cahn together for the first time. Sammy even demonstrated one of the songs he had in mind for the film and Fred thought it was outstanding. The tune was 'Call Me Irresponsible', arguably Sammy Cahn's best ever, but Fred never did it. The film was finally made with Jackie Gleason taking over the part intended for Fred.

Paramount eventually came to the rescue and he signed to do a couple of films with them over the next three years. He was unenthusiastic about one, but when Paramount told him that in the other he would be teamed with Bing Crosby, Astaire was happy with the deal. In the end, both projects fell through, one because Crosby left Paramount shortly after, and the other because Astaire temporarily opted out in favour of the Crosby replacement picture at Paramount. This was to feature the elfin-like Audrey Hepburn and Astaire was particularly flattered when he discovered that Hepburn had especially asked for him as her co-star. She was at this time one of Hollywood's most glittering stars and Astaire, for all his experience and fame, showed remarkable humility at the prospect of appearing with her. It is said, in fact, that he kept himself free, shunning any other possibilities which might have come along, when the project with Hepburn became difficult to organize. She was heavily in demand all round and it seemed at one time that the film would be lost forever as negotiations stuck in an almost unbelievable tangle involving agents, studios, foreign commitments and Hepburn's and Astaire's own representatives. Determined not to lose the possibility of working with Audrey Hepburn, Astaire kept himself available and it worked out satisfactorily in the end.

The film was finally shot at Paramount and took the title of one of Fred and Adele Astaire's stage musical successes, *Funny Face*. The Gershwins had produced the music and lyrics for the stage show, which ran for 250 performances on Broadway in 1927 and 263 performances in London a year later, and some of their best material was carried forward to the new film with Hepburn. Among them were ''S Wonderful' and 'He Loves and She Loves'. Other numbers came from Roger Edens and Leonard Gershe. 'Think Pink', 'How Long Has This Been Going On?', 'Funny Face', 'Bonjour Paris' and 'Clap Your Hands' were also in the score. The story was about a librarian from New York's Greenwich Village (Audrey Hepburn) who becomes a glamorous cover girl for a sophisticated magazine and has a romance in Paris with a top photograher, played by Astaire. Much of the ground work was done in the Hollywood studios, but a lot of the finished shooting took place in Paris. Because of the bad weather, scheduling became heavy, but Astaire, despite the pressure, was thrilled working with

Audrey Hepburn and was sorry when it was all over. His appetite for filming, and his general zest for life, seemed to be returning, though his great friend Hermes Pan once said that he didn't think he would ever really get over Phyllis's death. But his family was growing up, he acquired an attractive daughter-in-law when Fred junior got married, and his mother finally agreed to come and live with Astaire once more. It all helped the feeling that life must go on.

Best of all during this period, Astaire *was* kept busy. He was soon back at MGM where he was reunited with his old friend and producer Arthur Freed for a musical version of the vintage Garbo film *Ninotchka*. Cole Porter was brought in for the music and lyrics and Astaire was delighted to be working once more with dance director Hermes Pan. The beautifully leggy and loose-limbed Cyd Charisse took the part of a blue stockinged Russian girl commissar on a visit to Paris, fronting a Communist delegation comprising aides Peter Lorre, Jules Munshin and Joseph Buloff, whose comedy throughout the film was a delight. All come under the romantic spell of Paris, before which their rigid and blinkered life style wilts, and Charisse herself, despite a brave resistance, falls in love with American businessman Astaire, melting beautifully and seductively into his more relaxed way of life. Astaire fans might have hoped for a more riveting end to their hero's song-and-dance film career. On the other hand, it could have had a much less happy ending. By now and in comparison with his outstanding earlier successes, particularly with Ginger Rogers, it was difficult for the critics to be totally objective. Not for a decade perhaps had they been ecstatic about a Fred Astaire film, but many comments were less than fair to what was a very commendable and enjoyable film. *Silk Stockings* was following a classic which was stamped with the Garbo legend and therefore difficult to emulate. Maybe Cyd Charisse was a little bland and po-faced in her acting. Perhaps Cole Porter wasn't at his most creative. But even if it fell short of the *The Band Wagon, Silk Stockings* was still very good value for money.

The film was filled with music and some of the Cole Porter numbers became hot favourites. 'Stereophonic Sound' is still remembered. 'Fated to be Mated', 'Siberia' — a superb cameo spot for Lorre, Munshin and Buloff — and, of course, the evergreens 'You'd Be So Nice To Come Home To' and 'I've Got You Under My Skin' were all included in the film. Astaire and Charisse once again made an electrifying couple dancing, but undoubtedly one of the very best dance sequences in the movie was a Charisse solo when, alone in her hotel-room, she kicked herself clear of the drab clothing from her past in favour of the silk stockings and Paris fineries of Western society. Fred enjoyed dancing with Cyd and he considered her solo numbers positively outstanding. His famous quote about Cyd Charisse is well worth repeating. 'That Cyd! When you've danced with her you stay danced with.'

Astaire was now fifty-eight and he knew he couldn't go on making dance movies for ever. There were a number of attempts to persuade him to put on his dancing-shoes again, but nothing tempted him. Over the last two or three years he had been doing some television work and he wondered about moving into the medium. He could virtually have named his price for a weekly series, but that's not what he wanted. He didn't want to commit himself on a regular basis. He'd had enough of that during the Ginger Rogers years. So for a while, he just disappeared from public view, enjoyed his golf and racing, and went on trips abroad with Ava. It was a good life, but although he wasn't looking for a new career, he did have an urge to try one or two non-musical roles. He got the chance in a half hour American television comedy called *Imp on a Cobweb Leash* and followed this with more comedy in *Man on a Bicycle*. This led to his big-screen breakthrough in his first major dramatic role as the nuclear scientist who survives an atomic holocaust in *On the Beach*. This film, made by United Artists, took Astaire to Australia and included him in the star-studded cast list of Gregory Peck, Ava Gardner, Donna Anderson and the then almost unknown British actor Anthony Perkins. This epic tale, taken from Nevil Shute's story of the last days of the world, gave a worldwide audience the first chance of seeing the new, non-dancing, all-acting Fred Astaire . . . and he proved his talent wasn't all in his feet.

Two years later he was back at Paramount to make *The Pleasure of His Company,* in which he appeared with Debbie Reynolds, Lilli Palmer, Tab Hunter and Gary Merrill, and the following year he was cast with Kim Novak, Jack Lemmon and Lionel Jeffries in the Columbia picture *The Notorious Landlady,* a mystery thriller set in Britain. In 1968 Astaire returned to the world of the screen musical, but a musical with a difference, in Warner Brothers' *Finian's Rainbow,* in which he appeared with Britain's Petula Clark and former cockney skiffle king Tommy Steele. Among a collection of musical numbers, 'If This Isn't Love' and 'Old Devil Moon' were probably the best, though the most memorable for those who saw the film will almost certainly have been 'How Are Things in Glocca Morra?' Astaire played Finian McLonergan in a movie which had all the promise in the world but for most critics never quite made it, despite the commendable work of song-writer Burton Lane. By now

Fred had had enough of dancing professionally and announced that *Finian's Rainbow* would be the last film in which he would dance. Though the film was enjoyable, it was not a worthy or appropriate ending to such a remarkable career. Astaire had not only typified the Hollywood musical for more than thirty years, but he had stamped all these years with a talent and professionalism by which all other performances were judged. *Finian's Rainbow* had been a successful stage show with a good measure of fun, fantasy and satire, but it wasn't really the perfect film for Fred to end his screen dancing career. After *The Midas Run* (titled *A Run on Gold* in Britain), in which he appeared with Anne Heywood, Sir Ralph Richardson and Cesar Romero, Astaire was absent from the big screen for six years, but his return alongside Steve McQueen, Paul Newman and a host of other top stars in *The Towering Inferno* was powerful indeed. High drama runs through the film as guests present on the eve of a dedication ceremony of the world's tallest skyscraper are trapped inside the building when fire breaks out. It was a supreme disaster movie, with Fred, sporting slightly more hair than he had when he first appeared with Joan Crawford more than forty years before, cast as a confidence trickster who falls in love with his victim, Jennifer Jones, who dies in the inferno. Fred proved himself to be a surprisingly good dramatic actor, but there was just a slight tinge of nostalgia as he and Jennifer Jones take the dance floor and shuffle around a little. The joke has been with Astaire that, in spite of his excellent technique as a tap and stage dancer, his ability as a ballroom dancer was always mediocre.

It is not strictly true to say that Astaire's appearance in *The Towering Inferno* was his first big-screen showing after *The Midas Run,* because he had taken part a year before in MGM's film tribute to its own contribution to the film musical in *That's Entertainment,* a compilation offering which re-traced the history of MGM musicals from the beginning of the talkies in the early 1930s until the middle of the 1950s. Astaire was a host-presenter and appeared in a number of the film clips. Among several songs of his chosen for the tribute were 'They Can't Take That Away From Me', 'I Guess I'll Have to Change My Plan', 'Shoes With Wings On', 'Begin the Beguine, 'Dancing in the Dark' and 'By Myself'. Two years later, in 1976, MGM put out *That's Entertainment, Part 2,* a similar offering but adding some original musical sequences. Astaire film clips included 'That's Entertainment', 'I Wanna Be a Dancing Man', 'Easter Parade', 'Steppin' Out With My Baby' and 'A Couple of Swells'. Among the new numbers was 'Be a Clown'.

Later films were *The Amazing Dobermans* in 1976, and *Un Taxi*

Mauve in 1977, with Charlotte Rampling and Peter Ustinov also in
the cast, but with Fred now nudging seventy-eight, it is true to say
that his film career had been petering out over the last few years,
though with Astaire you could never be too sure where he might
pop up next. He gave a delightful performance in the 1980 movie of
The Man in the Santa Claus Suit, which was a superb offering full
of Christmas cheer. In it he took the part of numerous characters
— a New York cop, chauffeur, hot-dog seller, cab driver, a foot-
walker in Maceys, shop assistant, costumier and carollers' conductor. His phrase 'It being Christmas and all . . .' became a password
for the film which, incidentally, featured Nanette Fabray who had
starred with Astaire way back in *The Band Wagon.*

A girl who was in Astaire's other film he made with Cyd
Charisse, *Silk Stockings,* was also to prove significant to him later
in his career. Barrie Chase, attractive, lissome and a sensational
dancer, took a minor role in *Silk Stockings,* though Fred did
momentarily dance with her in the film, but in the late 1950s and
1960s she partnered him in a series of television shows in America.
She was Astaire's last outstanding dance partner and he considered
her sensational. Herbert Ross, who choreographed much of the TV
spectaculars, went so far as to say that Astaire considered her the
best partner he had ever had and only agreed to do the TV shows on
condition she would appear with him.

Fred Astaire seldom acted on impulse, even in his younger days.
He hadn't changed much in his late seventies. If Robyn Smith,
America's top female jockey, hadn't asked him out to dinner one
day in 1978, they may well have stayed just casual friends. But after
that, they dated from time to time, ignoring the gossips who pointed
out their age difference. Two years later, on 27 June 1980, at a small
secret ceremony at his Beverly Hills home, they were married.

It is a marriage they said would never last. The gossips doomed it
to failure. But more than ten years after they met and three years
after they wed, both Fred (eighty-five in 1984) and Robyn, forty-
one, still seem happy and contented.

It was eleven years before at Santa Anita racecourse near Los
Angeles that tycoon Alfred G. Vanderbilt unwittingly played
matchmaker between the world's best known dancer and the
world's top lady jockey. In the owner's paddock shortly before a
race he turned to Astaire and said, 'I want you to meet Robyn
Smith.' She was in racing silks preparing to mount her horse. 'I'd
heard of him but I'd never seen one of his movies and I knew
nothing about him,' she recalls. But Fred was taken by Robyn's

A tribute to Fred Astaire

dark-haired beauty to the extent of laying a small bet on her horse. And though it was a hopeless outsider called Exciting Divorce, it came first by a short head at twenty to one.

Afterwards, Fred said, 'She really drove that horse home. She had a hell of a ride.' Robyn wisecracks: 'When the horse won and Fred won his bet, that's when he fell in love.'

After that first meeting they met occasionally at the races or through mutual friends, but not for another five years did their relationship become a romance. Robyn lived in New York but had one day to fly out to Los Angeles to shoot a commercial. On impulse she telephoned Astaire and asked him out for dinner when she arrived. Fred admitted he was a little shocked, 'I was used to doing the asking myself.' Later Robyn said that it was during that dinner that she fell in love. 'He was so cute, humble and charming.'

When Fred asked Robyn to marry him she wondered if it might not be better if she just moved in with him, but Fred insisted, 'We're marrying and that's it.' The marriage licence cost twenty-three dollars and when Fred found out that the fee had more than doubled just a few days before, he joked, 'If we'd known, we'd have got married last week.' The marriage brought speculation, gossip and innuendo which still seems to break the surface from time to time. Fred conceded that the age difference means they're open to opportunists who want to see their marriage as a nine-day wonder. 'People who don't know us can't believe it's working out,' he says. Both insist firmly that it is, though there have been rumours that the couple have had their moments of discontent. Fred says they haven't had a cross word and Robyn admits to only a couple of small inconsequential rows at home. But when Fred went off to Vermont a couple of years ago for a film and the newspapers started talking about a young actress there, Robyn assured him she knew that what they were implying wasn't true. In a way she was relieved that the rumours suggested that it was Fred who was running around and not her. She points to the very special relationship she and Astaire have, reminding doubters that theirs wasn't a case of an older man chasing a younger girl. 'I pursued him,' she admits. 'It wasn't love at first sight, but it is now. He has all the qualities I want in a human being. He's so very easy to get along with. He will not fight me. I'm very moody but he's so mature. I want to be just like him.' Astaire agrees that Robyn has an artistic temperament and can be quick-tempered, but is relieved now that she has given up her riding career. 'It's a tough game and she has no fear,' he said. Robyn, apparently, hasn't found it easy to fill her retirement. She also has a restless temperament but she

142

insists that when she married Fred her one purpose was to make him happy and that she made up her mind to spend as much time with him as possible. Astaire admits, 'I'm happiest when I'm doing literally nothing.'

Both dislike socializing and only visit very old friends like Frank Sinatra or Gregory Peck. Most evenings they stay at home and go to bed early. They wake about 5.00 am. Robyn goes for a daily run while Astaire stays in bed for another hour, then breakfasts on a solitary boiled egg. His appetite is said to be frugal, but it keeps his 5 feet 9¾ inches frame down to around 134 pounds. He plays an occasional game of golf with Robyn but says, 'The courses seem to get longer while I get shorter.' In the daytime he is addicted to soap operas. He got hooked through his mother's interest in them. She watched regularly until her death in 1975, aged ninety-six. She lived with Fred for the last twenty years of her life and Fred says: 'She used to tell me the plots of the shows and I used to say, no mum, that can't be right, until I got hooked on them myself. I'm intrigued by those daytime shows. Some of those actors aren't bad.'

The house Astaire lives in with Robyn is modest by superstar standards. He built it for himself and his then teenage daughter Ava in 1960, some six years after Phyllis died. The house is carved out of Benedict Canyon with a huge terrace overlooking Pickfair, where Douglas Fairbanks and Mary Pickford once lived. On a clear day you can see Catalina Island over the ocean to the west. Palm trees overhang a medium-sized, crescent-shaped swimming-pool. Inside, Robyn now lives in what were Ava's rooms, including a bedroom. Fred's room has two pianos and he still doodles and writes occasionally. And he still dances from time to time. 'A few steps just for myself. If I hear music that moves me to.' But he admits that he is no longer agile though for his age he is still said to be light enough on his feet almost to glide around. His hair is fair, rather than grey and, although his hands and his face betray his age, he answers questions brightly and promptly. They live in the three-bedroomed house with a single female housekeeper.

A British journalist who recently talked to Astaire by telephone and who, from various close sources in the United States, managed to piece together much of his present-day lifestyle and living conditions, said: 'Next to the books on the long library shelves are a clutch of awards from his dazzling dancing career, but they aren't lined up or given pride of place to impress visitors, just casually placed on the shelves.' The atmosphere of the house is neat, but not stately or formal. 'Not a mansion is it? — but I've always liked it,' says Fred. He hasn't made a film for a few years now, but, retaining that sharp-eyed twinkle which was a hallmark of his smooth sophistication and jaunty screen persona, says he is still available. He often takes work on a whim, as when he appeared in *Battlestar Gallactica,* to please his young grandchildren.

'I don't like to think too much about the past,' he says. 'What's done is done. I never watch any of my old movies. If I had a favourite, I'd say it was *Top Hat.* That brought in a lot of bucks and you feel good about movies that do that and are a success. But when I think back to those dancing movies, I tend to remember what exceptionally hard work they were.' He said it seems strange to think of it now, but they used to spend an average of three months rehearsing the dance sequences even before shooting began. 'It had to take that long just to get them exactly right and to get into the sort of shape to do the movie,' he said. 'By the time shooting started we would be exhausted.'

His favourite routine is the one in *Top Hat* where he has a hotel-room above Ginger Rogers and he keeps her awake with his dance steps. Eventually he puts sand on the floor and shuffles quietly to allow her to sleep. Robyn jokes: 'I asked him to put down sand for me. It didn't work.' Responds Fred: 'It could have been something to do with the fact that we live in a one-storey home.'

Astaire rarely sees Ginger now. He says it's a 'few years' since they last met. His daughter Ava has been married twice. Fred gave Ava away though her first match with an interior decorator was said not to have been enthusiastically received by the family, especially Adele. Fred junior is a rancher living in California. Both attended a fairly recent major tribute to their father. This gives lie to reports that his marriage to Robyn had estranged him from his family, though Astaire admits that there was some concern in his family about his second marriage. 'Why should there be? What were they concerned about?' says Robyn. 'Well,' says Astaire gently, 'I had been a bachelor for twenty-five years, it's true, and when you hit your eighties that's a knock on the door of lateness. But it is just totally wrong and unfair to say that any of the family were alienated from each other.' None of the family went to the wedding, but Astaire insists that was because he and Robyn wanted as little fuss and ballyhoo as possible. Even so, many people say that sister Adele was infuriated when she was told that Fred was going to marry Robyn and the rift between them that this caused persisted. His children are still vitally important to him and Ava's second marriage seemed to be much more accepted by the family.

He loves his grandchildren, though, as a result, recently ventured onto a skateboard in his home and fell, breaking a wrist. 'I wouldn't go near one of those things again for all the tea in China,' he says.

He greatly misses sister Adele, who died three years ago aged eighty-four. Contrary to reports, he visited her in hospital in her final days. He says: 'We laughed a lot about the old days, as we always did, those old days in vaudeville.'

As always, Astaire is ever ready to dismiss his achievements, to put himself down. He's a hard man to compliment and now, in his eighty-sixth year, he remains as nonchalant as ever about the adulation that surrounds him and his life's work.

TWELVE

Entertainer of the century

Fred Astaire is still a phenomenon, fifty years after his legendary screen partnership with Ginger Rogers and in spite of having made his last recognized song-and-dance movie more than a quarter century ago. Unlike most of his contemporaries, his reputation transcends his own generation. Youngsters today may not be able to place him precisely in time and context, but few indeed would not recognize his name or know that he was at one time a big Hollywood dancing star.

For popular dance students bent on a career in show business he remains the ultimate inspiration. Twiggy is typical of a whole generation of modern dancers over whom the image of Astaire cast a spell. Once the world's highest paid model, she branched out into show business, starred in *The Boy Friend* and then, singing and dancing with Tommy Tune in *My One and Only,* took Broadway by storm. She was thrilled when they were called the new Noel Coward and Gertie Lawrence; but ecstatic when critics hailed them as the 1980s answer to Fred Astaire and Ginger Rogers. In a glittering career Twiggy still counts her first meeting with the ageing Astaire as a specially prized highlight and the remarkable Cockney girl obviously had an effect on the grand old man of dance. Astaire's daughter Ava revealed in 1975: 'If he likes a piece of music at home he will dance around. I remember two years ago after we had had dinner with Justin de Villeneuve and Twiggy, on the way back to the parking lot Daddy just twirled down the pavement!'

Astaire's reputation is so solid that other enormously talented dancers find no threat to themselves in recognizing him as the greatest of them all. Gene Kelly said: 'There was no one to touch Fred when it came to popular dance.' He told *Newsweek:* 'In the 1930s when I was a Depression kid, Fred Astaire represented American dance to the world. David Selznick brought me out to Hollywood and said: "Is there anyone you'd like to meet?" I said, "Two people. Carole Lombard and Fred Astaire".' It was in the 1930s, too, that a studio casting director, after seeing an Astaire screen test committed the howler of the century and told the same legendary film studio boss Selznick: 'I can get a dancer like that anywhere for seventy-five dollars a week!'

At a royal occasion in 1983 graciously attended by Princess Anne, I managed to speak to Britain's popular television personality and former television and stage dancer Lionel Blair and asked him what Fred Astaire meant to him. 'Everything,' he said immediately, 'He was just the greatest.' He said the remarkable thing about Astaire was that he danced with his whole body and always kept a perfect line. At the same occasion, Dickie Henderson added: 'He was so great because he did more than just dance. He acted his dancing as well. That is why he later became such a good actor in more dramatic roles.'

Britain's all-round entertainer Bruce Forsyth said recently that movie musicals were his great love as a youngster and if Fred Astaire was showing he'd go three or four times in the same week. He told London's *TV Times:* 'Astaire had that extra something. He could just walk across the screen and it was magic to me. I don't think there'll ever be another dancer like him.'

Not for dancers alone is Astaire a legend. Tough, gritty British journalist Michael Parkinson's job as talk show host on BBC Television brought him face-to-face with many of the giant superstars of Hollywood, but he admitted that the moment when Fred Astaire walked down the steps to take his seat beside him was one of the most magical in the whole of his career. Said Parkinson: 'Here was a man I had worshipped as a kid. I had never imagined I would ever see him in the flesh, walking towards me to do my show.' After their breath-taking performance in winning the world ice dance championship with their spectacular Bolero routine in Ottawa in 1984, Jayne Torvill and Christopher Dean revealed that they watched Astaire's 1930 Hollywood musicals devotedly and drew inspiration from them.

In 1975 American television viewing figures started to drop alarmingly for the first time in history. In desperation, one of the major networks turned to Fred Astaire and a host of other Hollywood has-beens to get them out of trouble. They paid £1¼ million for just one showing of the previous year's movie *That's Entertainment,* which was even more than the film cost to make. But the gamble paid off. The film was watched by an astronomic seventy million. Later, executives were looking for something to fill a late night spot on television and screened one of the old Astaire-Rogers movies. There was a huge demand for more. They showed them, and ratings soared. Other networks jumped on the bandwagon. As simple as that, a remarkable Fred Astaire-Ginger Rogers revival started. There was a similar reaction to a series of Astaire films shown on British television. Before long, both in America and Britain, youngsters were turning up at dance classes wanting to learn how to tap. This led to a whole new nostalgic song-and-dance movement. Tap-dancing was fashionable again. Investigating the phenomenon for the London *Daily Mail* David Lewin found that in California there was a twenty per cent increase in the number of people taking private tap-dance lessons compared with a year before. Many switched from ballet to tap; others added tap to their classical dancing. The popularity of *Fame* on television added to tap dancing's growing popularity. Old music movies shown on television were watched avidly by young people as well as by those who remembered them first time round, and exciting new musical shows once more dominated Broadway and London's West End. *Forty Second Street* attracted phenomenal business, *Cats* was a sellout and other musical offerings included Rodgers and Hart's *On Your Toes, Song 'n' Dance, Singing in the Rain,* Bob Fosse's *Dancin'* and *A Chorus Line.*

Years after Astaire's famous top hat was given away to a friend and his tails were sold by his daughter Ava with the labels taken out, some of the biggest selling videos were said to be his old film musicals. Yet one of the most interesting discoveries on looking closely over his film career is how little actual tap-dancing he did in his later films, despite being synonymous with the art form in movies. It is perhaps the most absorbing and fascinating aspect of his career in terms of its development. His first film appearances were almost pure tap, with Fred and Ginger marking virtually every note with their feet. With some of his other partners it was still there, in flashes, but as his routines with Ginger developed, to match more complicated stories, twirls, spins and flowing movement across the floor played an increasing part as a means of expressing the romance which developed between them.

The song-and-dance revival was accompanied by murmurings to bring some of the old stars out of cold storage. Astaire had been persuaded by Kelly to do *That's Entertainment,* but *Wizard of Oz* star Ray Bolger was astonished to find himself, at seventy-one, offered an engagement at swank Las Vegas. Eleanor Powell was wanted for television spectaculars and, at fifty-two, Ann Miller, who claimed she had never really been away, was back in the public eye. Ginger, however, did not reappear in a nostalgic dancing comeback and Astaire, too, *That's Entertainment* apart, has steadfastly refused to involve himself in such a circus. The sight of aged stars being trotted out largely to satisfy public curiosity is not often an altogether happy or tasteful experience. It is surely an endearing quality to be found in Astaire that, despite his unique place in the history of movie song and dance, he is more than willing to hand over to a new generation. 'I just don't like wallowing in the past,' he said.

One side of Astaire which sadly has largely been lost on his enthusiastic public is his talent at writing songs. With more time and greater incentive he could well have developed into a remarkably good and successful composer. He doesn't waste time on regrets, as he points out most emphatically to almost every interviewer who somehow manages to get to see him, but if he does have a niggle lodged in the back of his mind it is almost certainly that he didn't get more opportunity for song composition. Even when he was hitting the big-time on stage with Adele he spent a lot of his spare time composing and over the years had many songs published. 'I'm Building Up to an Awful Let-down', a tune he had published with a Johnny Mercer lyric in 1938, actually got into the Hit Parade. Others had potential, among them 'Hello Baby' and 'Just Like Taking Candy From a Baby', the latter which will still be remembered by many Astaire fans, but didn't quite make the big-time. Fred's output of songs over a period of about twelve years from 1924 was quite prolific. He was often at his happiest rummaging through music publishers' offices looking for material, chatting with the song-writers and lyricists and absorbing the atmosphere. He admits that at one time he would have been prepared to give up all other branches of show business to concentrate on composing, but he never considered himself good enough.

It was at music publisher Jerome H. Remick's office that he first met George Gershwin, when both were unknown, and from which a solid friendship developed. It was also there that he struck up a firm friendship with his then favourite composer Dick Whiting, father of 1940s singing star Margaret Whiting, and whose numerous famous standards include 'Beyond the Blue Horizon', 'She's Funny That Way' and 'Louise'. Though his nagging ambition to be a composer was not fulfilled, his ability to put a song together undoubtedly went some way to placing him in a class of his own as a popular dancer. For his instinctive feel for melody, harmony and musical form were applied to good effect when, with Hermes Pan, he came to choreograph those historic film dance sequences.

He was underestimated, too, as a musician and singer. His phrasing, timing and feeling for a lyric were remarkable and even on his later recordings when his voice, never strong at best, was noticeably frailer, his sheer natural ability to sell a song was exceptional. An in-depth assessment must conclude that Astaire was much more than a dancer who could sing. His vocal limitations were obvious, but his light voice was always rhythmic, full of melody, and his personal commitment to the lyric and his impeccable taste were unsurpassed. You can't name an outright singer, not to say a singer-dancer, who introduced so many songs which became all time standards. Little wonder Irving Berlin once said, 'I'd rather have Astaire introduce my songs than any other performer.'

If he couldn't really take his place alongside them, he must have found some consolation in being able to work closely with the composers he admired most of all, George Gershwin, Jerome Kern, Irving Berlin and Cole Porter. Way back during his stage days with Adele, when they were scheduled to do *For Goodness Sake* with Alex Aarons producing, he said that one thing that disappointed him was that George Gershwin was not going to do the music. He genuinely considered himself privileged to have had scores written by George and Ira Gershwin for several of his pictures and that he was able to introduce, as he put it, 'the wonderful material' of Irving Berlin, including many songs which Berlin wrote especially for his pictures.

At another time he said that his association with Cole Porter had been one of the highlights of his career. This was not the great performer being gracious or patronizing. That wasn't Fred's style. He admired them all, probably more than he revealed publicly, and according to some of his closest associates would gladly have forsaken some of his own career to have joined in with them to share some of theirs.

Had Phyllis Astaire lived to grow old with her husband it is anybody's guess whether Fred would have bothered with television. Never prone to think in terms of careers, he was always inclined to move with the wind, to take off and do a film, or a personal appearance, or a radio show, as the mood dictated. And having done one successfully was no guarantee that he would be prepared to accept another. Challenges for their own sake did not appeal to Astaire. So it's possible that had Phyllis lived, they might have spent a quiet retirement together, playing golf, attending race-meetings, going on extended holidays, and drifting through days happily with very little thought for anything else.

But at that time Fred found work a form of therapy and later, his romantic style of screen dancing having run out of fashion, he hit the jackpot in a totally new medium with several stupendously successful television spectaculars. The widespread appeal, his magnetic qualities and the sheer artistry and charisma of the man, proved as strong as ever. Dancing with Barrie Chase, he captivated an enormous audience and a whole new generation, and carved out a new career for himself on television, without ever intending seriously to do so.

The first show was in 1958 with Astaire approaching sixty but showing the figure, style, energy and flair of a man thirty years his junior. It was the legendary Ed Sullivan, the doyen among American talk show hosts, who first persuaded Fred to try television. That was in 1955, not long after Phyllis's death, and just after completing work on *Daddy Long Legs* with Leslie Caron. Astaire agreed to appear in order to promote the film and it has been said that he didn't get paid for it. Appearances on other shows followed, but there was nothing really significant until 1957, when he starred in a CBS television comedy with Charles Laughton, *Imp on a Cobweb Leash.*

For the first time he now began to think about television seriously, though not, curiously enough, as a dramatic actor which was where his big screen career had terminated, but in a song-and-dance format. All the strands came together neatly as Fred and the Chrysler Corporation reached agreement for a Fred Astaire special, in colour and presented live. Through Fred's new company, Ava Productions, he also produced the show and the highly respected and talented musician and conductor David Rose, of *Holiday for Strings* fame, and fronting a fifty piece orchestra, was engaged as musical director. There was also plenty of opportunity to chat over old times — had Fred wanted to — as the evergreen Hermes Pan joined the team to help him with the dances.

The major speculation was over whom Fred would choose as his partner. The young and beautiful Barrie Chase, who had appeared in a small way in *Silk Stockings,* was his selection. At twenty-two she was slim, blonde, small to the extent that Fred might have wished Cyd Charisse, Rita Hayworth and even Ginger Rogers at times might have been, and she proved delectable and hard working.

The dogged quest for perfection which had stamped his movie career was now carried over to television. He allowed no compromises. Telling Barrie Chase what a wonderful dancer she was in that inimitable and captivating way he had, didn't prevent him from shouting at her and pushing her to such frustratingly high standards that she at times would rush off the set in tears. When she returned, having composed herself, he would ignore the incident and carry on pleasantly as though her temporary departure, for all the inconvenience it caused, was an inevitable consequence of attaining the standards he had set himself.

Typically, Astaire insisted on working through to perfection every small detail of the dancing, music, singing and production; not so much the music, for David Rose appears to have been left a reasonably free hand once Fred had decided with him what was needed. But after several gruelling months, *An Evening with Fred Astaire* emerged as superlative television, setting new standards. It was fresh, innovative, individually distinctive and outstandingly professional, and it won no fewer than nine Emmy awards, with Fred collecting one for himself as the best actor of 1958. Viewing figures reached impressive proportions and soared even higher when the show was repeated three months later, in January 1959.

Not surprisingly, there was an immediate clamour for Fred and Barrie to be teamed again in another television special, but it was some years before it happened. After clearing away some film work, including Stanley Kramer's *On The Beach,* for which Fred had been on location in Australia, he agreed. *Another Evening with Fred Astaire,* screened in November 1959, and again with Barrie Chase, was a worthy follow-up and it all began to look like Fred and Ginger born again. The style, of course, had been updated, but it seemed that Fred and Barrie, for all except his most stuffy and die-hard followers who seemed reluctant to cloud the memories of the past with television pictures of their hero with a new partner, were as compelling and attractive a partnership as Fred and Ginger had ever been. This was despite Astaire being some forty-five years older than Ms Chase. Fred was again sensitive and almost embarrassed by the age differential, as he had been with some of his earlier dancing partners all those years before — notably Rita Hayworth and Joan Leslie. But Barrie Chase was so smooth and exciting and moved so beautifully that when they danced together, only the occasional critic, wanting to exploit an angle, bothered to tot up the years.

More than once in the late 1950s and early 1960s Astaire said he didn't want to do any more dancing pictures and he virtually kept his word in terms of the big screen. His fascination with television, however, kept his song-and-dance career going long after his natural instincts told him it ought really to have ended. By now he was enjoying doing things on a one-off basis, though after his break in Australia for *On The Beach* he didn't exactly jump at the chance to do another television spectacular. But at sixty, though exceptionally fit and in excellent general health, and having for many years had no real need to earn, it is perhaps understandable that psyching himself up for the rigours and demands of a major performance may not have been as easy as it had been ten years before. Even so, in both movies and television, he found himself almost as busy as he had been at the peak of his screen career. He seemed to revel in the combination. He did four major films in the 1960s, and the 1970s is distinguished for his performance in *The Towering Inferno,* for which he received an Oscar nomination. Around this schedule he fitted in a number of television appearances. There was another spectacular with Barrie Chase in 1960, again sponsored by Chrysler and with David Rose once more in charge of the music. Called *Astaire Time,* it was another outstanding success, winning two Emmys. Two years later he was fronting the popular *Fred Astaire's Premiere Theatre* and in some of these straight plays he took featured roles over a period of two years. In 1964 he appeared with Barrie Chase in the not highly-rated *Think Pretty* and in 1965 popped up surprisingly in a number of Dr Kildare episodes.

In the second half of the decade it seemed that Fred Astaire was as big a star as he had ever been, much in demand for television and films, though approaching seventy. He and Barrie Chase did yet another television special together, with Fred showing remarkable footwork and a fine sense of feeling for many of the newer musical rhythms as well as the recognized standards. He guested on a number of television shows and proved himself to be compulsive viewing, and into the 1970s took part in a number of offerings from ABC Television. When America paid tribute to George Gershwin in 1972, Fred was the natural choice as host.

Much of Astaire's professional work in the 1960s and 1970s, his movies apart of course, has been lost to his fans outside America. Sadly, only one of his television spectaculars with Barrie Chase was screened in Britain (*Astaire Time* by BBCTV in October 1961), and no one seemed to know why. Surely they would attract a massive audience even now if put out as a special attraction at peak times, for in the 1980s the revival of interest in Fred Astaire and his work appears remarkable.

It was his association with Barrie Chase which set the gossip writers' tongues wagging and typewriters clattering. While working on the television spectaculars they went out together and, according to reports, enjoyed one another's company. There was talk about an affair and speculation about a possible marriage. Fred countered by saying he was sure that she was not interested in him, though they had much in common. Long after he filmed *You'll Never Get Rich* and *You Were Never Lovelier,* there was similar speculation about his relationship with Rita Hayworth. There was newspaper talk about the gifts he was supposed to have given her while they were filming together. There is no doubt that Fred was incredibly fond of Rita and there is no doubt that he presented her with a gift. Before giving it to Rita he felt compelled to ask the advice of Helen Hunt, who was head of hairdressing at Columbia Pictures, if she felt it would be all right, because he didn't want to give the impression that he was pursuing her. At another time his name was linked with Tina Sinatra and yet again he was supposed to be infatuated with Twiggy. It was fertile ground, of course, for the gossip writers — an ageing man, extremely rich, still active and youthful, and extraordinarily attractive in many ways, and the gorgeous, shapely girl young enough to be his daughter, if not quite his granddaughter in the case of Barrie Chase. In some ways it was difficult for everyone, Fred included, to accept the realization of his age. He said in 1979 he didn't consider himself a professional octogenarian, nor felt anywhere near eighty. 'I can't believe I'm not fifty anymore,' he told Ross Benson in California. But Fred fooled them in the end. When years later he was seen going places with Robyn Smith, their relationship was again fair game for the press. They wrote about romance and the possibility of marriage, but when they got tired of speculating and had gone on to concentrate on others, Fred shook them by one day announcing that he and Robyn were to be married.

Those closest to Astaire maintain that the new match is happy, despite what the newspapers have reported from time to time about rifts and arguments. But, despite what Fred himself has said, it is a marriage which is believed by many to have infuriated Adele and created anxiety in Ava, whose own first marriage ended in divorce. Fred was attending an Emmy award ceremony when Ava married a second time, to an artist called Richard McKenzie, but he managed to spend some time with his daughter and new son-in-law to wish them well. Whether he is disappointed that neither of his own children nor Phyllis's own son followed him into showbusiness is not known, though Fred's view is likely to be that they have their own lives to lead and their decisions are of no concern to anyone else.

In the 1980s, dancing professionally, on either film or television screen, is long since behind him. Astaire packed it in, as one would have expected of him, when he could no longer perform to the high standards he set himself, but he could, and did, continue in character roles which appealed to him. In 1981 he was an old man, but gave a telling performance, as an old man, in the Universal picture *Ghost Story*. The magic was still there.

The circumstances of death can play games with reputations. In showbusiness, an unexpected death at an early age can create a legend overnight. It is doubtful, for example, that Glenn Miller would have been remembered in quite the same way had he not disappeared dramatically in the fog on a lonely wartime flight from England to Paris. The memories remain vivid and are not neutralized by a fading career, retirement and old age.

That is what is so remarkable about Fred Astaire. For all his long career in the movies and on television, radio and record, he has never been considered a 'has been' in the way many of his film contemporaries were, and you can never be quite sure where he might pop up next. His reputation is probably stronger now than at any time in the last ten years.

For a long time after his screen dancing career ended he received little official recognition, but in more recent years he has been widely honoured. While he still clings to that inherent tendency to play down his talent and reputation, it is obvious that he has mellowed in recent years and has quietly enjoyed the various honours which have justly come his way. In America he was labelled the 'Entertainer of the Century', but more specifically, in the 1970s, he became a member of the Entertainments Hall of Fame in Hollywood. In New York the Film Society of the Lincoln Centre held an important gala occasion in his honour, and extracts from twenty of his films were shown. Both were major distinctions. In 1981 the American Film Institute recognized Astaire's monumental contribution to the cinema. He joined a unique hall of fame as they presented him with their Life Achievement Award. Hollywood could not have given him greater honour and the presentation ceremony was attended by many top international stars, including his lifelong friend David Niven. It was a wonderful but very emotional occasion. He also has several Emmys, but the honour he may quietly treasure most of all is the special award he received from the American Society of Composers, Authors and Publishers, of which he has been a member for a great many years, for his 'contributions to the music industry'.

One of the most endearing qualities of Astaire is that, for all his outstanding success, he has changed little over the years. His strength of character is such that wealth, international recognition, film and television stardom have not inflated his ego, turned his head, or blurred ordinary accepted values. He is not flamboyant, he values friendships and relationships as much now as ever he did, and his personal lifestyle is simple and has changed little as one success tops another. And if you ask him why that is so, he will probably turn to you and say: 'Why should it change? I live the life

155

I enjoy, the same as I always have.' Not for Astaire the excesses of many superstars. As recently as 1981 he told David Lewin that he did a few loosening up exercises every day and would maybe run around the room a couple of times now and then. For someone aged eighty-two it was remarkable that he found the days too short for him to do everything he wanted to do. He'll still more often than not answer the telephone himself, go into town like any other citizen to pick up some groceries or do some shopping. The Rolls-Royce he and Adele dreamed of owning all those years ago has long since been achieved and Fred being chauffered quietly around Beverly Hills is a familiar sight. He's not stuffy, formal or cynical, and if sometimes he gives the impression of being remote and, to writers particularly who want to talk to him about the past, intolerant and abrasive, then that is no more than he has always been.

As an entertainer and dancer of course, Astaire has inevitably been compared with Gene Kelly. The debate has always irritated both men, more so Kelly perhaps who, being the younger man, has often been expected to be a second Astaire. He considers that ridiculous because his approach was very different from Fred's. 'I was the Marlon Brando of dancers and he the Cary Grant,' he once said. Kelly was right in his assessment of their individual styles. He told Clive Hirschhorn: 'Fred's steps were small, neat, graceful and intimate — mine were ballet-oriented and very athletic.' Their styles were related to their different physiques and while Kelly demonstrated remarkable qualities and enormous technique, he didn't use the whole of his body including head and hands as effectively or with such style as Astaire. Temperamentally they were very different. Gene has said that the things he wore like jeans, sweatshirts and sneakers, Fred wouldn't be seen dead in. Even at rehearsal Fred was always smart.

Fred Astaire did more than anyone to popularize tap-dancing and make it respectable for the general public. In those vintage pictures with Ginger Rogers he made tap-dancing something which, if the public couldn't emulate, they could certainly identify with in terms of the situations in which Fred used the dance to express emotion. It had never really been done this way before — and certainly not with such compelling attraction.

Fred Astaire is one of the most respected superstars of all time. His extraordinary talent is universally recognized and his skill and creativity is ageless. Without scheming or an excessive sense of ambition — almost at times it appeared with some reluctance — he conquered films during the heydays of the cinema and radio when it was perhaps the most powerful medium of all. He also conquered records in those exciting days when collectors made their choice from published catalogues and not after artists' work had been 'plugged' by DJs. He made a success of television, too, with a number of remarkable and spectacular performances. And he showed he could be an impressive dramatic actor as well as the world's number one song-and-dance man.

It is difficult to find an entertainer with more widespread, genuine acclaim among his fellow artists. When the Gershwins had the chance to write for *Shall We Dance,* Irving Berlin encouraged them, adding: 'There is no set-up in Hollywood that can compare with doing an Astaire picture.' Pandro Berman, Astaire's producer of those Fred and Ginger classics at RKO, recognized how fortunate he was in being able to get the best composers to work on the pictures. 'They all wanted to write for Fred Astaire,' he said.

His devoted associate and kindred soul Hermes Pan said that Fred has such a natural sense of rhythm that you only have to see him walking down the street to tell he is a dancer, and Gene Kelly said that Fred looks marvellous at whatever he does, even simply getting out of a chair and pouring a drink. Jack Lemmon paid tribute to his 'enormous talent', pointing out that as well as being possibly the greatest dancer he was also one of the finest singers of contemporary music. Screenwriter Betty Comden said that you couldn't compare Fred Astaire with anyone else because there'll never be anybody like him, while film director Michael Kidd said he had never come across anyone who was so innately graceful as Fred — even going out to lunch, said Kidd, that 'jaunty little bounce and the swinging of the arms is right out of a Fred Astaire movie'.

Fred's talent is unique, his unstudied sophistication is a sublime art. He tends to recoil from such adulation, and is almost irritated and annoyed by it. But although his contemporary artists might single out qualities of the man which he himself hasn't bothered to identify or analyse, the fact remains that, for millions of fans, he is a nice guy who could dance and sing and whose fairy-tale stories with Ginger and others remain an experience to treasure. With Ginger particularly, that special chemistry was always present. As a man he is uncomplicated, ordinary, emotionally perhaps the most balanced of all the 'Hollywood Greats' and fulfilled, even in old age. It is true, he and his dancing were of his time. He was undoubtedly the right man, in the right place at the right time; but to say that, and only that, does him gross injustice. When his time evaporated, he had the stature, resourcefulness, strength of character and will — not to mention talent — to transplant successfully to other art forms and other media. Who could argue that in his own special way, Fred Astaire was a genius on film.

A very special tribute came from Her Majesty Queen Elizabeth the Queen Mother. Through her Private Secretary she said that she and the late King greatly enjoyed the wonderful musicals that Fred Astaire and his sister Adele were in and that Their Majesties knew, liked and admired both of them and also their charming mother, Mrs Astaire.

What made Fred Astaire so much better than anyone else? His natural talent was important. The high standards he applied to himself and to all his associates; and the control he insisted upon having with anything with which he was involved professionally, including the filming and cutting of his dance sequences, were also vital. His vision, application and eagerness to work as hard and as long as it was necessary to reach perfection, can't be overlooked.

But perhaps what ordinary people will most remember, without any analysis, is Fred himself, his easy grace, friendly personality, infectious smile, sparkling dancing and singing and that indefinable quality which Fred Astaire has so abundantly . . . great *style*.

As journalist Richard Roud put it, 'As long as film exists, Fred Astaire will be remembered.'

Chronology

1896   Father (Frederic Austerlitz) and Mother (Ann Geilus) marry
1897   Sister born (Adele)
1899   Born in Omaha, Nebraska (10 May)
1903   Leave Omaha with mother and sister for New York City and stage school
1904   Change surname to Astaire for professional reasons
1917   Broadway debut with Adele in *Over the Top*
1918   *The Passing Show* (New York) with Adele
1919   *Apple Blossoms* (New York) with Adele
1921   *The Love Letter* (New York) with Adele
1922   *For Goodness Sake* (New York) with Adele
1922   First show built around the Astaires: *The Bunch and Judy* (New York) with Adele
1923   London debut. *Stop Flirting* with Adele
1923   First meetings with British Royal Family
1923   First recordings made in London
1924   *Lady, Be Good!* (New York) with Adele
1924   First song published
1926   Engagement with Adele at The Trocadero, New York, at 5,000 dollars a week
1926   *Lady, Be Good!* (London) with Adele
1926   Father dies while Fred and Adele in London with *Lady, Be Good!*
1927   *Funny Face* (New York) with Adele
1928   Adele burned in boat accident
1928   *Funny Face* (London) with Adele
1930   *Smiles* (New York) with Adele
1931   *The Band Wagon* (New York) with Adele/Vera Marsh. Adele's last show
1932   *Gay Divorce* (New York) with Claire Luce
1932   Phyllis Potter divorces her husband at Reno
1932   Adele retires (March, at Illinois Theatre, Chicago) on marriage to Lord Charles Cavendish

1933 *Gay Divorce* (London) with Claire Luce

1933 Marriage to Phyllis Potter (12 July)

1933 Film debut: *Dancing Lady* (MGM) with Joan Crawford

1933 Film: *Flying Down to Rio* (RKO) with Ginger Rogers

1933 Adele's premature daughter dies at birth

1934 Film: *The Gay Divorcee*

The Gay Divorce (UK) } (RKO) with Ginger Rogers

1935 *Roberta* (RKO) with Ginger Rogers

1935 Adele's twin sons die at birth

1935 Top billing for the first time. *Top Hat* (RKO) with Ginger Rogers

1935 First recordings on the Brunswick label

1936 *Follow the Fleet* (RKO) with Ginger Rogers

1936 *Swing Time* (RKO) with Ginger Rogers

1937 *Shall We Dance* (RKO) with Ginger Rogers

1937 *A Damsel in Distress* (RKO) with Joan Fontaine

1938 *Carefree* (RKO) with Ginger Rogers

1938 Listed for the first time in Who's Who in America

1938 An Astaire composition 'I'm Building Up to an Awful Let-down' (words by Johnny Mercer) makes the American Hit Parade

1939 *The Story of Vernon and Irene Castle* (RKO) with Ginger Rogers

1940 *Broadway Melody of 1940* (MGM) with Eleanor Powell

1940 *Second Chorus* (Paramount) with Paulette Goddard

1941 *You'll Never Get Rich* (Columbia) with Rita Hayworth

1941 Son, Fred Junior, born

1942 *Holiday Inn* (Paramount) with Bing Crosby

1942 *You Were Never Lovelier* (Columbia) with Rita Hayworth

1942 Daughter, Ava, born

1943 *The Sky's the Limit* (RKO) with Joan Leslie

1944 Adele's husband, Lord Charles Cavendish, dies

1944 Entertains American troops in Europe

1945 *Yolanda and the Thief* (MGM) with Lucille Bremer

1946 *Ziegfeld Follies* (MGM) with Lucille Ball, Lucille Bremer, Judy Garland, Gene Kelly, Kathryn Grayson, Lena Horne and others

1946 *Blue Skies* (Paramount) with Bing Crosby and Joan Caulfield

1946 Astaire's horse Triplicate wins the 100,000 dollar Hollywood Gold Cup

1946 'Officially' retired. Petition backs widespread call for his return to the screen

1948 *Easter Parade* (MGM) with Judy Garland and Ann Miller

1949 *The Barkleys of Broadway* (MGM) with Ginger Rogers

1950 *Let's Dance* (Paramount) with Betty Hutton

1950 *Three Little Words* (MGM) with Vera-Ellen

1951 *Royal Wedding*
     Wedding Bells (UK) } (MGM) with Jane Powell

1951 Receives special Oscar

1952 *The Belle of New York* (MGM) with Vera-Ellen

1953 *The Band Wagon* (MGM) with Cyd Charisse

1954 Wife Phyllis dies (13 September) aged forty-six

1955 *Daddy Long Legs* (Twentieth Century Fox) with Leslie
     Caron

1955 Television debut on the American *Ed Sullivan Show*

1957 *Funny Face* (Paramount) with Audrey Hepburn

1957 *Silk Stockings* (MGM) with Cyd Charisse

1957 TV show *Imp on a Cobweb Leash*

1958 First of Astaire/Barrie Chase TV spectaculars: *An
     Evening with Fred Astaire*

1959 Film debut as dramatic actor in *On the Beach* (United
     Artists) with Gregory Peck and Ava Gardner

1959 Autobiography published: *Steps in Time*

1959 TV spectacular with Barrie Chase: *Another Evening with
     Fred Astaire*

1960 TV spectacular with Barrie Chase: *Astaire Time*

1961 *The Pleasure of His Company* (Paramount) with
     Debbie Reynolds

1962 *The Notorious Landlady* (Columbia) with Kim Novak

1962 Featured in TV's *Fred Astaire's Premier Theatre*

1965 Appearances in TV's *Dr Kildare* series

1968 *Finian's Rainbow* (Warner Brothers) with Petula Clark
     and Tommy Steele

1969 *The Midas Run*
     A Run On Gold (UK) } (Selmur) with Anne Heywood

1969 First meeting with professional
     jockey Robyn Smith

1971 Two major TV appearances on the *Dick Cavett Show*

1973 Honoured with a Gala at the Lincoln Centre in New York

1974 *That's Entertainment* (MGM)

1975 *The Towering Inferno* (Twentieth Century Fox)

1975 Mother, Ann, dies aged ninety-six

1976 *That's Entertainment,* Part 2 (MGM)

1976 *The Amazing Dobermans* (Golden Films)

1977 *Un Taxi Mauve* (Sofracima/ Rizzoli Films) with
     Charlotte Rampling

1979 TV film: *The Man in the Santa Claus Suit*
1980 Marries Robyn Smith
1981 Cinema film: *Ghost Story* with Melvyn Douglas and Douglas Fairbanks Jnr.
1981 Adele dies aged eighty-four
1981 Receives the Life Achievement Award

Stage career

All shows, except both the New York and London productions of *Gay Divorce,* were with sister Adele.

Over the Top   1917 44th Street Theatre, New York
78 performances
Produced by the Shubert Brothers
Music by Sigmund Romberg and Herman Timberg
Astaires had 3 musical numbers

The Passing Show of 1918   1918
Winter Garden, Broadway, New York
125 performances
Produced by the Shubert Brothers
Music by Sigmund Romberg and Jean Schwartz
Included in the cast: Willie and Eugene Howard and
Charles Ruggles
Astaires had 5 musical numbers

Apple Blossoms   1919
Globe Theatre, Broadway, New York
256 performances
Produced by Charles Dillingham
Music by Fritz Kreisler and Victor Jacobi
Dance direction: Edward Royce
Astaires had 2 musical numbers

The Love Letter   1921
Globe Theatre, Broadway, New York
31 performances
Produced by Charles Dillingham
Directed by Edward Royce
Music by Victor Jacob
Dance direction: Edward Royce
Astaires had 3 musical numbers

For Goodness Sake   1922
Lyric Theatre, Broadway, New York
103 performances
Produced by Alex A. Aarons
Music by William Daly and Paul Lannin
Included in the cast: Vinton Freedley
Astaires had 5 musical numbers including 'Oh Gee, Oh Gosh'

The Bunch and Judy   1922
Globe Theatre, Broadway, New York
65 performances
Produced by Charles Dillingham
Music by Jerome Kern
Lyrics by Anne Caldwell
Astaires had 6 musical numbers

Stop Flirting   1923
Shaftesbury Theatre, London
418 performances
Produced by Alfred Butt

Lady, Be Good!   1924
Liberty Theatre, Broadway,
   New York
330 performances
Produced by Alex A. Aarons and Vinton Freedley
Music by George Gershwin
Lyrics by Ira Gershwin
Astaires had 7 musical numbers including 'Fascinating Rhythm'
   and 'The Half of It, Dearie, Blues'

Lady, Be Good!   1926
Empire Theatre, London
326 performances
Produced by Alfred Butt with Alex A. Aarons and
   Vinton Freedley

Funny Face   1927
Alvin Theatre, Broadway, New York
250 performances
Produced by Alex A. Aarons and Vinton Freedley
Music by George Gershwin
Lyrics by Ira Gershwin
Included in the cast: William Kent and Victor Moore
Astaires had 7 musical numbers including 'Funny Face',
   'He Loves and She Loves', ''S Wonderful', 'My One and Only'
   and 'The Babbitt and the Bromide'

Funny Face   1928
Prince's Theatre, London
263 performances
Produced by Alfred Butt and Lee Ephraim with Alex A. Aarons
  and Vinton Freedley
Included in the cast: Leslie Henson and Bernard Clifton

Smiles   1930
Ziegfeld Theatre, Broadway,
  New York
63 performances
Produced by Florenz Ziegfeld
Music by Vincent Youmans
Lyrics by Clifford Grey, Harold Adamson and Ring Lardner
Included in the cast: Marilyn Miller, Larry Adler, Bob Hope and
  Virginia Bruce
Astaires had 6 musical numbers

The Band Wagon   1931
New Amsterdam Theatre, Broadway, New York
260 performances
Produced by Max Gordon
Music by Arthur Schwartz
Lyrics by Howard Dietz
Included in the cast: Frank Morgan and Helen Broderick
Astaires had 7 musical numbers including 'I Love Louisa' and
  'White Heat'

Gay Divorce   1932
Ethel Barrymore Theatre, Broadway, New York
248 performances
Produced by Dwight Deere Wiman and Tom Weatherly
Directed by Howard Lindsay
Music and lyrics by Cole Porter
Included in the cast: Claire Luce, Betty Starbuck, Erik Rhodes
and Eric Blore (Adele Astaire, having retired, did not appear)
Fred had 4 musical numbers including 'Night and Day'

Gay Divorce   1933
Palace Theatre, London
108 performances
Produced by Lee Ephraim
Included in the cast: Claire Luce, Eric Blore, Erik Rhodes and
  Fred Hearne

165

Film career

Fred Astaire's movie career began in 1933 and lasted into the 1980s. His films with Ginger Rogers were between 1933 and 1939, though he was reunited with her for *The Barkleys of Broadway* in 1949. His own song-and-dance career on film lasted until 1957, though *Finian's Rainbow* was released in 1968. His dramatic roles were in numerous films which began with *On the Beach* in 1959.

Dancing Lady   1933
Metro-Goldwyn-Mayer
Producer David O. Selznick
Director Robert Z. Leonard
Music: Burton Lane, Jimmy McHugh, Richard Rodgers and
  Nacio Herb Brown
Lyrics: Harold Adamson, Dorothy Fields, Lorenz Hart and
  Arthur Freed
Dance directors: Sammy Lee and Eddie Prinz
Art director: Merrill Pye
Appeared with Joan Crawford, Clark Gable, Franchot Tone,
  Nelson Eddy and Robert Benchley
Musical numbers included 'Everything I Have Is Yours'

Flying Down to Rio   1933
RKO Radio Pictures
Producer Louis Brock
Director Thornton Freeland
Music: Vincent Youmans
Lyrics: Edward Eliscu and Gus Kahn
Dance director: Dave Gould
Assistant: Hermes Pan
Art directors: Van Nest Polglase and Carroll Clark
Appeared with Dolores Del Rio, Gene Raymond, Paul Roulien,
  Ginger Rogers and Eric Blore
Musical numbers included 'The Carioca'; 'Orchids in the
  Moonlight'; Flying Down to Rio'

The Gay Divorcee   1934
UK : **The Gay Divorce**
RKO Radio Pictures
Producer Pandro S. Berman
Director Mark Sandrich
Music: Cole Porter, Con Conrad and Harry Revel
Lyrics: Cole Porter, Herb Magidson, and Mack Gordon
Dance director: Dave Gould
Art directors: Van Nest Polglase and Carroll Clark
Appeared with Ginger Rogers, Alice Brady, Edward Everett
  Horton, Erik Rhodes, Eric Blore and Betty Grable (minor
  part)
Musical numbers included 'Night and Day'; 'The Continental'

Roberta   1935
RKO Radio Pictures
Producer Pandro S. Berman
Director William A. Seiter
Music: Jerome Kern and James F. Hanley
Lyrics: Otto Harbach, Dorothy Fields, Ballard Macdonald,
  Bernard Dougall and Oscar Hammerstein II
Dance director: Hermes Pan
Art directors: Van Nest Polglase and Carroll Clark
Appeared with Irene Dunne, Ginger Rogers, Randolph Scott
  and Helen Westley
Musical numbers included 'I Won't Dance'; 'Smoke Gets in
  Your Eyes'; 'Lovely to Look At'

Top Hat   1935
RKO Radio Pictures
Producer Pandro S. Berman
Director Mark Sandrich
Music and lyrics: Irving Berlin
Dance director: Hermes Pan
Art director: Van Nest Polglase
Appeared with Ginger Rogers, Edward Everett Horton,
  Helen Broderick, Erik Rhodes and Eric Blore
Musical numbers included 'No Strings'; 'Isn't This a Lovely
  Day'; 'Top Hat, White Tie and Tails'; 'Cheek to Cheek';
  'The Piccolino'

Follow the Fleet   1936
RKO Radio Pictures
Producer Pandro S. Berman

Director Mark Sandrich
Music and lyrics: Irving Berlin
Dance director: Hermes Pan
Art director: Van Nest Polglase
Appeared with Ginger Rogers, Randolph Scott,
   Harriet Hilliard; Lucille Ball and Betty Grable (in minor roles)
Musical numbers included 'We Saw the Sea'; 'Let Yourself Go';
   'I'm Putting All My Eggs in One Basket'; 'Let's Face the
   Music and Dance'

Swing Time   1936
RKO Radio Pictures
Producer Pandro S. Berman
Director George Stevens
Music: Jerome Kern
Lyrics: Dorothy Fields
Dance director: Hermes Pan
Art director: Van Nest Polglase
Appeared with Ginger Rogers, Victor Moore, Helen Broderick,
   Eric Blore, Betty Furness and Georges Metaxa
Musical numbers included 'The Way You Look Tonight';
   'A Fine Romance'

Shall We Dance   1937
RKO Radio Pictures
Producer Pandro S. Berman
Director Mark Sandrich
Music: George Gershwin
Lyrics: Ira Gershwin
Dance directors: Hermes Pan and Harry Losee
Art director: Van Nest Polglase
Appeared with Ginger Rogers, Edward Everett Horton,
   Eric Blore and Harriet Hoctor
Musical numbers included 'Slap That Bass'; 'They All Laughed';
   'Let's Call the Whole Thing Off'; 'They Can't Take That
   Away From Me'

A Damsel in Distress   1937
RKO Radio Pictures
Producer Pandro S. Berman
Director George Stevens
Music: George Gershwin
Lyrics: Ira Gershwin
Dance director: Hermes Pan

Art director: Van Nest Polglase
Appeared with George Burns, Gracie Allen, Joan Fontaine,
    Reginald Gardiner and Constance Collier
Musical numbers included 'A Foggy Day'; 'Nice Work If You
    Can Get It'

Carefree   1938
RKO Radio Pictures
Producer Pandro S. Berman
Director Mark Sandrich
Music and lyrics: Irving Berlin
Dance director: Hermes Pan
Art director: Van Nest Polglase
Appeared with Ginger Rogers and Ralph Bellamy
Musical numbers included 'I Used to be Colour Blind';
    'Change Partners'

The Story of Vernon and Irene Castle   1939
RKO Radio Pictures
Producer George Haight
Director H.C. Potter
Dance director: Hermes Pan
Art director: Van Nest Polglase
Appeared with Ginger Rogers, Edna May Oliver,
    Walter Brennan and Lew Fields
Musical numbers included 'Waiting for the Robert E. Lee';
    'Little Brown Jug'; 'By the Light of the Silvery Moon';
    'Hello, Hello, Who's Your Lady Friend?'; 'Oh You Beautiful
    Doll'; 'Glow-Worm'; 'Row, Row, Row'; 'Cuddle Up a Little
    Closer'; 'Chicago'; 'Hello, Frisco, Hello'; 'Way Down Yonder
    in New Orleans'; 'It's a Long Way to Tipperary'; 'Keep the
    Home Fires Burning'; 'The Darktown Strutters' Ball';
    'Over There'

Broadway Melody of 1940   1940
Metro-Goldwyn-Mayer
Producer Jack Cummings
Director Norman Taurog
Music and lyrics: Cole Porter
Dance director: Bobby Connolly
Art director: Cedric Gibbons
Appeared with Eleanor Powell, George Murphy, Frank Morgan
    and Ian Hunter
Musical numbers included 'I've Got My Eyes on You';
    'I Concentrate on You'; 'Begin the Beguine'

Second Chorus   1940
Paramount
Producer Boris Morros
Director H.C. Potter
Music: Artie Shaw, Bernard Hanighen, Hal Borne, Victor Young
    and Johnny Green
Lyrics: Johnny Mercer, Will Harris and E.Y. Harbourg
Dance director: Hermes Pan
Art director: Boris Leven
Appeared with Paulette Goddard, Artie Shaw, Burgess Meredith
    (trumpet playing by Billy Butterfield) and Charles
    Butterworth. Astaire's trumpet playing by Bobby Hackett
Musical numbers included 'Sweet Sue'; 'I'm Yours';
    'Concerto for Clarinet'

You'll Never Get Rich   1941
Columbia
Producer Samuel Bischoff
Director Sidney Lanfield
Music and lyrics: Cole Porter
Dance director: Robert Alton
Art director: Lionel Banks
Appeared with Rita Hayworth and Robert Benchley
Musical numbers included 'Shootin' the Works for Uncle Sam';
    'Since I Kissed My Baby Goodbye'; 'A-stairable Rag';
    'So Near and Yet So Far'; 'Wedding Cake Walk'

Holiday Inn   1942
Paramount
Producer/Director Mark Sandrich
Music director Robert Emmett Dolan
Music and lyrics: Irving Berlin
Dance director: Danny Dare
Art directors: Hans Dreier and Roland Anderson
Appeared with Bing Crosby, Marjorie Reynolds (sung by
    Martha Mears) and Virginia Dale
Musical numbers included 'I'll Capture Your Heart Singing';
    'You're Easy to Dance With'; 'White Christmas';
    'Happy Holiday'; 'Holiday Inn'; 'Let's Start the New Year
    Right';   'Abraham'; 'Be Careful, It's My Heart';
    'Easter Parade'; 'Oh, How I Hate to Get Up in the Morning'

You Were Never Lovelier   1942
Columbia Pictures
Producer Louis F. Edelman

Director William A. Seiter
Music: Jerome Kern
Lyrics: Johnny Mercer
Dance director: Val Raset
Art director: Lionel Banks
Appeared with Rita Hayworth (sung by Nan Wynn),
    Adolphe Menjou and Xavier Cugat
Musical numbers included 'Dearly Beloved'; 'I'm Old
    Fashioned'; 'Shorty George'; 'You Were Never Lovelier'

Yolanda and the Thief   1945
Metro-Goldwyn-Mayer
Producer Arthur Freed
Director Vincente Minnelli
Music: Harry Warren
Lyrics: Arthur Freed
Dance director: Eugene Loring
Art directors: Cedric Gibbons and Jack Martin Smith
Appeared with Lucille Bremer (sung by Trudy Erwin) and
    Frank Morgan

Ziegfeld Follies   1946
Metro-Goldwyn-Mayer
Producer Arthur Freed
Director Vincente Minnelli
Dance director: Robert Alton
Art directors: Cedric Gibbons, Merrill Pye and Jack Martin
    Smith
Musical numbers included 'Sunny'; 'If You Knew Suzie';
    'This Heart of Mine'; 'Limehouse Blues'; 'The Babbitt and
    the Bromide'

Blue Skies   1946
Paramount
Producer Sol C. Siegel
Director Stuart Heisler
Music and lyrics: Irving Berlin
Dance director: Hermes Pan
Art directors: Hans Dreier and Hal Pereira
Appeared with Bing Crosby, Joan Caulfield, Billy de Wolfe and
    Olga San Juan
Musical numbers included 'A Pretty Girl is Like a Melody';
    'Puttin' on the Ritz'; 'A Couple of Song and Dance Men';
    'You Keep Coming Back Like a Song'; 'Blue Skies'; 'The
    Little Things in Life'; 'Not For All the Rice in China';
    'Russian Lullaby'; 'Everybody Step'; 'How Deep is the

Ocean?';
'Getting Nowhere'; 'Heat Wave'; 'Any Bonds Today?'; 'This is
the Army, Mr Jones'; Tell Me, Little Gypsy'; 'White Christmas';
'Nobody Knows'; 'Mandy'; 'Some Sunny Day'; 'When You
Walked Out'; 'Because I Love You'; 'How Many Times?';
'Lazy'; 'The Song is Ended'

Easter Parade   1948
Metro-Goldwyn-Mayer
Producer Arthur Freed
Director Charles Walters
Music and lyrics: Irving Berlin
Dance director: Robert Alton
Art directors: Cedric Gibbons and Jack Martin Smith
Appeared with Judy Garland, Peter Lawford and Ann Miller
Musical numbers included 'It Only Happens When I Dance
   With You'; 'Everybody's Doin' It'; 'I Love a Piano';
   'When the Midnight Choo-Choo Leaves for Alabam'';
   'Shakin' the Blues Away'; 'Steppin' Out With My Baby';
   'A Couple of Swells'; 'Easter Parade'

The Barkleys of Broadway   1949
Metro-Goldwyn-Mayer
Producer Arthur Freed
Director Charles Walters
Music: Harry Warren
Lyrics: Ira Gershwin and Arthur Freed
Dance directors: Robert Alton and Hermes Pan
Art directors: Cedric Gibbons and Edward Carfagno
Appeared with Ginger Rogers and Oscar Levant
Musical numbers included 'My One and Only Highland Fling';
   'Shoes With Wings On'; 'They Can't Take That Away
   From Me'; 'This Heart of Mine'

Let's Dance   1950
Paramount
Producer Robert Fellows
Director Norman Z. McLeod
Music and lyrics: Frank Loesser
Dance director: Hermes Pan
Art directors: Hans Dreier and Roland Anderson
Appeared with Betty Hutton, Roland Young, Ruth Warwick and
   Lucile Watson
Musical numbers included 'Oh, Them Dudes'; 'Why Fight the
   Feeling?'; 'Tunnel of Love'

172

Three Little Words   1950
Metro-Goldwyn-Mayer
Producer Jack Cummings
Director Richard Thorpe
Music: Harry Ruby, Herman Ruby,
   Ted Snyder, Harry Puck, Herbert Stothart and Nacio Herb Brown
Lyrics: Bert Kalmar, Edgar Leslie and Arthur Freed
Dance director: Hermes Pan
Art directors: Cedric Gibbons and Urie McCleary
Appeared with Red Skelton, Vera-Ellen, Arlene Dahl, Keenan
   Wynn, and Debbie Reynolds (minor role)
Musical numbers included 'She's Mine, All Mine'; 'Who's Sorry
   Now?'; 'Nevertheless'; 'I Wanna Be Loved by You'; 'You Are
   My Lucky Star'; 'Three Little Words'

Royal Wedding   1951
UK : **Wedding Bells**
Metro-Goldwyn-Mayer
Producer Arthur Freed
Director Stanley Donen
Music: Burton Lane
Lyrics: Alan Jay Lerner
Dance director: Nick Castle
Art directors: Cedric Gibbons and Jack Martin Smith
Appeared with Jane Powell, Peter Lawford, Sarah Churchill and
   Keenan Wynn
Musical numbers included: 'How Could You Believe Me When I
   Said I Love You When You Know I've Been a Liar All My
Life?';
   'Too Late Now'

The Belle of New York   1952
Metro-Goldwyn-Mayer
Producer Arthur Freed
Director Charles Walters
Music: Harry Warren
Lyrics: Johnny Mercer
Dance director: Robert Alton
Art directors: Cedric Gibbons and Jack Martin Smith
Appeared with Vera-Ellen (sung by Anita Ellis), Marjorie Main,
   Keenan Wynn and Alice Pearce
Musical numbers included 'When I'm Out With the Belle of
   New York'; 'Let a Little Love Come In' (Roger Edens);
   'Seeing's Believing'; 'I Wanna Be a Dancin' Man'

The Band Wagon   1953
Metro-Goldwyn-Mayer
Producer Arthur Freed
Director Vincente Minnelli
Music: Arthur Schwartz
Lyrics: Howard Dietz
Dance director: Michael Kidd
Art directors: Cedric Gibbons and Preston Ames
Appeared with Cyd Charisse, Oscar Levant, Nanette Fabray and
    Jack Buchanan
Musical numbers included 'By Myself'; 'A Shine on Your Shoes';
    'That's Entertainment'; 'Beggar Waltz' (from Giselle);
    'Dancing in the Dark'; 'You and the Night and the Music';
    'Something to Remember You By'; 'I Love Louisa';
    'I Guess I'll Have to Change My Plan'; 'Louisiana Hayride';
    'Triplets'; 'The Girl Hunt Ballet' (narrative: Alan Jay Lerner)

Daddy Long Legs   1955
Twentieth Century-Fox
Producer Samuel G. Engel
Director Jean Negulesco
Music and lyrics: Johnny Mercer
Dance directors: David Robel and Roland Petit
Art directors: Lyle Wheeler and John DeCuir
Appeared with Leslie Caron, Terry Moore, Thelma Ritter and
    Fred Clark
Musical numbers included 'History of the Beat'; 'Daddy Long
    Legs'; 'Dream'; 'Sluefoot'; 'Something's Gotta Give';
    'Dancing Through Life Ballet'

Funny Face   1957
Paramount
Producer Roger Edens
Director Stanley Donen
Music: George Gershwin and Roger Edens
Lyrics: Ira Gershwin and Leonard Gershe
Dance director: Eugene Loring
Art directors: Hal Pereira and George W. Davis
Appeared with Audrey Hepburn, Kay Thomson and
    Michael Auclair
Musical numbers included 'How Long Has This Been Going On?';
    'Funny Face'; 'Bonjour, Paris!'; 'He Loves and She Loves';
    'Clap Yo Hands'; ''S Wonderful'

Silk Stockings 1957
Metro-Goldwyn-Mayer
Producer Arthur Freed
Director Rouben Mamoulian
Music and lyrics: Cole Porter
Dance directors: Hermes Pan and Eugene Loring
Art directors: William A. Horning and Randall Duell
Appeared with Cyd Charisse, Janis Paige, Peter Lorre, Jules
  Munshin, George Tobias and Joseph Buloff
Musical numbers included 'Paris Loves Lovers'; 'Stereophonic
  Sound'; 'It's a Chemical Reaction'; 'That's All'; 'All of You';
  'Satin and Silk'; 'Silk Stockings'; 'Fated to be Mated';
  'Josephine'; 'Siberia'; 'I've Got You Under My Skin'; 'Close';
  'You'd Be So Nice to Come Home to'; 'You can Do
  No Wrong'

On the Beach 1959
United Artists
Producer & director Stanley Kramer
Screenplay by John Paxton from the novel by Nevil Shute
Art director: Fernando Carrere
Appeared with Gregory Peck, Ava Gardner, Anthony Perkins
  and Donna Anderson

The Pleasure of His Company 1961
Paramount Pictures
Producer William Perlberg
Director George Seaton
Music directed by Alfred Newman
Screenplay by Samuel Taylor from a play by Cornelia Otis
Skinner and Samuel Taylor
Art directors: Hal Pereira and Tambi Larsen
Appeared with Debbie Reynolds, Lilli Palmer, Tab Hunter and
  Gary Merrill

The Notorious Landlady 1962
Columbia Pictures
Producer Fred Kohlmar
Director Richard Quine
Music director: George Duning
Screenplay by Larry Gelbart and Blake Edwards from a novel by
  Margery Sharp
Art director: Cary Odell
Appeared with Kim Novak, Jack Lemmon, Lionel Jeffries and
  Estelle Winwood

Finian's Rainbow 1968
Warner Brothers
Producer Joseph Landon
Director Francis Ford Coppola
Music: Burton Lane

Lyrics: E.Y. Harbourg
Dance director: Hermes Pan
Art director: Hilyard M. Brown
Appeared with Petula Clark, Tommy Steele, Don Francks and
    Keenan Wynn
Musical numbers included 'How Are Things in Glocca Morra?'
    'If This Isn't Love'; 'Old Devil Moon'; When I'm Not Near
    the Girl I Love'; 'Rain Dance'

The Midas Run 1969
UK : **A Run on Gold**
Selmur Pictures
Producer Raymond Stross
Director Alf Kjellin
Screenplay by James Buchanan and Ronald Austin from a story
    by Berne Giler
Art directors: Arthur Lawson and Ezio Cescotti
Appeared with Anne Heywood, Richard Crenna,
    Roddy McDowell, Sir Ralph Richardson and Cesar Romero.
    Also Fred Astaire Jr.

That's Entertainment 1974
Metro-Goldwyn-Mayer
Produced, directed and compiled by Jack Haley Jr.
Appeared with a host of MGM musical stars

The Towering Inferno 1975
Twentieth Century-Fox/Warner
Producer Irwin Allen
Director John Guillermin
Screenplay by Stirling Silliphant
Art director: Ward Preston
Appeared with Steve McQueen, Paul Newman, William Holden,
    Faye Dunaway, Susan Blakely, Richard Chamberlain, Jennifer
    Jones, O.J. Simpson, Robert Vaughan and Robert Wagner

That's Entertainment Part 2 1976
Metro-Goldwyn-Mayer
Producer Saul Chaplin and Daniel Melnick
A second compilation with extracts from MGM's musicals, and

some original musical sequences
Music arranged and conducted by Nelson Riddle
Dance director: Gene Kelly

The Amazing Dobermans   1976
Golden Films
Producer David Chudnow
Director Byron Chudnow
Screenplay by Richard Chapman from a story by
  Michael Kariake and William Goldstein
Appeared with James Franciscus, Barbara Eden, Jack Carter,
  Charlie Bill, James Almanzar and Billy Barty

Un Taxi Mauve   1977
Sofracima/Rizzoli Films
Producer Catherine Winter and Gisele Rebillion
Director Yves Boisset, who also wrote the screenplay from the
  novel by Michel Deon
Music: Philippe Sarde
Art director: Arrigo Equini
Appeared with Charlotte Rampling, Philippe Noiret,
  Agostina Belli, Peter Ustinov and Edward Albert Jr.

Ghost Story   1981
Universal Studios
Producer Ronald G. Smith
Director John Irvin
Screenplay by Lawrence D. Cohen
Appeared with Melvyn Douglas, John Houseman and
  Douglas Fairbanks Junior

Recording career

More than eighty recordings of Fred Astaire were made available between 1923 and 1978 with a wide variety of artists from sister Adele to George Gershwin; the orchestras of Ray Noble, Bob Crosby, Benny Goodman, Johnny Green, John Scott Trotter and David Rose; Delta Rhythm Boys, Bing Crosby, Judy Garland, Ginger Rogers, Jane Powell, Petula Clark and Jack Buchanan. A number of compilation albums have been produced including *Three Evenings with Fred Astaire, Starring Fred Astaire,* and the *Golden Age of Fred Astaire,* re-recorded in 1976 and including such Astaire standards as 'Top Hat, White Tie and Tails', 'A Fine Romance', 'Cheek to Cheek', 'A Foggy Day', 'They All Laughed', 'They Can't Take That Away From Me', 'Isn't This a Lovely Day', 'Night and Day', and 'That's Entertainment'.

Television career

Fred Astaire made his television debut on the *Ed Sullivan Show* in 1955. He agreed to appear in order to gain valuable publicity for his film *Daddy Long Legs*. Among his numerous appearances since then have been the following:

1957 *Imp on a Cobweb Leash* with Charles Laughton
1958 *An Evening with Fred Astaire* with Barrie Chase, Arlene Francis and Art Linkletter Shows, *Person to Person*
1959 Repeat of *An Evening with Fred Astaire*
1959 *Another Evening with Fred Astaire* with Barrie Chase
1960 *Astaire Time* with Barrie Chase
1962-63 *Fred Astaire's Premiere Theatre*. Hosted the series and appeared in five titles
1964 *Think Pretty* with Barrie Chase
1965 Appeared in a number of episodes of the *Dr Kildare* series
1966 Hosted a number of *Hollywood Palace* shows
1967 Television Spectacular with Barrie Chase
1969 Appeared in a number of episodes of *It Takes a Thief*

In the 1970s Astaire appeared variously in television shows and films including the *Dick Cavett Show, Make Mine Red, White and Blue, Battlestar Galactica* and *The Man in the Santa Claus Suit*.

Index

Aarons, Alex A., 24, 25, 30, 31, 34, 36, 37, 65, 66, 150
Adler, Larry, 38
'Alexander's Ragtime Band', 69
Allen, Gracie, 91
Allyson, June, 115, 116
Alton, Bob, 108, 112
Alvienne, Claude, 18-19
Amazing Dobermans, The, 140
American in Paris, An, 118, 135
Anderson, Donna, 139
Apple Blossoms, 23, 24
Arden, Vic, 31, 35
Arlen, Harold, 100, 107
Asher, Jerry, 50
Astaire, Adele,
  early talent, 17-20
  Fred's relationship with, 130-1, 144, 154
  influence of, 14, 131-2
  leaving the act, 13
  marriage, 41, 80
  miscarriage, 44
  personality, 22, 40
  retirement, 39
  success, 26, 31-2
Astaire, Fred
  and the Royal family, 33, 46, 129
  broadcasting, 88, 91
  childhood, 17-21
  film debut, 48-50
  marriage to Phyllis, 44, 48, 50-51, 114, 126, 127
  marriage to Robyn, 141-5, 154
  partnership with Ginger Rogers, 91, 95-6, 98, 112, 133, 151
  partnership with Rita Hayworth, 105
  perfectionism, 15-16

  personality, 16, 26, 132, 155-8
  racing, 32-3, 128-30
  relationships, 133, 153-4
  singing, 78-9, 149-50
  song writing, 149
  success, 21, 31-2
  television, 139, 141, 151-3
Astaire, Phyllis, 14, 39, 42, 44, 48, 49, 50-51, 93, 120
Astaire Time, 153
Austerlitz, Ann (nee Geilus), 14, 17-18
Austerlitz, Frederic, 17-18, 19, 20, 21, 29

'Babbitt and the Bromide, The', 35, 109
Babes in Arms, 108
Babes on Broadway, 108
Bachelor Mother, 96
Bacon, Lloyd, 67
Ball, Lucille, 60, 81, 98, 101, 108
Band Wagon, The,
  film, 14, 102, 114, 117-19, 121-5, 134, 141,
  show, 38-9, 41, 44, 119
Bankhead, Tallulah, 26
Barkleys of Broadway, The, 98, 111-14
Baxter, Warner, 67
'Be a Clown', 140
'Be Careful, It's My Heart', 106
'Begin the Beguine', 103, 140
Bellamy, Ralph, 94
Belle of New York, 109, 117
Benchley, Robert, 34, 50
Bennett, Constance, 62
Berkeley, Busby, 47, 51, 53, 67, 74
Berlin, Irving, 15, 54, 78, 92, 96,

100, 107, 130, 150, 157
Blue Skies, 109, 111
Carefree, 93, 94
Follow the Fleet, 82-4
Holiday Inn, 106
Lady, Be Good!, 31
Top Hat, 68-9, 72, 73, 74-5
Berman, Harry M., 78
Berman, Pandro S., 54, 78, 98, 157
Carefree, 92-5
Damsel in Distress, 90
Follow the Fleet, 81, 83-4
Gay Divorce, 55
Gay Divorcee, The, 57-8
Roberta, 59-61
Shall We Dance, 88-9
Swing Time, 84, 85-7
Top Hat, 68, 69, 73, 74, 79
'Beyond the Blue Horizon', 149
Black Bottom, 33
Blair, Lionel, 147
Blondell, Joan, 67
Blood and Sand, 104
Blore, Eric, 56, 68, 85, 88, 107
Blue Skies, 109-10, 129
'Bojangles of Harlem', 85, 86
Bolger, Ray, 148
'Bonjour Paris', 137
Born to Dance, 102
Boy Friend, The, 146
Brady, Alice, 56, 68
Braggiotti, Mario, 35
Bremer, Lucille, 108, 109
Brent, George, 67
Bring on the Empty Horses, 51, 127
Broadway Melody of 1936, 102
Broadway Melody of 1938, 102
Broadway Melody of 1940, 97, 102, 103, 104, 106
Broadway Melody, The, 102
Brock, Louis, 59
Broderick, Helen, 68, 69, 85
Bromfield, Louis, 37
Brown, Nacio Herb, 102
Bruce, Virginia, 38
Buchanan, Jack, 14, 117, 119, 122-4
Bull, Henry, 39
Buloff, Joseph, 138
Bunch and Judy, The, 25

Burke, Billie, 108, 112
Burns, George, 91
Butt, Sir Alfred, 27, 128
Butterfield, Billy, 103
Butterworth, Charles, 97, 103
'By Myself', 119, 125, 140
'By the Light of the Silvery Moon', 96

Cagney, Jimmy, 72, 101, 107
Cahn, Sammy, 137-7
'Call Me Irresponsible', 137
Cansino, Eduardo and Elisa, 22, 104
Carefree, 89, 91, 92-5, 100
'Carioca, The', 13, 52-3, 75
Caron, Leslie, 14, 16, 126, 135-6, 151
Carson, Jack, 94
Catlett, Walter, 30
Caulfield, Joan, 98, 109
Cavendish, Lord Charles, 41, 42, 44, 131
Chance at Heaven, 67
'Change Partners', 94
Chaplin, Charlie, 103
Charisse, Cyd, 16, 99, 108, 110, 151
    Silk Stockings, 136, 138-9, 141
    The Band Wagon, 14, 114, 117-19, 122-5
Chase, Barrie, 141, 151, 152, 153
'Cheek to Cheek', 70, 71, 75
'Clap Your Hands', 137
Clark, Carroll, 75
Clark, Petula, 139
Coccia, Aurelia, 21
Cohn, Harry, 63-4, 104
Colbert, Claudette, 64
Comden, Betty, 112, 117, 119, 157
'Continental, The', 56-7, 75
Cooke, Alistair, 74
Cooper, Gary, 107
Cooper, Merian, C., 62, 63, 64
'Couple of Song and Dance Men, A' 110
'Couple of Swells, A', 140
Cowan, Jerome, 88
Coward, Noel, 24, 26, 29, 37, 146
Crawford, Joan, 14, 49-50, 140

Crosby, Bing, 76, 99, 101, 103, 106, 109-10, 137
Cukor, George, 62
Cugat, Xavier, 105
Cummings, Jack, 115
Cyrano de Bergerac, 18

Daddy Long Legs, 14, 126, 135-6, 151
Dahl, Arlene, 115
Dailey, Dan, 76
Dale, Virginia, 106
Damsel in Distress, A, 89, 90-91 92, 95
Danceland, 114
'Dancing in the Dark', 39, 123, 140
Dancing in the Dark, 117, 118
Dancing Lady, 14, 50, 51, 54, 55, 67
Daniels, Bebe, 67
'Dearly Beloved', 105
Del Rio, Dolores, 52
Depression, 62-3
Devine, Andy, 67
De Wolfe, Billy, 109
Dietz, Howard, 38, 39, 44, 100, 117
'Dig it', 103
Dillingham, Charles, 23, 24, 25
Donen, Stanley, 116
'Dream', 135
Duchin, Eddie, 66
Duer Miller, Alice, 60
Dunn, Irene, 60
Durban, Deanna, 20

Easter Parade, 110-12, 113, 140
'Easy to Dance With', 106
Edens, Roger, 137
Eddy, Nelson, 50
Ellis, Anita, 115
'Embraceable You', 65, 66
Evening with Fred Astaire, An, 152
'Everybody's Doin' It', 69

Fabray, Nanette, 14, 117, 119, 121, 123, 134, 141
Fairbanks, Douglas Jun., 92
Fairbanks, Douglas Sen., 22, 29, 45
Fallen Sparrow, The, 107

Farago, Alexander, 68
'Fascinating Rhythm', 30
'Fated to be Mated', 138
Fields, Dorothy, 60, 75, 78, 85, 86
Fifth Avenue Girl, 96
'Fine Romance, A', 85, 86, 100
Finian's Rainbow, 139-40
Finklea, Tula Ellice *see* Charisse, Cyd
Flying Down to Rio, 13, 14, 45, 48, 49, 51-5, 63, 67, 68, 98
'Foggy Day, A', 91
Follow the Fleet, 80, 83, 87
Fontaine, Joan, 90, 91
For Goodness Sake, 24, 25, 66, 150
'For He's a Jolly Good Fellow', 125
Ford, John, 84
Forsyth, Bruce, 147
Forty Second Street, 67
Foster, Allan, 24
Fred Astaire, 103
Fred Astaire's Premiere Theatre, 153
Freed, Arthur, 74, 98, 100, 102, 103, 107, 109, 110, 111, 112, 113, 115, 116, 117, 138
Freedland, Michael, 69
Freedley, Vinton, 30, 31, 34, 65
Frey, Jacques, 35
Funny Face,
    film, 48, 136,
    show, 34, 35, 36-7, 40, 66, 92
    song, 137
Furness, Betty, 85

Gable, Clark, 49-50, 87
Gardner, Ava, 139
Garfield, John, 107
Garland, Judy, 13, 16, 20, 98, 101, 102, 108, 110-12, 116
Gay Divorce, 13, 42-5, 48, 54, 55, 67
Gay Divorcee, The, 53, 55, 57-9, 63, 68, 75, 78
Gear, Luella, 94
Geilus, Ann *see* Austerlitz, Ann
Gelsey, Erwin, 85
George, Prince (later King George V1), 44-5

182

George White's Scandals, 102
Gershe, Leonard, 137
Gershwin, George, 24, 28, 36, 54,
    78, 92, 96, 149, 150, 153
    Damsel in Distress, 90
    Funny Face, 34, 137
    Girl Crazy, 65
    Lady, Be Good!, 30-31
    Shall We Dance, 88, 89
    Smarty, 34
Gershwin, Ira, 30, 31, 34, 65, 88,
    90, 112, 137, 150
Ghost Story, 154
Girl Crazy, 65, 66
'Girl Hunt, The', 102, 118, 119,
    124
Girl Who Dared, The, 68
'Give Me Something to
    Remember You By', 123
Gleason, Jackie, 137
Goddard, Paulette, 16, 97, 98, 103
Gold Diggers of 1933, 67
Golder, Lew, 21
Gould, Dave, 52, 53
Grable, Betty, 56, 63, 81
Graves, Lord Tommy, 126
Grayson, Kathryn, 101, 108
Green, Adolph, 112, 117, 119
Green, Benny, 16, 60, 77, 103, 115
Green, Johnny, 91
Greene, Grahame, 74

Hackett, Bobby, 103
'Half of It, Dearie, Blues, The', 31
Harbach, Otto, 60
Harmsworth, Esmond, 29
Harris, Phil, 63
Harvey Girls, The, 118
Having Wonderful Time, 92
Hayes, Max, 21
Hayward, Leland, 48, 54, 109
Hayworth, Rita, 16, 22, 98, 99,
    103-4, 105, 151, 152, 153-4
'Heat Wave', 110
'Hello Baby', 149
'Hello, Frisco, Hello', 96
'He Loves and She Loves', 137
Henderson, Dickie, 147
Henson, Leslie, 35
Hepburn, Audrey, 16, 136,
137-8
Hepburn, Katherine, 85, 89, 90
Herbert, Hugh, 101
Heywood, Anne, 140
Hilliard, Harriet, 81, 83
Hirschhorn, Clive, 109, 156
'History of the Beat', 136
Hoctor, Harriet, 83
Holiday for Strings, 151
Holiday Inn, 69, 76, 103, 106, 108
Hope, Bob, 38
Horne, Lena, 108
Horton, Edward Everett, 56, 68,
    69, 88
'Hot and Bothered', 65
Howard, Sidney, 35
Howard, Willie and Eugene, 23
'How Are Things in Glocca
    Morra?', 139
'How Could You Believe Me
    When I said I Loved You
    When You Know I've Been a
    Liar All My Life?', 116-117
'How Long Has This Been Going
    On?', 137
Hunter, Ian, 97
Hunter, Tab, 139
Hutton, Betty, 101, 114, 115, 116

'I Can't Tell a Lie' 106
'I Concentrate on You', 103
'I'd Rather Lead a Band', 82
'If This Isn't Love', 139
'I Guess I'll Have to Change My
    Plan', 102, 119, 123, 140
'I'll Build a Stairway to Paradise',
    28
'I'll Go My Way By Myself', 121
'I Love A Piano', 111
'I Love Louisa', 123
'I Love to Quarrel With You', 69
'I'm Building Up to an Awful Let-
    Down', 149
'I'm Old Fashioned', 105
Imp on a Cobweb Leash, 139, 151
'I'm Putting All My Eggs in One
    Basket', 83
'Isn't This a Lovely Day to be
    Caught in the Rain', 70

'It Only Happens When I Dance With You', 111
'I used to be Colour Blind', 94
'I've Got My Eyes on You', 103
'I've Got You Under My Skin', 138
'I Wanna Be a Dancin' Man', 117, 140
'I Wanna Be Loved by You', 115
'I Won't Dance', 60, 85

Jeffries, Lionel, 139
Jenkins, Alan, 35
Jenkinson, Philip, 53, 56, 94-5
Jolson, Al, 23, 67
Jones, Jennifer, 140
Jordan, Dorothy, 63
'Just Like Taking Candy From a Baby', 149

Kalmar, Bert, 65, 115
Keeler, Ruby, 67, 90
Kelly, Gene, 13, 14, 16, 77, 108-9, 110-111, 118, 135, 146, 148, 156, 157
Kent, Duke and Duchess of, 97
Kent, William, 35
Kern, Jerome, 31, 54, 60, 75, 78, 85, 86, 92, 96, 100, 105, 118, 150
Kibbee, Guy, 67
Kidd, Michael, 157
Kildare, Dr, 153
King George V, 33
Kitty Royle, 112
Kolb, Clarence, 94
Kreisler, Fritz, 24

Lady, Be Good!, 30-34, 35, 66, 92, 128
La La Lucille, 24
Lane, Burton, 100, 116, 139
Laszlo, Aladar, 68
Laughton, Charles, 151
Lawford, Peter, 13, 107, 110, 111
Lawrence, Gertrude, 26, 146
Leach, Jack, 128-30
LeMaire, Rufus, 22
Lee, Sammy, 50
Lemmon, Jack, 139, 157
Leonard, Bob, 50

Lerner, Alan Jay, 100, 116, 119
Le Roy, Mervyn, 48, 67
Leslie, Joan, 16, 98, 99-100, 106-7, 152
'Let's Call the Whole Thing Off', 89
Let's Dance, 115-16
'Let's Face the Music and Dance', 82, 83
'Let's Find Out', 122
'Let's k-k-nock K-nees', 56
'Let Yourself Go', 83
Levant, Oscar, 14, 112, 117, 119, 121, 123
Lewin, David, 132, 133, 148, 156
'Limehouse Blues', 108
Lindsay, Howard, 43, 85
Little Boy Blue, 116
'Little Brown Jug', 96
Loesser, Frank, 100, 116
Loring, Eugene, 109
Lorre, Peter, 138
'Louise', 149
'Louisiana Hayride', 119, 124
Love Letter, The, 24, 25, 28
'Lovely to Look At', 60, 75, 85
Luce, Claire, 42-3, 44-5, 58
Lussier, Dane, 116

McCrea, Joel, 67
McGuire, William, 37, 41
McIlvaine, Eddie, 48
McQueen, Steve, 140

MacDonald, Gertrude, 35
'Man I Love, The', 31
Man in the Santa Claus Suit, The, 141
Man on a Bicycle, 139
Martin, Tony, 81
Massey, Ilona, 100
Matthews, Jessie, 90
'Maxixe, The', 96
Mayer, Louis B., 106, 110
Melody Cruise, 63
Melville, Alan, 131
Menjou, Adolphe, 89, 105
Mercer, Johnny, 100, 105, 107, 117, 135, 136, 149

Meredith, Burgess, 97, 103
Merkel, Una, 67
Merman, Ethel, 65
Merrill, Gary, 139
Midas Run, The, 140
Miller, Ann, 13, 98, 110, 111, 148
Miller, Glenn, 101, 155
Miller, Marilyn, 37, 41
Minnelli, Vincente, 108, 117, 118
Mission to Moscow, 118
Modern Times, 103
Moore, Terry, 14
Moore, Victor, 35
Morgan, Frank, 97
Morse, Ella Mae, 107
Morrison, Charles, 65
Mountbatten, Lord and Lady
    Louis, 29
'Mr and Mrs Hoofer at Home', 115
Munshin, Jules, 138
Murphy, George, 76, 97, 103
Mutiny on the Bounty, 127
'My One and Only', 35, 146
'My One and Only Highland
    Fling', 112-3
'My Shining Hour', 107

'Never Gonna Dance', 87
'Nevertheless', 115
Newman, Al, 135
Newman, Paul, 140
'Nice Work If You Can Get It', 91
Nicholas Brothers, 76
'Night and Day', 43, 56, 57
Ninotchka, 138
Niven, David, 51, 96, 126-7, 155
Notorious Landlady, The, 139
Novak, Kim, 139

O'Brian, Virginia, 108
'Oh Gee, Oh Gosh, Oh Golly,
    I Love You', 26
Ohman, Phil, 31, 35
'Oh, Them Dudes', 116
'Old Devil Moon', 139
'One For My Baby and One More
    For The Road', 107
Only Angels Have Wings, 104
On the Beach, 84, 114, 139, 152
'Oompah Trot', 28

'Orchids in the Moonlight', 52
Osborne, Hubert, 80, 81
Over the Top, 23

Packard Motor Car Company, 88,
    91
Palmer, Lili, 139
Pan, Hermes, 15, 76, 96, 138, 149,
    151, 157
    Blue Skies, 109
    Carefree, 94
    Damsel in Distress, 90, 91
    Flying Down to Rio, 52-3
    Gay Divorcee, The, 58-9
    Let's Dance, 116
    'Night and Day', 57
    Roberta, 60-61
    Shall We Dance, 88, 89
    Silk Stockings, 86-7
    Swing Time, 86-7
    The Barkleys of Broadway, 112,
        113
    Three Little Words, 115
    Top Hat, 68, 71, 75
    Top Speed, 65
Pangborn, Franklin, 94
Parkinson, Michael, 147
Passing Show of 1918, The, 23
Payson, Charlie, 39
Peck, Gregory, 139, 143
Perkins, Anthony, 139
Phillips, Clyde, 129
'Piano Dance', 116
'Piccolino, The', 70, 75
Pickford, Mary, 29
'Pick Yourself Up', 85
'Please Don't Monkey with
    Broadway', 103
Pleasure of His Company, The, 139
Polglase, Van Nest, 61, 75, 79, 88,
    90, 94, 96
Porter, Cole, 31, 54, 78, 96, 100,
    103, 150
    Gay Divorce, 42-4
    Gay Divorcee, The, 55-6
    'Night and Day', 57
    Silk Stockings, 138
    You'll Never Get Rich, 105
Portrait of John Garnett, 85
Potter, Phyllis *see* Astaire, Phyllis

Powell, Dick, 67, 101
Powell, Eleanor, 16, 97, 98, 99, 102-3, 105-6, 148
Powell, Jane, 114, 116-17
Powell, William, 108
Power, Tyrone, 104
'Pretty Girl is Like a Melody, A', 110
Previn, André, 115
Prince of Wales, 27, 33
'Putting on the Ritz', 110

Queen Elizabeth, the Queen Mother, 27, 46, 129, 158

Rainbow Corner, 101
Rampling, Charlotte, 141
Randall, Carl, 43
Raymond, Gene, 52
Remick, Jerome H., 149
Reynolds, Debbie, 115, 139
Reynolds, Marjorie, 98, 106
Rhodes, Erik, 56, 68, 70
Richards, Dick, 57, 70, 94
Richardson, Sir Ralph, 140
Roberta 53, 59-61, 63, 68, 76, 85
'Robert E. Lee', 96
Robinson, Bill 'Bojangles', 22, 86
Rodgers and Hart, 118, 148
Rogers, Ginger
  Carefree, 92-5
  Flying Down to Rio, 13, 51-4
  Follow the Fleet, 82-4
  Gay Divorcee, The, 57-9
  In Person, 82
  life of, 64-6
  moving into films, 48, 58
  moving into straight acting, 89
  partnership with Fred Astaire, 14, 16, 66-7, 77, 84, 87, 89, 95, 98, 138
  Roberta, 60-61
  Shall We Dance, 87-90
  Stage Door, 90, 92
  Swing Time, 85-7
  The Barkleys of Broadway, 112-14
  Top Hat, 69-75
  'Waltz in Swing Time', 15
Rogers, Lela, 64-5, 66

Romero, Cesar, 140
Rooney, Mickey, 20, 101, 108
Rosalie, 102
Rose, David, 151, 152, 153
Ross, Herbert, 141
Roud, Richard, 158
Royal Family, 46
Royal Wedding, 115-17
Royce, Edward, 23, 24, 28
Ruby, Harry, 65, 115
Ruggles, Charles, 64
Run on Gold, A see *Midas Run, The*

Sandrich, Mark, 55, 68, 79, 81, 88, 90, 93-4, 95, 106
San Juan, Olga, 109, 110
'Say, Young Man of Manhattan', 37
Schwartz, Arthur, 38, 39, 44, 100, 117, 119
Scott, Allan, 68, 79, 81, 85, 116
Scott, Randolph, 60, 81
Second Chorus, 97, 99, 103, 104
'See a New Sun', 124
Selznick, David O., 15, 48, 62, 64, 78, 147
Sergeant York, 107
Schaefer, George, 78
Shall We Dance, 87-90, 91, 92, 95, 113, 157
Shaw, Artie, 97, 103
'She's Funny That Way', 149
'Shine on My Shoes, A', 119, 122
'Shoes With Wings On', 112, 113, 140
Shore Leave, 80, 81
'Shorty George', 105
Shubert, Lee and John, 22, 23
'Siberia', 138
Silk Stockings, 108, 136, 138-9, 141, 151
Sinatra, Frank, 143
'Since They Turned Loch Lomond Into Swing', 94
Singing Fool, The, 67
Singin' in the Rain, 118
'Singin' in the Rain', 16
Sitting Pretty, 67
Skelton, Red, 108, 115

186

Sky's The Limit, The, 99-100, 106-7
Slack, Freddie, 107
'Slap That Bass', 89
'Sluefoot', 136
Smiles, 37, 38, 66, 71
Smith, Robyn, 14, 141-5
'Smoke Gets in Your Eyes', 60
'Something's Gotta Give', 136
'Something to Remember You By', 119
Spillane, Mickey, 124
Steele, Tommy, 139
Steiner, Max, 79, 81
'Stepping Out With My Baby', 111, 140
Steps in Time, 16, 21, 26, 49, 58-9, 91
'Stereophonic Sound', 138
Stevens, George, 79, 85, 90
Stewart, James, 92
Stop Flirting, 26, 27, 28, 29, 32
Story of Vernon and Irene Castle, The, 78, 92-3, 95-6, 100
Strike Up The Band, 108
Sullivan, Ed, 151
Swing Time, 78, 84, 85-7, 88-9
'Swing Trot', 113-14
'S'Wonderful', 137

'**Tango, The**', 96
Taylor, Dwight, 68, 79, 81
Temple, Shirley, 22, 87
'Texas Tommy, The', 96
'That's Entertainment', 119, 122, 140, 147, 148
    Part 2, 140
'They All Laughed', 89
'They Can't Take That Away From Me', 89, 100, 102, 113, 140
'Think Pink', 137
Think Pretty, 153
'This Heart of Mine', 108
Three Little Words, 115
Three Wise Fools, 118
Till the Clouds Roll By, 118
Tone, Franchot, 50
'Too Late Now', 116
Top Hat, 15, 37-8, 63, 68-75, 79, 87, 144

'Top Hat, White Tie and Tails', 16, 70, 76
Top Speed, 53, 65, 66
Torvill and Dean, 147
Towering Inferno, The, 140, 153
'Triplets', 119, 124
Tucker, Sophie, 22
Twiggy, 146, 154

Under the Pampas Moon, 104
Un Taxi Mauve, 140-41
Ustinov, Peter, 141

Vanderbilt, Alfred G., 141
Vanderbilt, Mrs Graham Fair, 39
Variety, 22
Vera-Ellen, 16, 114, 115, 117
Vine, Brian, 133
Vivacious Lady, 92

'**Waiting for the Robert E. Lee**', 111
Walters, Charles (Chuck), 116, 117
'Waltz in Swing Time', 15, 86
Warner, Jack, 48, 67
Warren, Harry, 100, 109, 112, 113, 117
'Way You Look Tonight, The', 78, 85
Wayburn, Ned, 20
Weatherly, Tom, 43
Webb, Clifton, 117
Wedding Bells see *Royal Wedding*
Wells, George, 115
'We're a Couple of Swells', 111,113
'We Saw the Sea', 82,
'When the Midnight Choo-Choo leaves for Alabam', 111
'When You Wore a Tulip', 96
'White Christmas', 106
Whiting, Dick, 149
'Who's Sorry Now?', 115
'Why Fight The Feeling', 116
Williams, Esther, 108
Wiman, Dwight Deere, 43
Wodehouse, P.G., 90
Words and Music, 118
Wragg, Harry, 33
Wyler, William, 128

'Yam, The', 94
Yankee Doodle Dandy, 107
Yolanda and the Thief, 103, 108, 109
'You and the Night and the Music', 119, 122, 123
'You Are My Lucky Star', 115
'You'd Be So Nice To Come Home To', 138
You'll Never Get Rich, 103, 104-5, 153

Youmans, Vincent, 37, 48, 52
Young Man of Manhattan, 64, 71
You Were Never Lovelier, 103, 105, 153

Zanuck, Darryl, 14, 135
Ziegfeld, Florenz, 36, 37, 41-2, 108
Ziegfeld Follies, 108, 109, 118, 131
Zolotow, Maurice, 116

188